Interpretation and Social Knowledge

ISAAC ARIAIL REED

INTERPRETATION AND SOCIAL KNOWLEDGE

On the Use of Theory in the Human Sciences

THE UNIVERSITY OF CHICAGO PRESS

Chicago & London

ISAAC ARIAIL REED is assistant professor of sociology at the University of Colorado at Boulder.

The University of Chicago Press, Chicago 60637
The University of Chicago Press, Ltd., London

Printed and bound by CPI Group (UK) Ltd, Croydon, CR0 4YY
20 19 18 17 16 15 14 13 12 11 1 2 3 4 5

ISBN-13: 978-0-226-70673-3 (cloth)
ISBN-13: 978-0-226-70674-0 (paper)
ISBN-10: 0-226-70673-7 (cloth)
ISBN-10: 0-226-70674-5 (paper)

Library of Congress Cataloging-in-Publication Data
Reed, Isaac (Isaac Ariail)
Interpretation and social knowledge : on the use of theory in the human sciences / Isaac Ariail Reed.
p. cm.
Includes bibliographical references and index.
ISBN-13: 978-0-226-70673-3 (cloth : alkaline paper)
ISBN-10: 0-226-70673-7 (cloth : alkaline paper)
ISBN-13: 978-0-226-70674-0 (paperback : alkaline paper)
ISBN-10: 0-226-70674-5 (paperback : alkaline paper)
1. Knowledge, Theory of. 2. Knowledge, Sociology of. 3. Social sciences—Philosophy. 4. Social sciences—Methodology. 5. Interpretation (Philosophy) I. Title.
BD175 .R37 2011
121—dc22 2011010293

∞ The paper used in this publication meets the minimum requirements of the American National Standard for Information Sciences—Permanence of Paper for Printed Library Materials, ANSI Z39.48-1992.

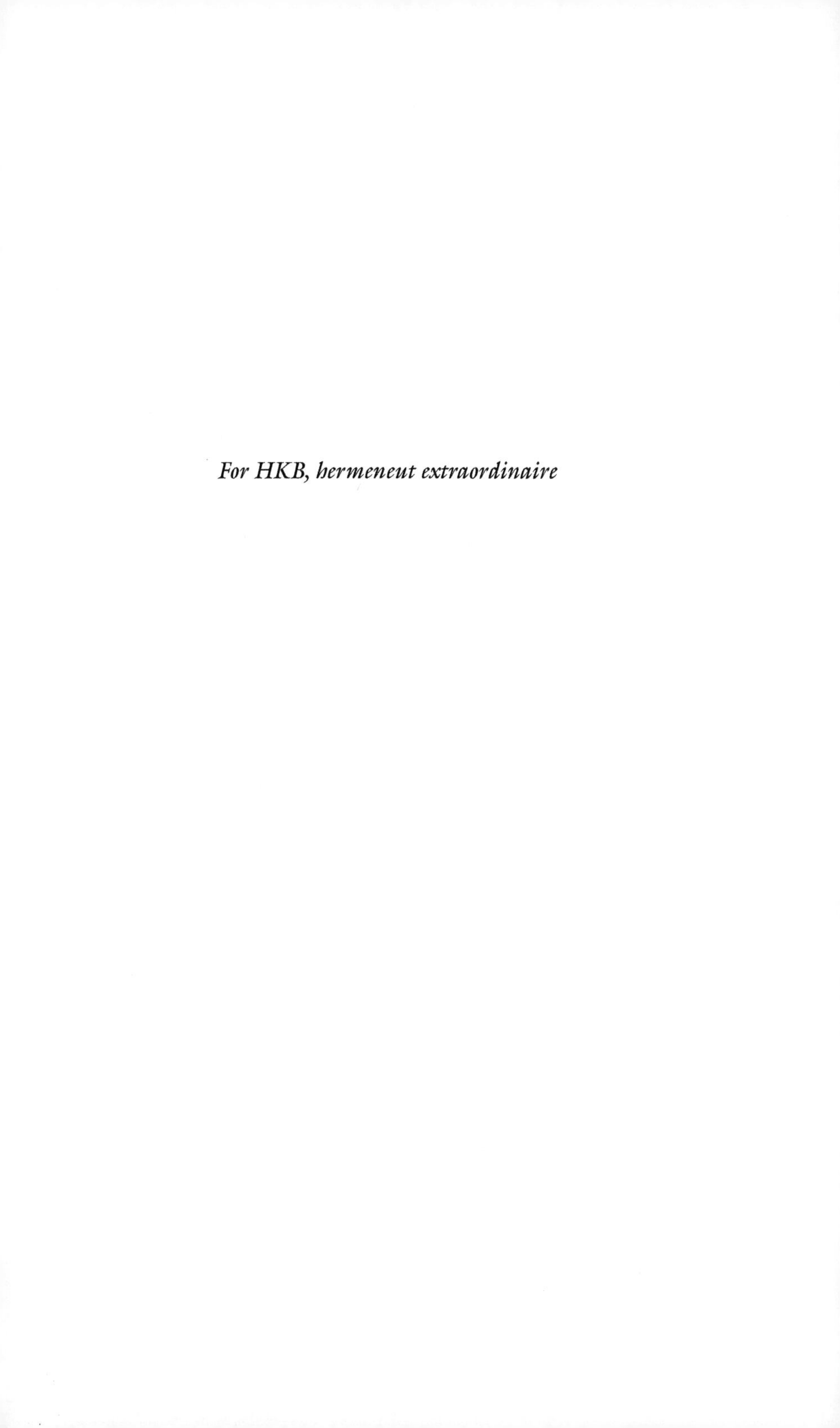

For HKB, hermeneut extraordinaire

Contents

Illustrations

Introduction

I

Our understanding of social knowledge is due for a massive transformation. A generation's worth of arguments about postmodernism and science, relativism and objectivism, have obscured our view; a consistent connection has been drawn between the study of discourse and the adoption of philosophical skepticism and ironic distance; a repeated disavowal of the possibility of causal explanation has crippled the interpretation of cultures; an overwhelming tendency to frame the problem of social knowledge as the problem of how social science can be like natural science has eliminated essential questions from our minds. The space of epistemological argument in social theory, then, comes to be defined by "posts" and their opponents: postpositivism, poststructuralism, postmodernism, postcolonialism. Regardless of what the "posts" actually are or are not, thinking about social knowledge is, in this Manichean account, a dispute about whether science (and perhaps modernity) is good or bad.

For the researcher intent on actually producing some sort of social knowledge, the disputations of social theory and philosophy are often experienced less directly, sublimated into distorted communiqués about methodology: qualitative against quantitative; unscheduled interviews against scheduled interviews; participant observation against survey research; in a phrase, depth against generality. And so, metatheoretical arguments about the construction and justification of social knowledge reappear as debates about lived social realities, and the research design that is necessary to grasp them.

The debates about method are, without a doubt, real: they denote significant divergences in the practice of gathering and colligating evidence in social research. But in their connotations, they encode the same paralyzing epistemological dilemma. From one point of view, there are clearheaded and rigorous producers of quantifiable, verifiable truths about social phenomena, and those who, for whatever reason, prefer to impose their own interpretive flights of fancy on idiosyncratic data gathered in idiosyncratic ways. From the opposite point of view, "objectivists" or "positivists" do not work for their objectivity but rather perform it. The ongoing scientism of large sectors of the human sciences is, in this latter view, the bane of a true understanding of social life, which can only be achieved through the careful humanism of attending to what people actually do, say, think, and tell their interviewer.[1]

But perhaps the heavy feeling of despair and déjà vu brought on by such dilemmas is not necessary. We can reconsider. So let us begin by asking: are all of our problems, as researchers and as theorists, understandable in terms of differences in method, practically conceived as that which we do to establish factual statements, broad or narrow,

1. The term "human sciences" has a historical referent in the intellectual project of the *Geisteswissenschaften*, literally "sciences of the spirit," and thus the nineteenth-century German philosophies of history that formed an important part of the intellectual context for Max Weber's definition of sociology. But it is also intended to evoke more recent arguments about the (sometimes nefarious) effect of disciplinary self-conceptions on research into how human beings live together in social groups. In particular, the sociologist Mayer Zald has developed an incisive analysis and critique of the ways in which the social sciences generally, and sociology in particular, can benefit from recognizing their historical-intellectual debt to both the humanities and the natural sciences, and from correcting their overemphasis on the latter as a model for the construction of knowledge. His open-ended paper invites, in my view, arguments of the kind found in this book. See Mayer Zald, "Sociology as a Discipline: Quasi-Science and Quasi-Humanities," *American Sociologist* 22, nos. 3–4 (1991). For a historical account of the conditions that led to the formation of the social scientific disciplines as we now know them in the United States, and an argument that this organization of intellectual labor is no longer appropriate, see Immanuel Wallerstein et al., *Open the Social Sciences: Report of the Gulbenkian Commission on the Restructuring of the Social Sciences* (Stanford: Stanford University Press, 1996).

about social life? Or do disputes over method, when considered carefully, reveal other problems, problems not reducible to measurement and technique, problems that point to deep divides in our fundamental conception of how a community of inquiry can expect to know something about other human communities and their various dynamics?[2] I am continually left to wonder whether the world of social researchers is really divisible into those who believe in the existence of social facts in some quantitative sense and those who do not, or whether this divide has lost even its heuristic utility. Is it at the level of facts, in other words, that the great controversies over the nature and purpose of research in the human sciences should be fought out? In one sense, yes: before doing anything, we have to find a way to "establish the phenomenon."[3] But in another sense, no: debates about method often carry implicit disagreements about the nature and purpose of inquiry, the structure of social life itself, and the role of the critical intellectual or social researcher in comprehending it. If we render these disagreements explicit, we find that they are not only about method, strictly understood, but also about how knowledge claims are built out of conceptual innovation, justified in publication, and criticized as inaccurate and untrue (or, to use that infuriatingly ambiguous word, "problematic").

We have disagreements, that is, not only about how we establish the sheer existence of this or that social phenomenon, but also about how we can claim to correctly and effectively explain, criticize, or interpret it. In my view it is these latter disagreements, rather than disagreements about whether or not there are, in some sense, social facts, that are at the core of controversies about social knowledge. And so, it is to these disagreements that we must address ourselves if we are to move beyond the world of posts.

2. Sandra Harding has usefully distinguished between method ("a technique for (or way of proceeding in) gathering evidence"), methodology ("a theory and analysis of how research does or should proceed"), and epistemology ("a theory of knowledge"). The analysis of this book could be said to address the latter two, if we consider that Harding's definition of methodology includes how theory is used and applied in specific disciplines and fields. But there is another way of framing this, which is to say that evidentiary method must be accompanied by a conceptual method, whereby evidence is ordered and comprehended as part of a larger knowledge claim. Sandra Harding, "Is There a Feminist Method?" in *Feminism and Methodology: Social Science Issues*, ed. Sandra G. Harding (Bloomington: Indiana University Press, 1987), 1–14.

3. Robert K. Merton, "Three Fragments from a Sociologist's Notebooks: Establishing the Phenomenon, Specified Ignorance and Strategic Research Materials," *Annual Review of Sociology* 13 (1987).

II

In the discourses in and around contemporary social theory, post-positivism has a somewhat clear historical meaning—the term refers to the break with certain taken-for-granted assumptions about the unity of the natural and social sciences that, like so many other breaks, happened sometime in "the sixties."[4] Given the academic penchant for overdramatizing our own intellectual disputations, it should not surprise us that this break is narrated in vaguely heroic terms, especially in casual academic conversation. "Positivist" is used pejoratively in certain sectors of the human sciences because the positivist is the antagonist to the heroic protagonist, the postpositivist, who broke his chains and challenged the dragon. In this frame "positivist" refers to someone whose addiction to reductive quantification causes him to miss the real stuff of social life—villains, in scholarship, are always associated with untruth.

But what could positivism mean, in some general and yet practically significant way, if it is not just a pejorative signifier, applied to work that lacks the sacred values of the researcher who casually uses the term? Probably postpositivists mean one of two things when they say "positivist." First of all, positivism can refer to an underlying philosophical commitment to certain methods for ascertaining social facts—descriptive positivism. Here the core positivist axiom is that the social sciences are rendered scientific by the use of specific methodological techniques for handling data, and in particular by an agreement about the superiority of certain ways of establishing reliability and validity through quantification and statistical inference. In the context of contemporary social research, the most immediate objection to descriptive positivism is in terms of the methods used to produce accurate descriptions of social phenomena. Is quantification and, more specifically, correlational analysis adequate to the task of producing facts about social life? It is a quite common argument, in fact, that social research should be empiricist, but that the methods

4. This break is documented and advocated for, in classic form, in Richard J. Bernstein, *The Restructuring of Social and Political Theory* (New York: Harcourt Brace Jovanovich, 1976). See also Sherry Ortner, "Theory in Anthropology since the '60s," *Comparative Studies in Society and History* (1984). For a good analysis of "the sixties" as it has become a construction relevant to intellectuals in the West more generally, see Eleanor Townsley, "'The Sixties' Trope," *Theory, Culture, and Society* 18, no. 6 (2001).

for achieving empirical validity differ significantly from those found in either the natural sciences or the (perhaps misguided) quantitative branches of social science. For example, one could value the descriptive production of truth above all else, but insist that this description must be qualitative and particularistic. Thus the tendency toward empiricism in social research extends far beyond quantitative methodologies taken from the natural sciences.[5] Positivism, as an approach to method, and empiricism, as a resistance to theory, are by no means coextensive. Empiricism can be "antipositivist." Furthermore, "positivism" can also refer to a way of building and using theory to guide research.

In particular, the second meaning of positivism refers to how one can use theory to construct explanations. Here we find the philosophical arguments of the logical positivists, the various attempts to put their covering-law model of explanation to work in the human sciences, and the increasingly sophisticated inheritors of the ambition to construct a truly universal science of the social. Explanation, in this view, is the logical result of combining a general law about social life with particular circumstances, thus enabling the investigator to predict or retrodict the resultant outcome. What we want, according to what we could call theoretical positivism, is a social physics, with theory leading the way by positing general laws of social behavior.[6]

Should we have a social physics? Can we have a successful one?

5. John Goldthorpe has written that ethnography, in so far as it is not "irrationalist," shares many of the epistemological assumptions of survey research. He then argues for a "common logic of inference" across both qualitative and quantitative research in social science, and indeed across the social and natural sciences, in John H. Goldthorpe, "Sociological Ethnography Today: Problems and Prospects," in *On Sociology, Volume 1: Critique and Program* (Stanford: Stanford University Press, 2007). Goldthorpe's own vision could hardly be called empiricist, however. Rather, he proposes a compelling synthesis of rational action theory and the quantitative analysis of data, which would fit the second meaning of positivism ("theoretical positivism") I discuss below. For an analysis, see Isaac Reed, "Review Essay: Social Theory, Post-post-positivism, and the Question of Interpretation," *International Sociology* 23, no. 5 (2008).

6. Jonathan Turner, drawing on the original vision of August Comte, argues that the goal of social physics "is to uncover abstract laws, and the fewer laws the better," and thus that the goal of "science is to seek understanding of the universe, and the vehicle through which such understanding is to be achieved is theory. Sociology has allowed poor philosophers to usurp theoretical activity and 'statistical packages' to hold social science hostage." (Jonathan Turner, "Returning to 'Social Physics': Illustrations from the Work of George Herbert Mead," *Current Perspectives in Social Theory* 2 [1981]: 188, 187). For Turner's classic defense of theoretical positivism in sociology, see Jonathan Turner, "In Defense of Positivism," *Sociological Theory* 3, no. 2 (1985).

Successful or not, we have it: there are, in the contemporary social sciences, extended and well-articulated attempts to develop a hypergeneralized approach to social explanation. In theoretical positivism, then, we find highly general hypotheses and propositions that are to be verified or falsified through empirical testing, and, simultaneously, a strong argument that social research must find a way to move beyond merely producing correlations and instead produce theory-informed explanations. Theoretical positivism, in other words, has deep suspicions about descriptive positivism. Perhaps the goal for theoretical positivism is a set of social sciences, all of which look like neoclassical economics, in which the basic assumptions are agreed upon, and metatheoretical debate about human nature, social structure, and the problems inherent in the very possibility of knowing something about either is left to philosophers and the occasional book on microfoundations.

It must be said: if one wants to understand, on its own terms, the philosophical underpinnings of positivism, or logical positivism, or the combination of the quantitative analysis of data with the testing of universal propositions, the resources are ample. The empiricist philosophy of science has developed in radically new directions since Carl Hempel ruled the scene,[7] and if one wants to grasp the presuppositions and conceptual how-to of strictly "objectivist" quantitative research, myriad books on research design in social science put previous generations' manuals to shame. And yet, simultaneously, such research has been subjected to ongoing, relentless attack for what is seen as its tendency to distort and reduce human social life—to sacrifice understanding for a form of mathematical precision that is, in the end, illusory. These arguments are, by now, exceedingly well known.

Thus this book is not another attack on positivism, either in the substance of its text or in the goals that it outlines for how we use theory in research. Rather, it is a reconsideration of two fundamental

7. Consider how Wesley Salmon's work extending the analytic tradition in the philosophy of science has moved beyond the logical positivists' initial aversion to theorizing causality outside Humean confines, and thus brought theories of causality and (neopositivist) theories of scientific explanation together. Indeed, the entire conversation between Salmon and his critics reveals how the analytic philosophy of science has had its own positivist/postpositivist conversation. See Wesley Salmon, *Scientific Explanation and the Causal Structure of the World* (Princeton: Princeton University Press, 1984), and Wesley Salmon, *Causality and Explanation* (New York: Oxford University Press, 1998).

and interrelated questions: how do, and how should, theory and evidence interact? For there is much objection, in postpositivism, to the positivist answer to these questions (in short, that theory generates hypotheses and evidences tests them), but little agreement as to how this intersection should happen outside the positivist mold.[8] What is this so-called dialogue between theory and evidence? How are we to construct and use theory if we are not formulating hypotheses? This is the curiosity that led to this book: I want to know how nonpositivist research works, and to build a constructive theory of knowledge claims made by nonpositivists. To do this, I have constructed a text that works at the intersection of practice and prescription: in-depth textual analysis of actual truth claims in social research is combined with epistemological reflection.

I call the different ways of bringing theory and evidence together "epistemic modes." The term is intended to indicate the relative autonomy of these modes from substantive commitments to theoretical programs, research agendas, or specific methods. Epistemic modes dictate the *conceptual* method by which theory is brought into contact with evidence, structure the expectations about what such contact can accomplish, and provide more or less well-formed criteria of validity that are used to evaluate the knowledge that is thereby produced. Epistemic modes can also be articulated in abstract argumentation about the possibilities and limits of social knowledge, and can be interrogated about their premises. But they do not map neatly onto substantive research programs, or onto any particular intellectual history of social theory or any particular account of paradigms of social research.[9]

Thus, while the epistemic modes I examine—realist, normative, and interpretive—have elective affinities with great thinkers and grand traditions of social analysis (affinities some readers will immediately recognize, and which I discuss throughout the text and especially

8. Isaac Ariail Reed, "Epistemology Contextualized: Social-Scientific Knowledge in a Postpositivist Era," *Sociological Theory* 28, no. 1 (2010).

9. There is one work, however, whose mapping of social thought and social research seems particularly relevant to this text. That is John R. Hall, *Cultures of Inquiry: From Epistemology to Discourse in Sociohistorical Research* (Cambridge: Cambridge University Press, 1999). Certainly this book is written in a similar interpretive spirit to Hall's project and shares some of its arguments, as will become clear. I argue herein, however, for a return to epistemology. I do not see this as incommensurate with Hall's map per se, but rather as a theoretical project for which Hall's map of sociohistorical investigation reveals the need, or calls forth.

in the footnotes), their truth and utility as terms for understanding what is going on when a researcher constructs a knowledge claim stand or fall with what makes up the core of each chapter in the book: the analysis of, and reflection upon, actual truth claims made in the human sciences. Here I briefly introduce the three epistemic modes that I examine.

III

In the realist epistemic mode (chapter 2), theory points to the fundamental forces and relations of social life that lie beneath the surface phenomena that we observe, narrate, experience, and/or measure. Thus when the investigator uses theory, what she does is connect an underlying social reality to the social phenomena or outcomes that she desires to explain. The entities referred to by theory give order to her data and a causal force to her conclusions. Revolutions are explained by the fundamental processes that bring them about; conversations and interactions, in which identities are established and dissolved, are explained by the underlying tendencies of human cognition; moves in a marriage market are explained in terms of the ways in which individuals maximize utility; the emergence of a cultural phenomenon, such as *Star Wars*, is explained by the way in which it hews to the fundamental binaries that structure the human mind.

Realism reignites the possibility that social science, post-Kuhn, is still an embodiment of a generalized scientific rationality. That rationality, however, is defined and guaranteed by the way in which social theory directly references social reality, revealing the social forces that structure the world. The core conceptual problem of realism, then, is this: how can the efforts of the experimental scientific laboratory be reconfigured and transformed for the science of society and history? The opening text of the contemporary critical realist intellectual movement, Roy Bhaskar's *A Realist Theory of Science*, begins with a philosophical analysis of what must be true about the world if natural scientific experiments are intelligible and rational.[10] Bhaskar's next book, perhaps even more important for that movement, considers how social science can and cannot imitate the logic of natural science that he originally derived from the analysis of experi-

10. Roy Bhaskar, *A Realist Theory of Science* (New York: Verso, 2008), chap. 1, esp. 23–26.

ment.[11] The problem, of course, is the way humans bring a certain "concept-dependence" to social reality, which is a nice way of saying that subjectivity messes everything up. Human subjects, moreover, have a rather irritating tendency to aspire to ideals, be motivated by outrageously unrealistic ideas, and pass judgment on each other. This issue—that human social life is full not only of concepts but of judgments—is what brings the argument of this book to the second epistemic mode I consider.

In the normative epistemic mode (chapter 3), theory is what enables research to be a dialogue between investigator and investigated—between an ethnographer and her subjects, between a historian and the lives he recreates, between a critic and the text she reconsiders and reframes. Theory brings to bear the critical force of well-articulated utopia upon the empirical world, but in doing so, it brings together the intellectual's political philosophies with the utopian capacities immanent in social life as lived and experienced. In normative social knowledge, then, two modes of consciousness come to inform each other, and thus theories of the good get better—while at the same time striving for some sort of practical effect. The possibilities for resisting a hegemonic cultural formation are revealed; the nascent democratic instincts of volunteers are articulated and made sharper; the deeply pathological implications of a seemingly liberatory set of cultural practices are brought to light. And thus the conversation about the good and the should is expanded.

What normative research does is reconfigure the terrain of normative argument by producing interpretations of actual social life. Ideals for a better social order are salvaged from conversations in coffee shops, solidaristic town hall meetings, anti-imperial campaigns, and so on. Visions of dystopia also anchor normative research, sometimes in the genre of tragic irony: the normative projects of humanist reformers are revealed to be norming projects in the service of a new format of domination (for example). But the core conceptual problem, for normativism, is how this operation of critique, which *is* grounded in actuality and fact, can or cannot be grounded in a more explanatorily powerful use of theory. A town hall meeting identifies a problem, but how can the solution be tested, if there is no laboratory? Normativism, in other words, either points back to realism, or toward a different

11. Roy Bhaskar, *The Possibility of Naturalism: A Philosophical Critique of the Contemporary Human Sciences*, 3rd ed. (New York: Routledge, 1998).

way to ground truth claims in social research. And it is to discerning what this "different way" could be that the latter part of this book is dedicated, in its study of interpretive social knowledge.

In what I call the interpretive epistemic mode (chapter 4), the primary focus of the investigator is on the arrangements of signification and representation, the layers of social meaning, that shape human experience. The investigator reconstructs the meaningful context of social action, and to do so she draws upon a plurality of theoretical abstractions; these different theoretical tools need not—pace realism—add up to a coherent, general, and referential theory of social reality in the abstract. Rather, the investigator combines bits of theory with bits of evidence, and then these theory-fact pairs are brought together into a meaningful whole. This meaningful whole is the deep interpretation that the investigator constructs, and it gives coherence to her case. Cockfights are reinterpreted as a performance of status, masculinity, and what it means to be human; a revolution is analyzed in terms of how the advance guard constructed, and propagated, a worldview; the actions of a whole cohort of politicians or scientists is traced back to a formative experience and the narrative construction of collective identity that emerged from it.

Interpretive social research, I argue, must push beyond the surface reports of actors and the immediate meanings available in the investigator's evidence to grasp some deeper set of meanings that inhere in the action under study. This is what the use of theory allows the hermeneutically sensitive researcher to do. But even deep interpretations are typically constructed—by friends and foes alike—as ***interpretations and not explanations.*** Overcoming this problem is the core conceptual difficulty for the interpretive epistemic mode. Consider, very briefly, an example.

An interpretivist sets out study the Salem Witch Trials. In his interpretation, he attempts to grasp the meaningful world of Puritan life and, in particular, how witches and witchcraft played an emotionally charged role in the Puritan social imaginary, encoding a socially powerful metaphysics of God, sex, and patriarchy.[12] What sort of knowledge claim is this interpretation? The point, with Salem at least, is that this metaphysics was *threatened* in 1692 by the possibility of witches meddling with the cosmos, thus turning the

12. Isaac Reed, "Why Salem Made Sense: Gender, Culture, and Puritan Persecution of Witchcraft," *Cultural Sociology* 1, no. 2 (2007): 209–34.

trials into a countrywide crisis, ending in the murder of nineteen men and women. Who felt threatened by the witches? What did fear motivate those people to do, and what social processes were they able to trigger to get done what they were certain needed to be done? What were the unintended effects of these developments? These are causal, explanatory questions, and they force us to consider whether or not, and if so how, interpretations of social meaning can possess explanatory torque.

In other words, if realism derives from the logic of the lab, and normativism from the logic of the democratic meeting or social movement, interpretivism derives from the logic of reading and disputing different readings of a text,[13] which raises the question—reading for what? How do symbols enter the social world, and have an effect on social action—an effect, moreover, that the investigator can comprehend and communicate by building an explanation? The idea of interpretive explanation is the subject of chapter 5. In it, I continue my attempt to recast the interpretive way of making social knowledge claims. Meaning-centered research in the human sciences, I argue, is not only theory-intensive (chapter 4) but also constructs causal explanations, albeit in a way that departs from the typical ways of thinking about social causality. By revealing the way social meanings act as *forming*, as opposed to *forcing*, causes, the interpretive epistemic mode can offer a synthetic approach to social knowledge, and enable the researcher to build social explanations and deliver social critique.

IV

These reconstructions of epistemic modes are intended to be an intervention in, and a symptom of, what I view as a new epistemological era for social research—the era after the posts. After debates about culture, interpretation, and the linguistic turn; after innovative

13. The issue is how much reading a text can be fruitfully compared to analyzing social action. Ultimately, in chapters 4 and 5, I move toward an image of the interpretive social researcher as more akin to a theater critic than a reader of texts. However, the whole question of action and text is one of the key debates of the cultural turn, which opens up many of the questions that this book attempts to address. The classic meditation on text and social action is Paul Ricoeur, "The Model of the Text: Meaningful Action Considered as a Text," *Social Research* 38 (1971). See also Susan Hekman, "Action as a Text: Gadamer's Hermeneutics and the Social Scientific Analysis of Action," *Journal for the Theory of Social Behavior* 14, no. 3 (1984).

recastings of standpoint theory and the politics of knowledge; after extended discussions of power/knowledge, interpellation, and subject production; after all this, what is the producer of social knowledge to do? Is it possible to believe a great deal of what is written and said in postpositivist social theory to be true, and yet to proceed with the goal of explaining social action? I think that it is, and this possibility is what I intend my account of social knowledge to render visible.

Yet if this book is a symptom of a specific epistemic moment, and the product of a certain generational experience—of being trained in social theory long after the fiercest battles over "postmodernism" had burned bright—its sympathetic engagements and reconstructions are less aimed at the august history of social theory and philosophy, and more at the inner workings of texts that have, often very successfully, attempted to say something about the world—or at least some small piece of it. For, when social theory is presented in the form of competing schools, when research programs are assessed for their fecundity, or when the basic traditions of philosophical thought about social science are set out, the result is often exigetically honest but repetitive. It is also bewildering. Not only are there a plurality of theoretical positions and research programs, but every such program of necessity involves combinations of methodological tendencies, theoretical presuppositions, and political implications or valences—along with answers to the more explicitly epistemological questions considered here. When one includes, furthermore, the codified empirical claims that often belong (or are seen to belong) to this or that research program, the result is a sprawling catalogue or encyclopedia of what are, ultimately, different subject positions in a complex and dynamic discourse.

Training in social theory involves learning how to map this discourse in useful ways, and to pay close attention to the way in which theoretical discourses encode their own historical conditions of production. Yet these maps, as they become their own extended apparatus of intersecting denotations and connotations, can be exhausting. At a certain point in my own intellectual biography, I came to view this exhaustion about mapping the field of social theory to be connected to a different problem—the problem of the metatheoretical frame within which one makes strong, empirically responsible, theoretically informed knowledge claims in social research itself. For both myself and the historians, anthropologists, sociologists, and scholars of communication I trained with, our metatheoretical frames were much more precise in their negative aspects. We did not have an integrated Marxist theoretical structure to contain and connect social explanation, political judgment, and the interpretation of cultures. We did not have the calm and settled scientific frame of variables and their various effects, or even the frame of a truly general sociological theory (almost everyone I trained with was, in a rather disturbingly certain way, a "postpositivist"). We did not have the warrant to simply head out into the world (or into the archives) to pursue value-free social research. I interrogated my friends, colleagues, and teachers on the matter. We all knew for sure what we were not. We were not positivists, not Marxists, not "reductionists," and so on and so forth. But what was the negation of the negation? What were we?

I have come to view this question as essential, and as answerable only in an epistemological register. That register must resist the twin temptations of formal logic, permanently distant from the messiness of social investigation, and the reductive sociology of knowledge, insensitive to how internal and impersonal imperatives, combined with informal argumentation and scholarly communication, can make communities of inquiry more than just clubs or networks.[14] A theory of social knowledge should, instead, be built through critical reflection upon what it is that researchers do when they call on social theory to help them comprehend their evidence. That, at least, is the starting point for chapter 1.

14. For the classic criticism of formal logic as distant from the sorts of argument that carry weight in different areas of inquiry, see Stephen Toulmin, *The Uses of Argument* (New York: Cambridge University Press, 2003). For a critique of how strong programs in the sociology of science, and more broadly the sociology of knowledge, themselves reify social structure in a contradictory way, see James Bohman, *New Philosophy of Social Science* (Cambridge, MA: MIT Press, 1993), 40–49.

Chapter One

Knowledge

I

The construction of social knowledge occurs at the intersection of two meaning-systems, one of theory and one of fact. Let us begin, briefly, with the latter.

The problems that surround what Robert Merton called "establishing the phenomenon"[1] have long been the subject of methodological disputation in social research. Methodology is a reflection on the efficacy of our various techniques for establishing facts—survey data and in-depth interviewing, quantitative versus qualitative approaches to the historical archive, and so on. All of these methodologies (and the disputes about them) are, however, confronted by the problem that, in the case of human affairs, many of the most essential facts of the matter—the *social* facts—are not immediately observable. Rather, they are observable through what Émile Durkheim called their "individual manifestations."[2]

1. Robert K. Merton, "Three Fragments from a Sociologist's Notebooks: Establishing the Phenomenon, Specified Ignorance and Strategic Research Materials," *Annual Review of Sociology* 13 (1987).

2. Émile Durkheim, *Suicide: A Study in Sociology* (New York: Free Press, 1966), 277.

Why is this the case? Certainly much of what human beings who live in societies ***do*** is observable, recordable, etc. And there are many behaviors that we do not observe or record directly that we can, nonetheless, be fairly sure happened. It is not our spatial or temporal distance from social facts that makes them a difficult category. It is that reporting on the carryings on of human beings requires a reference to the meaning of their actions, in a very minimal yet fundamental way. The telling of the facts of the matter, in human affairs, already involves a structure of meaning and intention, and, therefore, of inference on the part of the investigator toward aspects of life that are not visible, and never were nor will be visible. Social facts understood in this manner can never be fully stated in protocol sentences that are verifiable by literal observation, but must be inferred and understood in a dialogue about what is happening or has happened, at a certain time, in a certain space, in a given society.

For example, when one states that, in 1692, after examination by the village doctor, it was determined by a set of adults in Salem Village, Massachusetts, and its environs that the fits and screams of "afflicted" girls were due to their being under an "evil hand," one is stating a rather uncontroversial fact. We know this happened—that these adults made this determination. But understanding this fact already involves understanding the possible meanings for the people of seventeenth-century Massachusetts of the physically observable behavior of the girls, the meaning of the utterance "evil hand," the meaning of the term "doctor," and the expectations that other people had of doctors, and so on. It is in this way that social facts are "thick."

Dispute already reigns here. However, the "thickness" of human facts[3]—that is, the way in which they already contain inferences to

3. Concerning the gathering and interpretation of evidence in the human sciences, Carlo Ginzburg writes that "It is one thing to analyze footprints, stars, feces, sputum, corneas, pulsations, snow covered fields, or cigarette ashes; it is quite another to examine handwriting or paintings or conversation. There is a basic difference between nature, inanimate and living, and culture—certainly greater than the infinitely more superficial and mutable differences that exist between individual disciplines." Ginzburg constructs an extended argument that the "evidential paradigm" in the human sciences requires specific attention to the semiotics of facts. I agree. In particular, I agree with Ginzburg's embrace of an anthropocentric approach to evidence in the human sciences, and thus his idea that there is a commonality in the way in which detective work, art history and painting attribution, and psychoanalysis look closely at minute traces that reveal the characteristics of a in individual, action, or historical moment. In this book, however, I take a cue from a comment at the end of Ginzburg's essay

meanings that are, technically speaking, invisible—is but one aspect of a much larger problem of interpretation in social research. For, while establishing the phenomenon may be the most important and most difficult task a social researcher faces, it is neither the task that produces the most controversy in social science nor the final step in the production of social knowledge. For, as soon as we have established the phenomenon—or, some would say, thickly described it—then we ask the next question: how are we to understand it?

In other words, it is the responsibility of the social researcher not only to report the facts,[4] but to propose a deeper or broader comprehension of them. When investigators attempt to do this, we reach for our theories. We do this because we need some way of comprehending what is, to speak colloquially, "underneath" the facts. We want to know what generates them, determines them, what their consequences are, how we should think about them politically, what their connection to the here and now is, and so on. To do this, it is very seldom enough to continue to gather more facts, no matter how

---

"Clues: Roots of an Evidential Paradigm." There, he writes that "[t]hough pretentions to systematic knowledge may appear more and more far-fetched, the idea of totality does not necessarily need to be abandoned. On the contrary, the existence of a deeply rooted relationship that explains superficial phenomena is confirmed the very moment it is stated that direct knowledge of such a connection is not possible. Though reality may seem to be opaque, there are privileged zones—signs, clues—which allow us to penetrate it." Ginzburg writes that this idea is the "crux of the conjectural or semiotic paradigm." What this indicates to me is the need to recognize not only the way in which evidential reasoning relies upon an "anthropocentric" view of the human sciences, but also how the success of those sciences depends upon the use of social theory to penetrate the clues that have been gathered, so as to generate deep interpretations of sociohistorical episodes. After all, to follow Ginzburg's argument about the emergence of the evidential paradigm in the work of Sigmund Freud, Arthur Conan Doyle, and Giovanni Morelli, all three may have been interested in the clues left unintentionally behind by humans, but their *theories* of what drives individuals to do this, and of the relationship between the motives of individuals and larger forces and forms of social life, are rather different. Carlo Ginzburg, *Clues, Myths, and the Historical Method* (Baltimore: Johns Hopkins University Press, 1986), 118, 123.

4. Here I use the term "report" in direct reference to W. G. Runciman's concept of *reportage*. In a series of theoretical arguments beginning with a critique of Max Weber's epistemology, Runciman has developed the position that interpretation is a problem for the human sciences at the level of description, but not at the level of explanation. I disagree, and the argument of this book runs directly counter to Runciman's proposed solution to the problem of interpretation and social knowledge. See W. G. Runciman, *A Critique of Max Weber's Philosophy of Social Science* (New York: Cambridge University Press, 1972), and W. G. Runciman, *A Treatise on Social Theory*, 3 vols. (New York: Cambridge University Press, 1983). I take up the problem of interpretation and explanation explicitly in chapter 5.

thickly we comprehend them and present them to our colleagues. We need theory to help us explain and evaluate social life.

Our theories are, by their very nature, meaningful human constructions. They exist primarily in the heads of investigators and the pages of their books and journals. Sometimes they consist of a vast, abstract architecture of interrelated and highly consistent terms, sometimes they attempt to specify in the abstract a single mechanism, sometimes they propose a new way to think about something we all already think about, such as democracy. But the world of social theory is meaningful in the basic human sense of providing a coherent model for and model of the (social) world. The hope is that this meaningful world is also a useful one, so that our attempts to develop a deeper understanding of social phenomena are sometimes successful.

Our facts are thus a set of meanings, and our theories are a set of meanings. When we bring theories and facts together, then, we are bringing two meaning-full worlds, or meaning-systems, together. To a certain degree, of course, our theories may indeed influence our use of evidence to construct the facts, or our emphasis on different facts. But this happens less than we think, and at the level of bare social facts—the level of understanding required to *report what happened*—we quite often can achieve a good deal of consensus, despite our theoretical, or even epistemological, differences. (This is not always the case, and I will consider an example of a disputation over facts below.) Rather, the influence of theory on our knowledge claims most often comes in a much more conscious and controlled form—when we deliberately bring terms foreign to our subjects of study (e.g., "mode of production," "episteme," "ideological state apparatus," "habitus") to bear on our facts, in an effort to grasp some essential aspect of social life that is not given up easily by the facts.

So, by bringing our theoretical terms to bear on what happened at the Salem Witch Trials, we might come to understand that rather horrendous set of actions as an expression of the economic transformation of early America and the politico-economic interests of the parties involved. Or we might grasp it as one of the last violent episodes in the vast formation of early modern European patriarchy, in which the inner resentments and fears of men found their grisly public resolution. Or we might understand Salem as an early expression of American populism, a willingness of some actors, some of the time, to speak outside of the legal structures established by elites, whatever the risks—and thus as a story that should be recuperated by those interested in the establishment of a more democratic United States today. Each of these proposals gains in power what it loses in obviousness, and each incorporates into its interpretation the basic reports of what happened at Salem. The results of this incorporation are very different, however, and that is what makes them exciting and valuable.[5]

II

To say that theory and fact are both meaning-systems is not to say that they are meaning-systems that work in exactly the same manner. Indeed, the intellectual disciplines dedicated to the study of meaning—hermeneutics and semiotics—are flush with typologies, dichotomies, and elaborate theoretical artifices all designed to work out the different ways in which language—or, more generally, signification—can work in its various social contexts. And needless to say there are surely many ways of gathering evidence and thus producing factual reports on what happened in social life, and many genres of theoretical exploration and imagination. But let us stick to the basics, at least at first. What is the difference between theory and fact as meaning-systems?

I think the central difference is that in the meaning-system of fact, we expect evidence to function *referentially or indexically* when indicating what happened, and in the meaning-system of theory, we expect theoretical terms to function *relationally or conceptually.* Some evidence is directly indexical—we think of it as a trace of a physical act that happened at a certain point in time and space.[6] But,

5. These different sorts of interpretations crisscross the literature on Salem and on early modern witchcraft. See in particular Paul Boyer and Stephen Nissenbaum, *Salem Possessed: The Social Origins of Witchcraft* (Cambridge, MA: Harvard University Press, 1974); Nancy Ruttenburg, *Democratic Personality: Popular Voice and the Trial of American Authorship* (Stanford: Stanford University Press, 1998); Evelyn Heinemann, *Witches: A Psychoanalytic Exploration of the Killing of Women* (London: Free Association, 2000). For a summary of the scholarly literature on witch hunts and its relationship to feminist concerns, see Elspeth Whitney, "International Trends: The Witch 'She'/the Historian 'He': Gender and the Historiography of the European Witch-Hunts," *Journal of Women's History* 7, no. 3 (1995).

6. Peirce writes that "an index stands for its object by virtue of a real connection with it or because it forces the mind to attend to that object" (Charles S. Peirce, "Of Reasoning in General," in *The Essential Peirce: Selected Philosophical Writings*, vol. 1 [Bloomington: Indiana University Press, 1998]: 11–26, 14), and Roy Rappaport ex-

as discussed above, most of the reality we are busy studying in the human sciences is not reducible to its biophysical supports. Thus it is safer to say that we expect the gathering, organizing, and presenting of evidence, as an active and dynamic meaning-system, to serve a primarily referential function—even if what it references is not (or is not only) a material object or biological person. In the language game of fact, there are myriad evidential signs—sentences, photographs, quotations, assertions, graphs, tables, charts—and we expect these signifiers to express a certain content that *is or was in the social world.* This means that meaningful facts result from the connection of evidential signs to a ground that emerges, from research, as the object of investigation—the selected set of social actions that happened. Evidential signs, colligated together, connect the sociological investigator, and the people who read her text, to a set of social actions that are the ground of factual signification (see fig. 1).[7]

The English locutions "evidence for" and "theory of" hint at how differently theoretical meaning works. In theory, meaning develops to a great degree by the ways in which contrasts between expressions—e.g., "forces of production" and "relations of production"—create conceptual contrasts in the minds of researchers. This is not to say that those concepts cannot, in turn, reference something else, perhaps something in the world. But if they do (and this book is, in part, an effort to figure out what, if anything, theory references) it is surely reasonable to point out that we do not expect theory to reference the social world in the same concrete manner that we expect evidence to reference the social world. Indeed, the *whole point* of theory is to be abstract and conceptual. The necessary result of this is that what theory "references," first and foremost, is not really a referent at all

plains that "A true index is a sign that is either an effect of, or an aspect of, or a part of its object" (Roy A. Rappaport, *Ritual and Religion in the Making of Humanity*, Cambridge Studies in Social and Cultural Anthropology [Cambridge: Cambridge University Press, 1999], 63).

7. As I explain below, I think that all signs function both referentially and relationally, and thus the difference between the tendencies of evidential signs and theoretical signs is a matter of degree, not a strict distinction. To use Peircian language, most signs have elements of the symbolic, the indexical, and the iconic (and especially the first two), and thus the difference between theory and fact is the tendency of the latter to foreground the indexical dimension of signification, and the former to foreground the symbolic dimension. (As Rappaport comments, "The terms 'index,' 'icon,' and 'symbol' should be taken to be possible aspects of signs rather than labels for necessarily separate and distinct signs." Rappaport, *Ritual and Religion in the Making of Humanity*, 66).

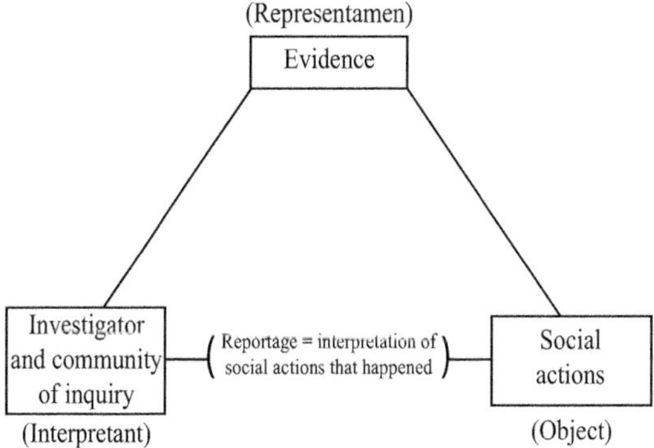

Figure 1: The factual sign

in the concrete sense of ***meaningful social actions that actually happened***. Rather, the immediate reference of theoretical expressions is, as far as I can tell, (1) other theoretical expressions and (2) imagined societies, social actions, and social relations whose primary existence is in researchers' heads.

This may seem a strange thing to say, but anyone who has recently had the experience of being initiated into a group of theoretically informed social researchers (or, even worse, into a group of social theorists) probably has an intuitive sense of its truth. The disputations of the early and the late Wittgenstein aside, if there is one language you *cannot* learn by asking, at each turn in the conversation, "can you point to what that word refers to?" it is the language of social theory. This does not, however, make theory irrelevant to or useless for understanding social reality. Quite the opposite is the case. It is precisely because theory is abstract that it enables analysis of facts, and, ultimately, the construction of knowledge. Furthermore, this distinction between theory and evidence is relative; there are relational aspects of evidence as a language, and referential aspects of theory as a language.[8] As an example of the former, consider how gender history must, even at its most empirical and evidential, use the binary of male/female as source of meaning. As an example of the latter, think

8. For an explanation from the philosophy of science for how the theory/data distinction can function as a matter of degree, see Mary Hesse, "The Hunt for Scientific Reason," *PSA: Proceedings of the Biennial Meeting of the Philosophy of Science Association* 2 (1980).

of the referential importance of Speenhamland for Polanyi's abstract theories of economy and society. Here reference to a set of quite actual processes enabled the development of highly abstract definitions and elaborations of the historical prerequisites for the institutionalization of a "market society"—a theoretical term understood in relation to the abstractions of Marx, Weber, and others.

Still, the point holds, especially when push comes to shove: the most effective way to criticize another researcher's evidence is to suggest that it fails to accurately represent the phenomenon it claims to represent—that it is referentially incorrect; theory, when it is taken to task on its own, separate from any evidence, can be devastated if the critic can show conceptual incoherence. However, perhaps more frequent than either of these criticisms is the critique of a social knowledge claim as suffering from a *disjunction* between theory and evidence: the evidence does not bear out the theory, the theory does not fit the evidence, this is the wrong theory to use to interpret this evidence, etc. This sort of response, by an audience, to a failed knowledge claim gives us a clue as to what happens when theory and evidence do come together successfully.

III

In most of its contacts with actual happenings in the social world (represented by evidence), theory is *metacommentary*. It proposes to rethink, reframe, and recast facts that have already been established; it proposes to set up a research question to be investigated; it hypothesizes about a cause whose traces can be either measured quantitatively, confirmed comparatively, or perhaps verified via testimony and interview; it creates the conditions for critique by denaturalizing the inevitable, reopening the possible, and exhorting for the radically democratic. All of these functions are invaluable, but they are also supervenient upon the existence of referential evidence in a well-colligated meaning-system of fact. In this format, the sign-system of theory combines with the sign-system of fact in an obvious way: facts provide an "example of" a theory, theory provides "a new way to view" the facts.

The importance of these functions of theory should not be underestimated. However, they refer to a kind of discourse in which the difference between theory and fact remains obvious because the two meaning-systems remain to some degree in disjunction. The stakes are higher when the meanings of theory and the meanings of fact mix in a more extensive and effective manner to produce the social knowledge claims that I will call *maximal interpretations.* In maximal interpretations, theory and fact articulate in such a way that the referential functions of evidence and the relational functions of theory are subsumed under a deeper understanding. No longer is evidence used merely to shore up a factual "example" of a theoretical expression. Rather, the signs of evidence become themselves intertwined with the signs of theory, such that both come to express a deeper social force, a longstanding democratic imperative, or an underlying discursive formation. They become part of a maximal interpretation.[9]

In other words, while "establishing the phenomenon" requires interpretation at the level of evidence and method—the arrangement of evidential signs—such work tends toward one end of a spectrum that runs from *minimal* to *maximal* interpretation. At the minimal end of the spectrum, the frequency of theoretical terms is slight (or . . . minimal), and the claims tend to be less controversial—though they can, on rare occasions, be startlingly new. The maximal end of the spectrum involves statements that mix, in a consistent and deep way, theoretical and evidential signification, in an effort to produce a powerful comprehension of the matter at hand. Here is a minimal interpretation: 'On the night of August 4, 1789, feudal privileges in France were abolished.' Here is a maximal interpretation: ' The French Revolution was a social revolution with political consequences.'

To believe the first statement to be true, one has to understand the meaning of certain basic terms (most notably 'feudal privileges'),

9. The concept of maximal interpretation could be compared to (and indeed draws inspiration from) Arthur C. Danto's account of "deep interpretation," and in particular his article of that name from 1981. However, while Danto works to situate and comprehend a format of "deep interpretation" that is quite distinct from the "routine acceptance of the term," and even compares it to the "divination anciently practiced by the Greeks," I attempt to use the distinction between minimal and maximal interpretation as more of a matter of degree, which enables me to comprehend the sorts of truth claims actually made in texts written by social researchers. Still, Danto makes absolutely clear something essential to understanding maximal interpretations, namely that "the distinction between depth and surface cuts at right angles across the philosophically more commonplace distinction between inner and outer." It is precisely because the distinction between minimal and maximal interpretation cuts across the distinction between inner and outer (or "subjective" and "objective") that I can distinguish between maximal interpretations that pay a great deal of attention to subjectivity and meaning, and those that pay less attention to these "inner" phenomena. But this should become clear in my discussion of Marx below. See Arthur C. Danto, "Deep Interpretation," *Journal of Philosophy* 78, no. 11 (1981): 691, 695, 694.

and one has to agree that a series of actions took place at a specific time and place that can be adequately described as the 'abolition' of feudal privileges (and that that place can be adequately described as something called 'France'). This can, of course, be disputed in a variety of ways, including looking empirically into what demands aristocrats still made on the peasants who worked on their land after August 4, 1789, and whether these demands were fulfilled. Still, this statement can inspire a certain degree of agreement, primarily because of its status as a relatively minimal interpretation—there is nothing in the statement to suggest *why* feudal privileges were abolished, or *what it meant* to the future of France that they were abolished.[10] No social research can exist without minimal interpretations, but very few works in the human sciences limit themselves to them, and even those have to choose some statements over others. Minimal interpretation is necessary but not sufficient for powerful social research.

To believe the second statement to be true, one has to understand that the term "social revolution" is given meaning partially by the language of social theory, and in particular one must understand the contrast between 'social' and 'political' as a fundamental theoretical disagreement about the causes and consequences of social action in many times and places. Furthermore, to believe the second statement one has to agree that all sorts of statements of the first kind (i.e., that feudal privileges were abolished, that a national assembly was constituted, that the army began taking directions from the new government) have their *explanation* in the underlying social conflict between the bourgeoisie and the aristocracy in France. And here social scientists dip their pens in the venom of polemic; if we know one thing from the scholarship on the French Revolution from the last century, it is that the disagreements about explanations of the Revolution always outrun the disagreements about its facts.

Maximal interpretations, then, are always organizing, explaining, judging—in a word, interpreting—minimal interpretations, drawing themselves into relationship with the facts, but also going "beyond"

10. I am aware that there are debates around the term 'feudalism' that could be characterized as involving the sorts of theoretically informed interpretive disputes that characterize maximal interpretations (see, e.g., Elizabeth A. R. Brown's classic, "The Tyranny of a Construct: Feudalism and Historians of Medieval Europe," *American Historical Review* 79 [1974]). However, particularly in the context of debates about the French revolution, I think the phrase 'feudal privileges in France' can be said to have a relatively clear set of manifest historical referents.

the facts. This is not to say that, given a maximal interpretation, one cannot go out in search of minimal interpretations that support it. Undoubtedly one can. It is only to say that, in engaging these maximal interpretations, we are relying on a language that is *not only* the language of fact—it is the language of theory fused with the language of fact to produce the social knowledge that we tend to value highly.[11]

IV

Maximal interpretations result from bringing theory together with minimal interpretations. They are what we want theory to get us to—an explanation or evaluation of the phenomenon at hand, and perhaps a proposal for explaining other, as yet unexplored, cases, outcomes, events, etc. And so theoretical differences become more and more relevant as we move up the spectrum from minimal to maximal interpretation. Consider an example.

In the 1990s, an academic conflagration swept through American anthropology concerning what happened in Hawai'i in 1778 and 1779.[12] Was Captain James Cook received by the Hawai'ians as the god Lono? And why did several Hawai'ians kill Cook when he and his

11. Thus the spectrum of minimal to maximal interpretation could be described as an attempt to capture the degree of theory-ladenness of truth claims. In maximal interpretations, then, one uses a relatively greater amount of abstract terms that *could* be combined conceptually ("in theory") but which are, in the maximal interpretation, articulated with the minimal interpretations that describe, in a more indexical way, people's behaviors. The result of this articulation is an *in-depth* truth claim about social life. This definition of theory-ladenness and its implications for the opposition of minimal to maximal interpretation emerged in a conversation with Mayer Zald about the issue.

12. Gananath Obeyesekere, *The Apotheosis of Captain Cook: European Mythmaking in the Pacific* (Princeton and Honolulu: Princeton University Press and Bishop Museum Press, 1992). Marshall Sahlins, *How "Natives" Think: About Captain Cook, for Example* (Chicago: University of Chicago Press, 1995). For reviews of the dispute, see Ian Hacking's chapter "The End of Captain Cook," in *The Social Construction of What?* (Cambridge, MA: Harvard University Press, 1999), and Robert Borofsky, "Cook, Lono, Obeyesekere, and Sahlins," *Current Antrhopology* 38, no. 2 (1997). The shorter reviews of Obeyesekere's and Sahlins's books are numerous, but for a brief and strongly pro-Sahlins review, see David R. Stoddart, "Captain Cook and How We Understand Him," *Geographical Review* 87, no. 4 (1997). For a more ironic account of the continuing battles over Cook's memory, see Greg Dening, "Review," *William and Mary Quarterly* 54, no. 1 (1997). Obeyesekere's original article is indispensable for understanding the precise nature of his objections; see Gananath Obeyesekere, "'British Cannibals': Contemplation of an Event in the Death and Resurrection of James Cook, Explorer," *Critical Inquiry* 18, no. 4 (1992).

sailors, due to a broken mast, returned to the island of Kealakekua Bay shortly after they left it? Finally, what is the source of insight or obliviousness that aids or hinders anthropologists who attempt to answer these questions? In this controversy, minimal interpretations about what happened in Hawai'i all those years ago were made controversial, but that was not the end of the story. The dispute invoked and relied upon the meanings of theory, and thus quickly became a dispute about maximal interpretations, which is to say, a polemic about why what happened happened and what its significance is for "us."[13]

"How did the Hawai'ians receive Cook?" is a question that can be answered, initially at least, minimally. There is a great deal of evidence that suggests that they referred to him as "akua"—sometimes translated as "god." But how the Hawai'ians related to "gods" is itself a question that has to be established through interpretation and inference—calling a person a "god" is a social fact in this case, and indeed, debates over the translation of "akua" tend to center on whether the social organization that results from recognition of an akua is such that the better translation might be "chief." Marshall Sahlins had been questioned on this matter before Ganneth Obeyesekere wrote *The Apotheosis of Captain Cook*,[14] and he had responded then, as he did in his reply to Obeyesekere, with a wealth of evidence—drawn from many shipmen's journals—concerning the terms the Hawai'ians used when they received Cook, what these terms meant in that context, and so on.[15] In other words, he responded to some of the initial criticisms of his work on Hawai'i by attempting to solidify his minimal interpretation of the case.

But whether, ultimately, the term "akua" should be translated in English as "god" or "chief," or understood as meaning something in between, the issue was not to be left there. Indeed, the battles over Cook in Hawai'i had never been limited to the facts—in 1982

13. What constitutes the "us" as a community of inquiry dedicated to comprehending social behavior and human history is precisely what much careful postcolonial theory has rendered problematic. Conflicts over the authors and audiences of scholarly work, as well as what sorts of knowledge they take for granted, are one of the underlying tensions sublimated into the discursive battles of social theory, in my view. See Dipesh Chakrabarty, *Provincializing Europe: Postcolonial Thought and Historical Difference* (Princeton: Princeton University Press, 2000).

14. Jonathan Friedman, "Captain Cook, Culture, and the World System," *Journal of Pacific History* 20 (1985).

15. Marshall Sahlins, "Captain Cook at Hawaii," *Journal of the Polyneisan Society* 98 (1989).

Greg Dening, and in 1988 Jonathan Friedman, challenged Sahlins's explanation of why the Hawai'ians did what they did[16]—and, with Obeyesekere's book, the debate quickly moved beyond what could be minimally established by, and argued about, using the evidence. And this makes sense: when it comes to the relationship of Hawai'i to the British Empire at the end of the eighteenth century, we do not just want to know a small tidbit of what happened during that time. We do not just want to know *that* the Hawai'ians killed Cook, we also want to know *why* they killed him, and furthermore, what this violent action means to us today. (For example: was it a valiant adumbration of the anticolonial revolutions of the twentieth century?) These "maximal" questions cannot be answered by the evidence alone, though they can never leave the evidence behind. Theory must be mobilized, and a fusion of theory and fact must be attempted by bringing together theoretical signifiers with evidential ones, in search of a new interpretation. In this case, two different theoretical schemas became intertwined with the evidence and thus confronted each other, as it were, on the beach in Hawai'i: Marshall Sahlins's theories of culture and mythology, and of structure and history, and Ganneth Obeyesekere's theories of practical rationality, and of the knowledge-politics of colonialism and postcolonialism. Both are highly abstract meaning formations that purport to say something general about what drives social action. They are both meaningful human creations that were brought to bear upon the evidence, in the attempt to create new and deeper knowledge about the British, the Hawai'ians, and "us."

Sahlins first explains the Hawai'ians' friendly treatment of Cook as an expression of the ritualized behavior called forth by Hawai'ian mythology. He advances much detail to show that a series of unlikely coincidences—including Cook arriving at the beginning of the time of the season of the Hawai'ian akua Lono, and Cook sailing around the island at a certain time in a certain direction—confirmed empirically to the Hawai'ians that their myth-guided interpretation of Cook was correct, and suggested to the Hawai'ians that Cook and his men were acting according to the same understandings as the Hawai'ians

16. Greg Dening, "Sharks That Walk the Land: The Death of Captain Cook," *Meanjin* 41 (1982); Jonathan Friedman, "No History Is an Island," *Critique of Anthropology* 8 (1988). I owe these insights into earlier critiques of Sahlins, and my original awareness of their existence, to Borofsky, "Cook, Lono, Obeyesekere, and Sahlins."

were. Then, argues Sahlins, Cook left at about the time when, in the mythological interpretation of the calendar, the akua Lono's season was over. And so, when Cook returned, this return was unexpected by the Hawai'ans in a mythological sense of the term 'unexpected.' Cook was outside the sense-making categories of their mythology, and thus a profanation who had to be eliminated. So, they killed him. But in doing so, they appropriated Britishness into their sacred mythological system. This explains why many British symbols were used by Hawai'ian chiefs after the initial encounter with Cook, and why several Hawai'ian leaders named their sons "King George."

Obeyesekere is incredulous about Sahlins's maximal interpretation of Cook's arrival and subsequent death (i.e., that its cause was Hawai'ian myth and the ritualized behaviors that enacted it), and highly skeptical about the theory that organizes the evidence to produce this maximal interpretation (namely, the structural study of myth). This leads him to reread the evidence and provide a quite different maximal interpretation. According to Obeyesekere, the Hawai'ians, like all humans, possessed a certain amount of practical rationality—that is, an ability to perceive the social and natural world realistically and solve impending problems. The Hawai'ians correctly perceived Cook as the representative of a colonial threat, and, as a result, killed him. Obeyesekere also proposes, as part of his maximal interpretation, an explanation for why many Europeans *thought* that the Hawai'ians had received Cook as a god. In the midst of constructing the colonial regime, Obeyesekere argues, Europeans could comfort their conscience by pretending that colonized peoples themselves felt Europeans to be superior. Finally, he offers a highly charged political interpretation of *Sahlins himself* as a participant in this Western ideology, which covers over the brutalities of the colonization of Hawai'i and other parts of the globe. So, we have two maximal interpretations:

> 'The Hawai'ians killed Cook because he was matter out of place, and they wanted to order the world according to their mythology. Ironically, however, in reaffirming this mythology in their encounter with the British, they also changed it. Such are the intersections between structure and history.'

and

> 'The Hawai'ians killed Cook because they knew the English were a threat to do violence to them and exploit them. Ironically, however,

because of colonial ideologies, Europeans and American anthropologists have continued to believe that the Hawai'ians thought Cook was a god, when the Hawai'ians knew quite well that he was a man. Such are the fallacies of ideology in the service of power and domination.'

We could produce more and more evidence—as indeed Sahlins did in his defense of himself—but the theoretical aspects of these maximal interpretations would not go away entirely. Our knowledge claims would continue to depend upon the successful resignification of a minimal interpretation into a maximal one. That is the bane and glory of maximal interpretation in social research. It is only because we, as investigators, have theory—or, better put, live in a meaningful world partially constituted by our theories—that we can propose to comprehend not just *that* the Hawai'ians killed Cook, but *why* the Hawai'ians killed Cook, and that we can propose to reflect, in a deep way, on how our knowledge of this episode from the eighteenth century is twisted, clarified, or unaffected by our politics. But how is this fusion of theory and fact, this resignification that takes us from minimal to maximal interpretation, to be accomplished?

V

To begin our answer to this question, let us consider a piece of social research that provides—for this author at least—the *ur*-example of maximal interpretation. In *The Eighteenth Brumaire of Louis Bonaparte*, Karl Marx wrote:

> When we think about this conjuring up of the dead of world history, a salient difference reveals itself. Camille Desmoulins, Danton, Robespierre, St. Just, Napoleon, the heroes as well as the parties and the masses of the old French Revolution, performed the task of their time—that of unchaining and establishing modern bourgeois society—in Roman costumes and with Roman phrases. The first one destroyed the feudal foundation and cut off the feudal heads that had grown on it. The other created inside France the only conditions under which free competition could be developed, parceled-out land properly used, and the unfettered productive power of the nation employed; and beyond the French borders it swept away feudal institutions everywhere, to provide, as far as necessary, bourgeois society in France with an appropriate up-to-date environment on the European continent. Once the new social formation was established, the antediluvian colossi disappeared and with them also

> the resurrected Romanism—the Brutuses, the Gracchi, the publicolas, the tribunes, the senators, and Caesar himself. Bourgeois society in its sober reality bred its own true interpreters and spokesmen in the Says, Cousins, Royer-Collards, Benjamin Constants, and Guizots; its real military leaders sat behind the office desk and the hog-headed Louis XVIII was its political chief. Entirely absorbed in the production of wealth and in peaceful competitive struggle, it no longer remembered that the ghosts of the Roman period had watched over its cradle.[17]

Written in 1852, this is a classic, well-known, and much toiled over combination of theory and fact. And, in this paragraph, one can witness how theoretical signifiers come together with evidential signifiers to produce new social knowledge. On the one hand, we have minimal interpretation of the most basic sort: the naming of individuals who existed at a certain time and place ("Danton, Robespierre . . ."). The reference to how French Revolutionaries used "Roman phrases" is also a relatively minimal interpretation. We can, indeed, show that those involved in the French revolution used such language. On the other hand, there are clear and distinct theoretical signifiers throughout, which stand out in their difference from the evidentiary ones: "modern bourgeois society," "unfettered productive power," "social formation," "free competition," "production of wealth." The true power of the paragraph, however, derives from the bringing to bear of these theoretical signifiers upon the evidential ones, the *combination* of phrases like "modern bourgeois society" with phrases like "cut off the feudal heads that had grown upon it."

This combination—so effectively researched and written—is what makes this paragraph part of a maximal interpretation of the French Revolution. Contained therein are the answers to a whole series of why and wherefore questions. Why were feudal privileges abolished and the heads of aristocrats removed from their bodies? (So as to establish a capitalist mode of production.) Why did the new French republic go to war so soon? (To create in all of Europe the conditions it had just created at home, that is, social relations that were no longer fetters for the forces of production, but rather enabled them.) Why did the French leaders after 1815 forget the Roman rhetoric of the

17. Karl Marx, *The Karl Marx Library, Volume 1* (New York: McGraw-Hill, 1977), 245.

1790s? (Because in an established capitalist society, such ideas are of no use; the effectiveness of rhetoric or ideology is conditioned by the social situation.) For an explicitly moral and political evaluation of the French *Revolutions* (1789–1814 and 1848–51) and for predictions of what is to come, we must reach beyond this paragraph, but not far beyond it. The evaluation of '89 and '48: "The first time as tragedy, the second time as farce." The exhortation for the next revolution: "The social revolution of the nineteenth century cannot take its poetry from the past but only from the future."

The first thing to note is the *reliance* upon theoretical understanding. None of this explanation and evaluation makes sense unless you understand Marx's (and to some degree Hegel's) theories—of modes of production, of social revolution, of dialectical materialism, of history, and so on. On the other hand, the theory here is almost perfectly fused to the social facts being interpreted—to the point that both fact and theory come together to say something about social *reality*. This paragraph is far more powerful than those theories are in and of themselves. Marx uses theory to understand a piece of social reality in a deep way. We can amass more and more facts about the French Revolution (and we have), but the gauntlet has been thrown down by this text of 1852; there is a deeper sense in which we must strive to *know* the French Revolution, or, for that matter, anything else. In Marx the minimal, relatively uncontroversial, interpretations of what happened in the French Revolution are *resignified* by the use of theory so as to produce maximal interpretations. This process of resignification, on splendid display in Marx, is the essence of the transition from the minimal to maximal interpretations, and is the central object of inquiry for this book.

VI

The maximal interpretations that emerge over the course of Marx's oeuvre grasp fundamental social realities, and thus produce social explanations; they anchor themselves in utopian aspirations, and thus enable critique; and they propose sophisticated historical interpretations of the twisting of human subjectivity by ideology. Perhaps such a synthesis of explanation, criticism, and interpretation will always remain the collective ego-ideal of social research. But there was a certain disequilibrium to this fusion: "History itself is a *real* part of *natural history*—of nature's coming to be man."[18] And so: "The *social* reality of nature, and *human* natural science, or the *natural science about man*, are identical terms."[19] Thus though Marx exemplified all three epistemic modes I examine in the chapters that follow, it must also be admitted that his naturalist ambitions for sociohistorical analysis tilted his synthesis in a particular direction. I think that because this tendency—toward a naturalistic approach to social science inflected by both scientific ambition and materialist sensibilities—is so well known, well entrenched, and well worked through in contemporary social thought, it is worth considering from a very general point of view before delving into the specific problems associated, in each epistemic mode, with producing maximal interpretations.

For much of the twentieth century—in both academic sociology and in the more wide-ranging and majestic discourse of Marxist social research[20]—explanation, critique, and interpretation moved backward from the synthesis proposed by Marx himself to a sheer separation based on misrecognition. However, there are now significant strands of intellectual discourse in the social sciences that propose rather explicitly to synthesize explanation and interpretation, and, in some cases, to connect this new synthesis to the goal of social critique.

That the explanation of social life is the stated goal of the social sciences can, in this emergent understanding, be squared with the

18. Karl Marx, "Economic and Philosophic Manuscripts of 1844," in *The Marx-Engels Reader*, 2nd ed., ed. Robert C. Tucker (New York: W. W. Norton, 1978), 90.

19. Marx, "Economic and Philosophic Manuscripts of 1844," 91.

20. Many of these issues were debated within the language of Marxism, since Marx was, to quote Foucault, a "founder of discursivity" (see Michel Foucault, "What Is an Author?" in *The Foucault Reader*, ed. Paul Rabinow [New York: Pantheon Books, 1984], 114). In particular, the problematic of explanation, critique, and interpretation expressed itself in the work of Georg Lukacs, and was taken up by successive generations of Marxist theorists. But note the radical disparities that emerge over the course of the twentieth century—between, for example, Athusserian "science" and E. P. Thompsons's approach to history, or between the "explanatory" study of the global economy (e.g., Wallerstein) and the "interpretive" study of culture (e.g., Jameson). Despite efforts to bring these aspects of Marxist discourse together (e.g., Harvey), it remains the case, I would argue, that the Marxist synthesis has been broken apart. See Louis Althusser and Etienne Balibar, *Reading Capital* (New York: Pantheon Books, 1971), E. P. Thompson, *The Poverty of Theory and Other Essays* (New York: Monthly Review Press, 1978), Immanuel Wallerstein, *The Modern World-System* (New York: Academic Press, 1974), Fredric Jameson, *Postmodernism; or, the Cultural Logic of Late Capitalism* (Durham: Duke University Press, 1991), David Harvey, *The Condition of Postmodernity: An Enquiry into the Origins of Cultural Change* (Cambridge, MA: Blackwell, 1989).

idea that the human sciences require the interpretation of subjectivity to accomplish their explanatory task. Thus John Goldthorpe argues that the theoretical schemas of rational action theory provide the most coherent approach to the problem of *verstehen*, and the most powerful source of explanations of collective behavior.[21] And, in his foundational writing on the philosophy of social science, Roy Bhaskar claimed, and other critical realists continue to claim, that the explanatory program of realism in social science of necessity starts with the hermeneutic task of interpreting the conceptions of the social world that actors carry with them; only by moving through this step can the social investigator ultimately grasp the real structures of the social that explain why people do what they do.[22] Meanwhile cultural sociology has produced countless investigations into symbolic structures as one aspect of the social that, supposedly having been neglected by a century of positivism, and supposedly misunderstood as ideology by a century and a half of historical materialism, are due some respect. Hence a new set of debates concerning what people do with symbols, how symbols intersect social networks and group processes, and, generally, how the study of symbols and their meanings for actors can help sociologists explain action. And symbols require human subjectivity to give them meaning. Add to this all of the talk about "habitus" and "structuration" in social theory, and we can say that the subjective element of social life has become a central focus of analysis for those who work in the human sciences.

However, there is something odd about this turn to subjectivity. In many cases, it turns out, engagement with the subjective or with the signs and symbols that humans use to make meaning does not connect to an engagement with the problem of interpretation and social knowledge. In rational choice theory, preferences are revealed and observable. In the formalist strands of semiotics and communication theory, the depth of meaning provided by human subjects is eschewed in principle—communication is manifest and thus in studying it we can avoid the entanglements of deep interpretation.

21. John H. Goldthorpe, *On Sociology*, 2nd ed. (Stanford: Stanford University Press, 2007).

22. Roy Bhaskar, *The Possibility of Naturalism: A Philosophical Critique of the Contemporary Human Sciences*, 3rd. ed. (New York: Routledge, 1998); Andrew Collier, *Critical Realism: An Introduction to Roy Bhaskar's Philosophy* (New York: Verso, 1994).

For much of cultural sociology, it is a question of measuring observable culture, not interpreting "other minds."[23] And, when the problem of interpreting others *is* recognized as part of the goal of social research, this recognition usually arrives via an argument according to which interpretation augments, enables, but ultimately folds into the much more fundamental, and still separate, project of social scientific explanation.

Thus we find throughout these arguments the idea that, since explanation uses understanding as one moment in a larger process, we can ultimately conclude that the logic of social explanation recalls and relates intimately to the logic of natural scientific explanation. To paraphrase Thomas Nagel, subjectivity exists as part of the objective world, and therefore to grasp the world objectively one must grasp, among other things, the subjective.[24] The turn to the subjective, then, is but an *expansion* of the "objectivist" point of view, a fuller comprehension of the social. This is the idea implicit in many of the most compelling and well-argued social scientific epistemologies of today: "critical realism";[25] "second-order empiricism";[26] and of course "the objective limits of objectivism" and "reflexive sociology."[27]

This view on social knowledge considers the new, stronger objectivity to be the dialectical supersession of positivism and its critics.

23. In a move iconic for a whole generation of American cultural sociologists, Robert Wuthnow argued that by interpreting discourse or communication, one could avoid interpreting subjectivity. Robert Wuthnow, *Meaning and Moral Order: Explorations in Cultural Analysis* (Berkeley: University of California Press, 1987). I discuss the issue of interpreting talk as opposed to interpreting people's motivations, with reference to C. Wright Mills and R. M. MacIver, in chapter 5.

24. Thomas Nagel, *The View from Nowhere* (New York: Oxford University Press, 1986). This is similar to John Searle's "one world" thesis. See John R. Searle, *The Construction of Social Reality* (New York: Free Press, 1995) and John Searle, "Social Ontology: Some Basic Principles," *Anthropological Theory* 6, no. 1 (2006).

25. For a selection of the key writings of critical realism, see Margaret Archer et al., eds., *Critical Realism: Essential Readings* (New York: Routledge, 1998). For an account of its importance for comparative-historical sociology, see George Steinmetz, "Critical Realism and Historical Sociology. A Review Article," *Comparative Studies in Society and History* 40, no. 1 (1998).

26. Geoffrey Brahm Levey, "Theory Choice and the Comparison of Rival Theoretical Perspectives in Political Sociology," *Philosophy of the Social Sciences* 26, no. 1 (1996).

27. Pierre Bourdieu, *In Other Words: Essays toward a Reflexive Sociology* (Cambridge: Polity, 1990); Pierre Bourdieu and Loïc J. D. Wacquant, *An Invitation to Reflexive Sociology* (Chicago: University of Chicago Press, 1992); Pierre Bourdieu and Loïc J. D. Wacquant, *Science of Science and Reflexivity* (Chicago: University of Chicago Press, 2004).

And it expects researchers armed with the new, postpositivist epistemology to arrive at intersubjectively verifiable explanations of why people do what they do, the premises of which are not, ultimately, different from those of any other truth-seeking activity whose primary orientation is empirical. Understanding is thus included in the project of explanation.

It is my view that this line of thinking—which elevates to a new level of sophistication and reflexivity our understanding of the social sciences as sciences—is exactly backward. Explanation, as a goal for the study of human beings, can only function as a subcategory of the larger category of understanding. And the strange human trait of subjectivity has a much deeper effect on the forms of understanding (including explanation) that are possible in the human sciences than is granted by the purveyors of "reflexive science."

Of course, it is the case that human subjects and human societies exist in a wider world, and that that wider world can to a very effective degree be comprehended under the schemas of the natural sciences. No social explanation can be reasonably proposed that, say, defies physics as we know it. Yet to remain at this level of understanding is to conflate the manifest fact that humans exist in, are of, and work upon nature with the philosophical position that the premises of the human sciences cannot be all that different from the premises of the natural sciences. I think this is a conflation that does not hold up under sustained reflection on what, precisely, social researchers claim when they claim to know something about what other people are up to. What if, before jumping to the naturalist metaphor, we took seriously Hegel's injunction that before getting to the "cognition of what truly is," we must first of all develop an understanding of cognition itself?[28]

This proposal brings us directly to the problems of interpretation, because in examining the process of knowledge production we are attempting to comprehend a very specific, perhaps in some ways privileged, form of meaning-making—the attainment and verification of knowledge. And since all knowledge involves human subjectivity as its instrument or medium, no form of knowledge can be said to exist outside of the problem of interpretation.

Thus I begin, here, from a position that recognizes the meaning-

28. Georg Wilhelm Friedrich Hegel, *Phenomenology of Spirit*, trans. A. V. Miller (New York: Oxford University Press, 1977), paragraph 73.

making nature of human endeavors to produce knowledge.[29] From this perspective, rather than seeing natural science as pure and true knowledge that emerges from the encounter of an unblemished subjectivity with unmediated Nature, we can see it as a specification of the interpretive process that, at a more general level, characterizes all human thought and communication.[30] It is a specification, furthermore, that required for its achievement a remarkable coincidence of sociohistorical circumstances, and that requires for its continuance a form of training and social organization whose details are still being worked out in sociological research, and whose philosophical basis has become the occupation of post-logical-positivist philosophy of science.

The interpretive capacities of natural science, that is, are of a specific kind. In natural science, the human capacity to interpret, to grasp the meaning of phenomena, is pointed to the reconstruction of sense-experience and observation in terms of a vast and precise set of theories and laws about the natural world. These laws themselves are constructed and justified through the work humans do on and through nature—the practical interaction of human beings with their environment, which is disciplined through scientific training.[31] If,

29. The critical realists recognize prima facie both the hermeneutic problems attending the human sciences and the possibilities and contingencies that "history" introduces to social life. They thus arrive at their version of explanation only after arguing their way out of the epistemic dilemmas of human knowledge. As I shall argue below, however, the realist solution is in need of radical reform.

30. Kurt Hübner in *Critique of Scientific Reason* argues that Weber's ideal types—and, more generally, work in the human sciences—in fact exemplify the relationship between a priori principles and facts that obtain in all of the sciences, both social and natural. Thus he argues that "the so-called hermeneutic circle, which is discussed so often today, does not really exist . . . this erroneously named 'circle' comes up not only in the historical and human sciences, but in every empirical science, since the relation between a priori assumptions and facts interpreted with their help is principally the same everywhere. Hence we are not dealing with something inherent to the historical and human sciences alone." My goal here is, by examining closely truth claims in the human sciences, to show that Hübner was wrong to find essentially the same "interpretive" operation at work when theory is used in natural science and in the human sciences. It is not clear (to me at least) how Hübner's philosophical account of scientific reasoning would change what natural scientists do and write; I hope to show that the peculiarities of interpretation *for the human sciences* are in fact of great consequence for how we imagine and practice social research. Kurt Hübner, *Critique of Scientific Reason* (Chicago: University of Chicago Press, 1983), 189.

31. Ian Hacking has considered these issues with extreme care, writing at the intersection of realist philosophies of natural science, pragmatist-influenced epistemology, and Foucauldian-historical studies of the human sciences. See in particular Ian Hacking, *Representing and Intervening: Introductory Topics in the Philosophy of*

indeed, this specific sort of interpretation has managed to achieve a certain kind of universality—to create forms of knowledge that can be explicated and compellingly communicated to humans (or perhaps one day, nonhumans!) who share very little linguistically, socially and culturally, and psychologically with the communicators, this is a remarkable achievement, but not one that belies the way that, at a very general level, the enterprise is interpretive. It suggests, rather, that in so far as the grammar of science is mathematics, and mathematics is a human creation whose intersubjective validity can be established with a remarkable amount of abstract certainty, science can have an objectivist outlook as its working format for making and criticizing knowledge claims, and a pragmatic-realist justification as its working format of philosophical self-reflection.[32] This speaks to an essential hermeneutic truth about science often ignored by positivists and antipositivists alike, but grasped in some philosophies of natural science and certain social-theoretical traditions: that the "scientific mindset" is just that—a specific manipulation of the human ability to assign meaning to certain manifest signifiers—and that scientific objectivity is something earned through labor and social organization, rather than something philosophically guaranteed. Certainly most natural scientists would agree that they work for their objectivity.

For social research, it is not at all clear that the interpretive capacities of the investigator can be channeled in the same way, and I will ultimately argue in this book that the epistemic synthesis that can be traced to Marx's naturalist inclination must be countered. Metaphors of standing on head or feet notwithstanding, this argument will not ultimately hinge on an inversion, but rather on a differentiation between ways of using theory, and a recognition of the limits, as well as the capacities, of social knowledge. To preview the anti-antirealist

---

Natural Science (New York: Cambridge University Press, 1983), and Hacking, *The Social Construction of What?*

32. The issues raised by the rather astounding way in which mathematics can serve as the language for physics and some other natural sciences are outlined in Eugene Wigner, "The Unreasonable Effectiveness of Mathematics in the Natural Sciences," *Communications in Pure and Applied Mathematics* 13, no. 1 (1960). But the larger issue here is the development of a sociological approach to natural scientific knowledge that does not associate "rationality" with individual knowers or philosophical certainty, and as a result oppose social determinants of knowledge to rational determinants of knowledge. This I take to be the central project of Helen Longino's philosophy/sociology of science, which she traces to C. S. Peirce's meditations on communities of inquiry and the attainment of truth. Helen Longino, *The Fate of Knowledge* (Princeton: Princeton University Press, 2002), 4–5, 77–96.

argument that follows: I think realism is correct that social investigation must reach beyond the surface of colligated facts to grasp causal explanations of action, and I will follow the critical realists in suggesting a connection between explanation and critique—I too hold that the critique of social life and its cultural products requires, at least implicitly, some sort of approach to social explanation. But I doubt whether these connections can be adequately established via the mode of theoretical resignification that is at the core of the realist epistemic mode. But to fully articulate both realism and its alternatives, we have to look at how theoretical resignification actually works.

How, in other words, does the use of the language game of social theory enable the construction of compelling historical narratives of cause, critique, and meaning? Let us pull apart these different conceptual methods. For we now work without the fetters—and thus without the supports—of the Marxian philosophy of history, which could connect in one compelling logical circle the explanation of society, the interpretation of culture, and the critique of systematically distorted communication. We have not yet fully understood the ways in which these intellectual tasks have become so radically different from each other.

It may in fact be that the synthesis of these modes will not—or not yet—be possible: that we live in an epistemically fallen age, yearning for the ultimate whole that once was guaranteed by the metanarratives of communism or modernization. However, consider this: the most outstanding versions of that synthesis were based upon an illusory equation of materiality and scientificity, the critique of which is by no means complete, and thus it might be a mistake to wager the possibility of synthetic social knowledge on their success.

Chapter Two

Reality

Philosophical men even have a presentiment that the reality in which we live and have our being is also mere appearance and that another, quite different reality lies beneath it.

—Friedrich Nietzsche, *The Birth of Tragedy*

I

In the last chapter, I argued that the signs of evidence have a ground in social actions that happened, and thus that these actions can be reported upon in minimal interpretations. The question is, then, how theory is brought to bear on this web of factual signification to resignify the evidence, and thus offer deeper knowledge of the "social actions that happened." When this is done, maximal interpretations are created.

The fundamental premise of realism is that theory has a ground in the basic structures of the social; and thus that theory draws its coherence from its referent. In realism, the problem posed in chapter 1 (what brings theory and evidence together?) is solved by insisting, realizing, or discovering that the language of theory, like the language of fact, draws meaning primarily from reference, and only secondarily from contrast. Theory, on this account, is an explicitly and exquisitely designed exercise in referencing and describing social reality, whose injection into the sign-system of evidence allows the discovery of the fundamental social realities that underlie and explain the social actions of interest. According to realism, the signs of theory come together effectively with the signs of evidence when and because they both point to the same real social entities as their ultimate referent. The ground of the theoretical sign becomes, in the course of turning a minimal interpretation into a maximal one, the ground of the evidential sign. The result of this process of resignification is, in realism, maximal interpretations that contain, as their central component, (claims to) causal explanations. To comprehend how this works, it is necessary to understand the way in which the realist philosophy of social science understands itself.

"Realism," as an intellectual movement of significance for social theory, the philosophy of social science, and, increasingly, social research itself, emerged in contrast to both positivism and postmodernism as ways of understanding social knowledge. From the point of view of realist epistemology, there is one thing that both of these "isms" suffer from: they dismiss, avoid, or condemn *depth interpretation.* In positivism—at least in its strict forms—sentences that cannot be checked by sensory observation are metaphysical nonsense. The only possible referents for terms are manifest, detectible persons or occurrences that can be measured. In postmodernism, the authority of the interpreter to go beyond what he is presented with by the social world is challenged as unwarranted and, often, reduced to an exercise in power. According to postmodernism (or so say the realists anyway), the use of theory—e.g., psychoanalytic theory, rational choice theory, Marxist theory—as a way to get behind the "surface" of social life is a way of dictating truth, not discovering it.

For realism, this emphasis on the surface and the corresponding distrust of attempts to know what is "underneath" evidence, data, or manifest social actions and events is an intellectual error of the highest order. It is incorrect, argue realists, to think that social researchers either do, could, or should stay on the surface, content to either inductively generate hypotheses from their data or to offer interpretations of that data that are "just" interpretations. It must rather be the case that the social world is layered, and that what social knowledge does is reveal the underlying layers of social life that explain the surface outcomes, events, and phenomena we want to understand. Much as it is the case that the natural world contains within it forces that we cannot see, but that we know exist, and that help us explain empirical events (e.g., gravity, electromagnetism), so it must also be the case that in society, there are underlying mechanisms or structures that explain what happens or has happened, thus granting social research the possibility of *in-depth knowledge*, and, indeed, the possibility of *causal explanation*.[1]

Realism is, then, a way of conceptualizing the construction of maximal interpretations in social research. It proposes a framework in which going beyond evidence is warranted and indeed necessary, and it provides a clear and distinct set of arguments for how the use of theory to interpret evidence can be guided appropriately, so as to produce valid social knowledge. The core of that argument—articulated in myriad ways by different sorts of realists—is that theory must reference social reality (hence, "realism"), while at the same time remaining general and abstract. The coherence and rationality of social theory (and, therefore, of maximal interpretations) derives from the correspondences developed between theory and social reality.

Social theory, in its classical form, contained a strong tendency toward this sort of theorizing—which we can call, in line with Roy Bhaskar's language, ontological. Durkheim explicitly and bluntly, and Marx carefully and implicitly, set out in abstract theoretical terms the nature of society or "the social" *as such*. In particular, Durkheim's final study, *The Elementary Forms of Religious Life*, was premised on ontology as the central project of social theory. Therein, Durkheim proposes to study the most "simple" or "primitive" form of religious activity because in doing so he will be able to grasp "the religious nature of man."[2] This is clearly ontological language. This legacy

1. Perhaps this instinct—that one must, in social research, go beneath the surface of both observable data and the invariant categories that are often used to name events or outcomes—is best expressed by Charles Tilly's attack on the implicit positivist logic of much historical and political sociology. This logic is objectionable, Tilly argues, in so far as it attempts to identify events and their invariant, easily observable properties (e.g., all revolutions have characteristics X, Y, and Z, thus, if event A is revolution, then it has characteristics X, Y, and Z). Instead, explains Tilly, "regularities in political life are very broad, indeed transhistorical, but do not operate in the form of recurrent structures and processes at a large scale. They consist of recurrent causes which in different circumstances and sequences compound into highly variable but nonetheless explicable effects. Students of revolution have imagined they were dealing with phenomena like ocean tides, whose regularities they could deduce from sufficient knowledge of celestial motion, when they were actually confronting phenomena like great floods, equally coherent occurrences from a causal perspective, but enormously variable in structure, sequence, and consequences as a function of terrain, previous precipitation, built environment, and human response." Charles Tilly, "To Explain Political Processes," *American Journal of Sociology* 100, no. 6 (1995), 1601.

2. Émile Durkheim, *The Elementary Forms of the Religious Life* (New York: Free Press, 1995), 1.

from "the classics" has been passed on to social theory today. So, for example, Anthony Giddens offers his "structuration theory" as a "social ontology"—that is, an account of what, exactly, agency and structure *are*;[3] extended debates occur about whether the assumptions of rational choice theory are methodological or ontological—that is, whether actors really *are* utility maximizers;[4] Bourdieu's relational sociology is interpreted, in American sociology at least, as a new general theory of social reality that overcomes a hidden individualism of sociological research.[5]

"Ontology" aside, this ambitious project for social theory can be articulated via three guiding principles for the use of theory in generating maximal interpretations. In the realist epistemic mode, theory creates a picture of the social world that is expected to apply widely (generality), be consistent with itself (coherence), and describe directly social reality (reference). A good example of this is the recent emphasis in certain sectors of sociology on theorizing a finite set of mechanisms as the essence of the social. To take an especially clear statement of this position: "A focus on mechanisms tends to reduce theoretical fragmentation. For example, we may have numerous different theories (of crime, organizations, social movements or whatnot) that are all based upon the same theory-within-the-theory, that is, they all refer to the same set of mechanisms."[6] While realism as an epistemic mode is certainly not reducible to the search for mechanisms,[7] this quotation shows well the ambition that theory be general ("all based upon the same theory-within-the-theory") and that it be referential ("they all refer to the same set of mechanisms"). Later in his text, Hedstrom insists

3. Anthony Giddens, *The Constitution of Society* (Berkeley: University of California Press, 1984); Anthony Giddens, *Social Theory and Modern Sociology* (Cambridge: Polity Press, 1987); Ira J. Cohen, *Structuration Theory: Anthony Giddens and the Constitution of Social Life* (Houndmills, Basingstoke, Hampshire: Macmillan, 1989).

4. Donald P. Green and Ian Shapiro, *Pathologies of Rational Choice Theory: A Critique of Applications in Political Science* (New Haven: Yale University Press, 1994).

5. Mustafa Emirbayer, "Manifesto for a Relational Sociology," *American Journal of Sociology* 103, no. 2 (1997).

6. Peter Hedström, *Dissecting the Social: On the Principles of Analytical Sociology* (Cambridge: Cambridge University Press, 2005), 28.

7. I will argue below, and in chapter 4, that "mechanism" is a very specific metaphor for understanding social life that can be complemented and encompassed by other useful metaphors. Thus, when I present the interpretive epistemic mode's approach to explanation, in chapter 5, I argue that interpretive explanations should, when appropriate, theorize mechanisms.

that the theory used in explanations should form a single, coherent ontology.[8]

Realism's claim, then, is that theory refers directly to entities or processes (or, to use that word again, "mechanisms") in the world that have the potential to cause events to happen. These entities have a coherent structure that is reproduced in the coherence of the theory that sets out what they are. Thus, in realism, social theory has in social reality what C. S. Peirce would have called a "ground" for the sign, which is stable and, for maximal interpretations, stabilizing. Now, the idea that the words on the page in a theory book—or even in the theory section of a research monograph—would conjure up, in the mind of the reader, a picture of "social reality" in the abstract is not what is at issue here. The point is, rather, that this signifier-signified relationship is backed up by the "ontological status of theoretical entities"[9]—that theoretical terms and the ideas they call forth in our minds have real referents, and that, moreover, these referents are essential pieces in the structure of social reality. Perhaps nowhere in contemporary social science is this expectation that theoretical terms have direct and real referents more viscerally and convincingly communicated than in what is surely one of the most impactful paragraphs in the history of comparative-historical sociology:

> Social revolutions in France, Russia, and China emerged from specifically political crises centered in the structures and situations of the old regime states. The events of 1787–9 in France, of the first half of 1917 in Russia, and of 1911–16 in China not only undermined autocratic monarchical regimes but also disorganized centrally coordinated administrative and coercive controls over the potentially rebellious lower classes. The revolutionary crises developed when the old-regime states became unable to meet the challenges of evolving international situations. Monarchical authorities were subjected to new threats or to intensified competition from more economically developed powers abroad. And they were constrained or checked in their responses by the institutionalized relationships of the autocratic state organizations to the landed upper classes and the agrarian economies. Caught in cross-pressures between domestic class structures and international exigencies, the autocracies and their centralized administrations and armies

8. Hedström, *Dissecting the Social*, 37.

9. Grover Maxwell, "The Ontological Status of Theoretical Entities," *Minnesota Studies in the Philosophy of Science* 3 (1962).

broke apart, opening the way for social-revolutionary transformations spearheaded by revolts from below.[10]

Herein all the elements of the maximal interpretation that makes up the first half of Theda Skocpol's *States and Social Revolutions* are present in powerfully reduced and lucid form. The second sentence ("The events of . . .") states the social actions that happened, the evidence for which is found throughout the book. But the paragraph as a whole revolves around its theoretical signifiers, and the immediate reality of the theoretical terms is affirmed by the clear implication of the text that, in every one of her cases (and also in the comparison cases mentioned later where revolutions did not occur), there were such things as an "old regime state"/"autocratic state organization," a "domestic class structure" and "landed upper class," and "international exigencies." But it is not just that these underlying social realities exist. Perhaps even more important is that the relations obtaining between the entities referred to by theory drive the causal narrative of each case forward. The "cross-pressures" of domestic class structures and international competition "broke apart" the state. This breaking apart, in turn, "open[ed] the way" for revolts from below.

When considering a statement with such obvious intellectual power, it is difficult (for this author, anyway) to avoid a sort of thinking-dilemma, wherein *either* such a text refers to social reality *or* it does not. But to think this way is to ignore the specific epistemic mode of these sorts of research texts, which so effectively unify general social theory with historical narrative.[11] They do so in a very particular way,

10. Theda Skocpol, *States and Social Revolutions: A Comparative Analysis of France, Russia, and China* (Cambridge: Cambridge University Press, 1979), 47.

11. Skocpol's stated epistemology is Millsian. She claims to be strictly inductive and thus could be labeled an "empiricist," giving her approach affinities with (some forms of) social scientific positivism. But, as many have noticed about her book, Skocpol's substantive investigations into the processes of social revolution and state consolidation that follow on the heels of her first chapter undercut any claims to a strictly "observational" or "inductive" approach. Indeed, it is increasingly becoming clear within comparative-historical sociology, I believe, that the implicit epistemology of the classics of small-N comparison is realist. See George Steinmetz, "Odious Comparisons: Incommensuarability, the Case Study, and 'Small N's' in Sociology," *Sociological Theory* 22, no. 3 (2004). For the specific argument that the epistemology of *States and Social Revolutions* is ultimately realist, see Philip Gorski, "The Poverty of Deductivism: A Constructivist Realist Model of Sociological Explanation," *Sociological Methodology* 34 (2004).

If Skocpol was already a realist without knowing it, then the recognition that her epistemic mode is in fact realism has come, in American sociology at least, with a shift

however: by revealing the general social reality that lies behind a series of particular cases. Let us, then, delve further into the workings of this semiotic for social knowledge.

Consider the following passages from the iconic text that preceded Skocpol's, Barrington Moore's *The Social Origins of Dictatorship and Democracy*:

A. The ways in which the landed upper classes and the peasants reacted to the challenge of commercial agriculture were decisive in determining the political outcome [of Britain].[12]

B. There is widespread agreement among historians that the period from about 1688 to the end of the Napoleonic Wars was the golden age of the great landed estate. In important parts of the country, the estates spread out over land, sometimes at the expense of the smaller gentry, and more significantly at the expense of the peasants. No one has yet arisen to deny the general importance of the enclosures or that innumerable peasants lost their rights on the common lands of the villages as the great landlords absorbed these lands.[13]

C. Thus over substantial parts of England, as the large estate became larger and was operated more and more on commercial principles, it finally destroyed the medieval peasant community . . . the wave of parliamentary enclosures during the eighteenth and early nineteenth centuries merely gave legal sanction to a process of eroding peasant property that had been going on for some time. We know from the experience of other countries that the intrusion of commerce into a peasant community generally sets in motion a tendency toward the concentration of land in fewer hands. This tendency had been noticeable in England at least as early as the sixteenth century. In the heart of an area heavily hit by enclosure, seventy percent of the land in one village had been withdrawn from the peasant economy before the village was enclosed

---

toward theorizing mechanisms—not only in the analytic sociology of Hedström, but most notably in the debates and commentary that exploded around Doug McAdam's, Sidney Tarrow's, and Charles Tilly's *Dynamics of Contention*, in which the authors advocated the view that "to explain contentious politics is to identify its recurrent causal mechanisms." To me, their work evidences a similar set of epistemic imperatives as found in Hedström's approach, quoted earlier in this chapter, even if their ontology of social process is different. Doug McAdam, Sidney Tarrow, and Charles Tilly, *Dynamics of Contention* (New York: Cambridge University Press, 2001), 13.

12. Barrington Moore, *Social Origins of Dictatorship and Democracy: Lord and Peasant in the Making of the Modern World* (Boston: Beacon Press, 1967), xxiii.

13. Moore, *Social Origins of Dictatorship and Democracy*, 23.

> by act of Parliament. By 1765 only three families in ten occupied land in this area of advancing industry. The rest were laborers, knitters, small tradesmen.[14]

Statement A is theoretical, though it contains within it a promise to—somehow—explain the "political outcome" of Britain and, as the preface to Moore's book makes clear, also France, the United States, China, Japan, and India (with gestures toward Germany and Russia). It sets out some abstract terms that will have to be defined *and* applied: "landed upper classes," "commercial agriculture," "determining," and "political outcome." Indeed, as Jonathan Weiner's review of reviews of Moore's book makes clear, each and every one of these terms was questioned, criticized, and debated.[15] Some criticized Moore's determinism, some criticized Moore's assumption that economically defined classes are the primary collective actors that make up society, and some criticized Moore's (supposed) economic determinism. But whether or not Moore is a Marxist in the substantive sense of expecting the handling of material resources by men to drive history is not precisely what interests us here. Rather, let us ask: what is the logic by which Moore's theoretical signs intersect with his evidential ones?

Statement B is primarily evidential. It is a report about something that happened, cobbled together from secondary evidence that was cobbled together from primary evidence. It is one instance of a type of writing that appears often in Moore's book: a first-order narrative of something that happened in history, which can of course be debated, but wherein the various signifiers of (1) words written by Moore, (2) texts referenced by Moore, and (3) archival evidence referenced by those texts referenced by Moore are all expected to point back to the same set of human actions, movements of materials, events, etc. Herein, certainly, there is dispute. But I would contend that statement B is primarily part of a minimal interpretation, and uses mostly factual signs. It is part of a report of *what happened*: there were a set of actions called the enclosures, by which men who farmed small bits of land (peasants) were prohibited from so doing by men who claimed control of large tracts of land (great landlords).

14. Moore, *Social Origins of Dictatorship and Democracy*, 25–26.

15. Jonathan M. Weiner, "The Barrington Moore Thesis and Its Critics," *Theory and Society* 2, no. 3 (1975).

But *why* did the enclosures happen and what was their significance? In statement C, theory and fact mix together: *We know from the experience of other countries that the intrusion of commerce into a peasant community generally sets in motion a tendency toward the concentration of land in fewer hands.* That is to say, what happened in England is explained by a *mechanism* that, once set in motion, produced the result of "enclosures." This mechanism is "commerce," or, to take the original theoretical formulation, "commercial agriculture," which is to say, the making of a market in land and the farming of land for the purpose of turning a monetary profit (as opposed to subsistence, or some combination of subsistence and profit). You could "notice" this tendency in England in the sixteenth century (either a historian or an Englishman of the sixteenth century, presumably, could do the noticing). Thus a general social mechanism enables Moore to *resignify* the evidence as a "process" or "tendency."

Statement C clearly shows how much causal power is attributed to this mechanism. Look at all of the things commercial agriculture does/did: "destroyed the medieval peasant community," "eroding peasant property," "sets in motion a tendency." And there is a result—we perhaps should say a clear causal effect—of all this process and motion, attested to in this case by a telling evidential example: "In the heart of an area heavily hit by enclosure, seventy percent of the land in one village had been withdrawn from the peasant economy before the village was enclosed by act of Parliament." Note also that statement C clearly and rather ironically disputes Parliament's lawmaking as itself the causal force in this case. Parliament "merely gave legal sanction to" the results of the forces of commerce; by the time Parliament got to the area that makes for Moore's example, the "enclosures" had taken place *because of commerce*, legality or illegality be damned.

Of course, the appeal and power of Moore's book derives to a great extent from the way in which this interaction of theoretical and evidential signs is repeated case by case. This is an important clue to what is going on in the realist mode. Comparative explanation, from within a singular, complex framework, of a variety of political outcomes (bourgeois democracy, fascist dictatorship, communist dictatorship), is a perfect example of realism in action. In each and every case, the evidential story (the reportage) is ultimately explained in causal language that invokes the same set of theoretical terms, referring to the same underlying social reality. To take just one further example:

> C2. As might be anticipated on the basis of the experience of other countries, the new commercial relationships produced some tendency toward the concentration of land in fewer hands and the breakup of older familistic relationships within the peasant community. The significant point about Japan, however, is that these tendencies did not go very far. After the rise of tenant farming as a solution to the problems of agriculture, property relationships underwent very little change for nearly a century. Despite a few incipient signs of an expropriation of the peasantry, no such expropriation took place. Nor did the peasants rise to expropriate the dominant classes in Japanese society.[16]

The *partial absence* or *insufficient strength* of the mechanism of "commerce," in this case, explains the divergent outcomes of England and Japan; Japan ended up with a coalition of the landed aristocracy and the industrialist bourgeois class that led to fascist dictatorship much like in Germany.[17] England, on the other hand, had a bourgeois/democratic revolution. In Moore, the same theoretical terms repeat themselves as they intersect with the reportage of different cases, providing in each case the causal joints upon which the evidential narrative turns. The theoretical terms provide the explanation of the events that happened and the outcomes of interest to the researcher.

Our distance from the substantive debates that swirl around Moore's text allows us to notice in his work an epistemic logic that is in fact found in a wide variety of social knowledge claims. It is evident in Randall Collins's construction of an interactional emotions-centered microsociology, which is the basis for all social expla-

16. Moore, *Social Origins of Dictatorship and Democracy*, 270.

17. In France, an initially weak ("in the latter part of the seventeenth century and the opening decade of the eighteenth") mechanism of commercial agriculture ultimately intensified certain feudal relationships, thus "feudalizing" the bourgeoisie, predisposing France, in Moore's view, to "modernization from above" on the model of Germany and Japan. The revolution, however, changed all this, as certain members of the bourgeoisie—never as strong as they were in England—rode the radicalism of the Sans-Culottes and peasant resentment into a position of partial power, resulting in the "long" road to French democracy (1789–1871). Moore, *Social Origins of Dictatorship and Democracy*, 45, 109. It is important to recognize that such contingencies can be accommodated by the realist mode, which is not reliant on a deterministic philosophy of history so much as it is on a general ontological framework for analyzing historical causality. See George Steinmetz, "Critical Realism and Historical Sociology: A Review Article," *Comparative Studies in Society and History* 40, no. 1 (1998): 170–86.

nation and into which all macro concepts can be translated.[18] It is evident in Claude Levi-Strauss's ambitious willingness to frame his investigations of myth as investigations into the timeless structure of the human mind.[19] It is evident in the Skocpol-led revolution in comparative analysis to "bring the state back in."[20] That logic is this: theory, when used in social explanation, points directly to the underlying structures, mechanisms, or forces of the social world. It is general, coherent, and referential, and these properties allow the construction of maximal interpretations that are causal.

This underlying social world, which is represented/revealed by perspicacious theoretical terms, becomes, in the research text, the underlying causal source of that which requires explanation. The claim is, implicitly or explicitly, that the theoretical signifiers used by the researcher point to an essential aspect of the social *as such*, and that this world exists underneath the time-space patch of social life to which their evidence refers. In Moore, for example, the signifier of "the relation between town and country" is taken to refer to an actually existing relation, which can vary in the direction and strength of its imbalance, which exists or has existed in England, France, the United States, China, Japan, and India (and Germany and Russia). The adding of these theoretical terms to narrative history is a process of weighing where and when they apply—as evidence is evaluated for and against their existence and character. However, when the theoretical signs pass this test—and it is, in some sense, a test, though it is not an experiment—they then make an appearance among the varied evidential signs. In doing so, they *resignify* that evidence in a particular way. The theoretical signifiers do causal things in the narrative of what happened: they "drive forward," "destroy," "bring about," "regulate," "determine," and so on.

The standard sociological account of "structural causation," inaugurated by Marx and exemplified by Skocpol, takes on this textual pattern. But, of course, the utilization of theoretical signifiers in this

18. Randall Collins, *Interaction Ritual Chains* (Princeton: Princeton University Press, 2004); Randall Collins, "On the Microfoundations of Macrosociology," *American Journal of Sociology* 86, no. 5 (1981): 984–1014.

19. Claude Levi-Strauss, *The Raw and the Cooked: Mythologiques*, vol. 1 (Chicago: University of Chicago Press, 1983).

20. Peter B. Evans, Dietrich Rueschemeyer, and Theda Skocpol, *Bringing the State Back In* (New York: Cambridge University Press, 1985).

way is not *only* a textual effect. It is a textual effect that attempts to reference and represent the social world; it is a truth claim. In so far as these texts claim to be *true*, then it must be that they claim that these theoretical signs drive forward the explanatory research text for the precise reason that the entities to which the theoretical signs point exist or existed, and, furthermore, that they do or did cause the actions, events, and outcomes pointed to by the evidential signs in the research text. In other words, for these texts to work as producers of true social knowledge, then it must be that the theories do what, implicitly or explicitly, these authors and their (sympathetic) readers contend that they do—reference the nature of the social in general, in a way that holds across time and space, and thus can be "applied" and "tested" in certain cases. How might one epistemologically justify this position on what theories do, and how they work with evidence to produce explanations?[21]

II

To answer this question, let us first propose a more formal account of what is happening in the realist mode. First, we can say that theoretical signs are "grounded" in a general and consistent social reality (see fig. 2).

Then (and here is the key point): in the realist epistemic mode, *every case or instance that grounds evidential interpretation is made to point back to the singular referent—social reality—to which theory points directly*. That is, the cases are "regrounded" by social theory. Ultimately, the social actions that happened become, as it were, signs that point back to the social reality identified by theory, which also, in many cases, is taken to have *causally produced* those social actions (see fig. 3).

The implication is that, according to realism, the knowledge of

21. In what follows, then, I examine and criticize the specific way in which realism develops and uses social theory to build these in-depth truth claims. This critique is intended to be different than the overarching philosophical critique of representational theories of truth. In this regard, I work with a modified representationalist theory of truth, much like Helen Longino's account of how various sorts of truth claims (including models, specific explanations, etc.) can be understood according to a "conformist" theory of truth that drops the strictly propositional theory of truth but preserves the idea that truth claims involve more or less correct claims about the world. The question, for me at least, is the degree to which very different ways of creating such truth claims animate social research. Helen Longino, *The Fate of Knowledge* (Princeton: Princeton University Press, 2002), 117–21.

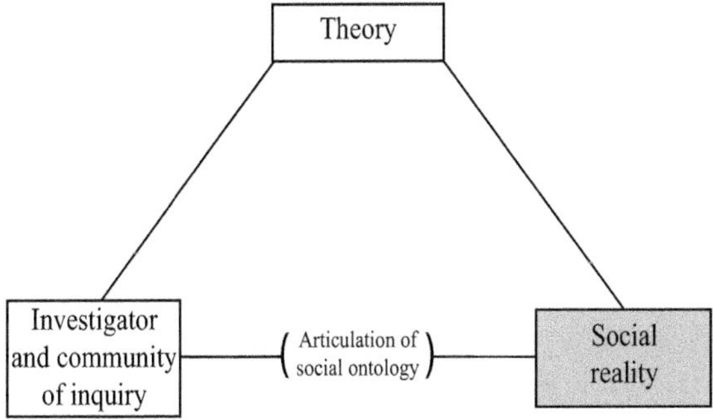

Figure 2: The realist theoretical sign

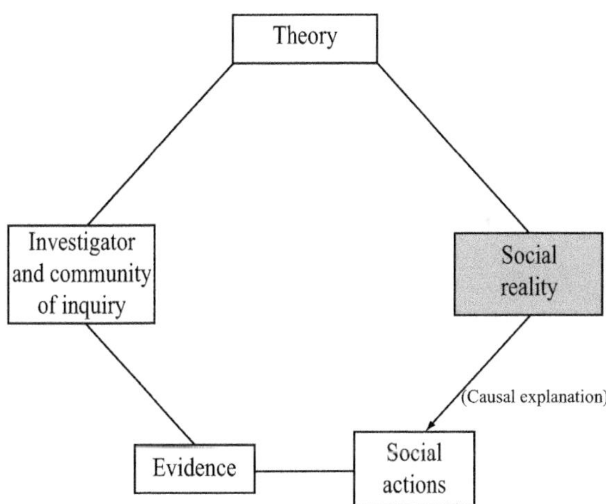

Figure 3: Realist maximal interpretation—causal explanation as social knowledge

social reality embedded in the theoretical sign-system completes the hermeneutic circle for the investigator. The referential meanings of this sign-system allow her to discover what is underneath her data. This does not imply that the interpretations produced proceed ***only and singularly*** from theory to evidence. But a clear and coherent framework for the evidence is provided, precisely because the underlying structures that will do the explaining are drawn from a coherently developed, general account of social life. And so, a highly effective and compelling semiotic circuit is constructed, whereby theoretical claims are posited and then tested in this or that case, and as a result are successively refined. It is easy, furthermore, to imagine that this circle of interpretation is not an interpretation at all; to imagine that what is happening is the verification or falsification of scientific hypotheses, and the linear accumulation of scientific knowledge of the social.

One of the most lucid defenses of the scientificity of comparative sociology evidences both this realist semiotic and the illusion of noninterpretation. Jack Goldstone separates "comparative historical analysis" (abbreviated CHA) from large-N statistical inferences, arguing that

> Analysts using CHA generally face a finite set of cases, chosen against a backdrop of theoretical interests, and aim to determine the causal sequences and patterns producing outcomes of interest in those specific cases. Generalization is certainly a goal, but that generalization is sought by piecing together finite sets of cases, not by sampling and inference to a larger universe.[22]

So, given the ways in which CHA does not work with the assumptions of large-N analysis, how is it that CHA can claim to accumulate objective knowledge? (Let us leave to the side, for the moment, whether large-N sociology does or does not accomplish this.) Goldstone answers this by arguing that the logic of CHA is implicitly the logic of Baysean analysis. That is to say, CHA also differs from large-N studies because it "rarely starts from ignorance of causal relationships. Quite the contrary; most CHA squarely targets strong prior beliefs about causal relationships. Indeed what makes case analyses compelling

22. Jack Goldstone, "Comparative Historical Analysis and Knowledge Accumulation in the Study of Revolutions," in *Comparative Historical Analysis in the Social Sciences*, ed. James Mahoney and Dietrich Rueschemeyer (New York: Cambridge University Press, 2003), 43.

is generally not that they pluck unknown causal relationships from behind a veil of ignorance, but that they are specifically designed to challenge prior beliefs."[23] This attests to the importance of theoretical knowledge, which stores in its signifiers such "prior beliefs" that are to be challenged or tested by evidence.[24]

For Goldstone, then, the analysis of a case does not enter into neutral intellectual ground constituted by a null hypothesis. Rather, cases are designed to speak to the knowledge already embedded in the research community. So how does this work? Here again, theory comes in. For Goldstone—like the realist philosophers of social science—eschews the mere citing of constant conjunctions. Rather, a case must be broken down into a series of events, and these events are then "plausibly linked given the interests and situations faced by groups or individual actors."[25] Crucially, this linking of events "involves making *deductions* about how events are linked over time, *drawing on general principles of economics, sociology, psychology, and political science regarding human behavior*" (emphasis added).[26] This linking occurs with the aid of quantitative and qualitative evidence that is marshaled "*within* complex cases." Then these processes are compared across "*particular cases of interest.*"

This is a perfect, if entirely internal, account of how realist maximal interpretations are constructed. Investigators come to a case bearing theory—indeed, they may choose a case because it is judged to be a sort of "crucial experiment" for a theory. These theories are general principles of human behavior, which articulate the processes that underlie and link together key events. Cases are then examined for the "existence/absence"[27] of causal chains or processes, on the basis of which the theory is refined. For this reason, argues Goldstone, the

> overall development of CHA in any particular field presents a research program . . . At any one time, a finite number of cases deemed to be

23. Goldstone, "Comparative Historical Analysis and Knowledge Accumulation in the Study of Revolutions," 45.

24. On the integration of "theoretical and substantive knowledge" into case-based work, see also Charles Ragin, *Fuzzy-Set Social Science* (Chicago: University of Chicago Press, 2000), 316.

25. Goldstone, "Comparative Historical Analysis and Knowledge Accumulation in the Study of Revolutions," 47.

26. Goldstone, "Comparative Historical Analysis and Knowledge Accumulation in the Study of Revolutions," 48.

27. Goldstone, "Comparative Historical Analysis and Knowledge Accumulation in the Study of Revolutions," 46.

> of interest to a research community are under investigation. Using process tracing, scholars seek to uncover sequences that produced the results or cases of interest. Using congruence testing, scholars make claims about the number of cases that "fit" a particular causal sequence or pattern (or "model").[28]

Several things are worth noting here. First it should be clear that realism can allow for a certain amount of flexibility about the "empirical scope" of its mechanisms, and can allow for causal complexity, or what George Steinmetz called, in his review of critical realism, "conjunctural determination."[29] Causal monism or strict universalism is not necessary. Rather, theory is expected to be *in principle* general, to work referentially, and to be consistent with itself in the abstract. That is the essence of the realist epistemic mode. The idea is that models are built and "tested" with cases. However, an implicit assumption here is that the amount of cases and amount of models is finite and manageable, and that the models that are provisionally taken as *true*—at least concerning a given object of study, like social revolutions—are not in contradiction with each other.

Goldstone uses the language of Bayesian analysis to articulate the logic of all of this. Comparative historical sociologists answer questions like this: "What would you bet that you would find certain conditions in a given case before a CHA of that case, and would you make the same bet after a CHA of that case?"[30] Presumably, here, Goldstone means to ask "would you make the same bet about the *next* case," after the CHA of the case at hand reveals, or does not reveal, the conditions predicted by theory. But this is just the thing—the commensurability of this case and the next is not a major problem for Goldstone, because the commensurability of the cases is guaranteed if they have the same object as defined by general social theory. This general social theory then proceeds gradually to refine itself and to store knowledge, thus creating the accumulation of knowledge that characterizes a research program on revolutions, or on whatever the theoretical object may be.

28. Goldstone, "Comparative Historical Analysis and Knowledge Accumulation in the Study of Revolutions," 51.

29. Steinmetz, "Critical Realism and Historical Sociology," 178.

30. Goldstone, "Comparative Historical Analysis and Knowledge Accumulation in the Study of Revolutions," 47.

III

We can now see the central problematic for research in the realist mode: although evidence provides a way to "test" for the presence and strength of certain mechanisms or social structures, the insistence on reference, coherence, and generality places tremendous weight on the theoretical frame that the investigator brings to the research situation. Theoretical "presuppositions" are in fact an incredibly consequential general theory of the social object—they articulate what exists in the social world, and how such basic social entities act.

But where should this general social theory come from? How should investigators establish the basis for the productive semiotic circuit outlined above? Where, according to Goldstone, is the first bet placed? Justin Cruickshank notes a common slippage in critical realist argumentation about the theoretical framework with which the investigator works—often referred to in realist circles as her social ontology. "On the one hand," Cruickshank notices, "ontology pertains to what critical realists refer to as the 'transitive domain' of fallible, theoretical interpretations of reality, whilst on the other hand, ontology is taken to be a direct representation of the 'intransitive domain,' meaning the reality beyond our knowledge."[31] This slippage reveals a problem in realism as imagined by Bhaskar, Mario Bunge, and others. If one did have direct knowledge of the "intransitive" social realm,[32] then one would be justified in offering that knowledge

31. Justin Cruickshank, "A Tale of Two Ontologies: An Immanent Critique of Critical Realism," *Sociological Review* 52, no. 4 (2004): 567. Cruickshank's critique is aimed primarily at critical realism as it exists in British sociology, and particularly the realism associated with Roy Bhaskar, Margaret Archer, and Tony Lawson, among others. But it could also apply, for example, to Christian Smith's account of realism and its importance for American sociology. Smith follows Bhaskar in prioritizing ontology over epistemology, and thus writes that "That which is cannot be immediately constrained by limits on the knowable of it. First we come to terms with what we believe is and what it is like, then we examine the possibilities for knowing about it." Christian Smith, *What Is a Person? Rethinking Humanitiy, Social Life, and the Moral Good from the Person Up* (Chicago: University of Chicago Press, 2010), 93.

32. The original purpose and utility of the transitive/intransitive distinction in Roy Bhaskar's account of *natural* science, and its relevance for social science will be discussed below. Briefly, however, we can follow Smith's summary: "Human knowledge has both *intransitive* and *transitive* dimensions that should not be conflated. The former concerns the real objects of scientific knowledge, the latter the content of our human knowledge of those objects in reality." Smith, *What Is a Person?* 94. The intransitive is that which is, and the transitive is what we (scientifically) know about that which is. Thus, to cite the *Dictionary of Critical Realism*, the intransitive dimension is

as *the* theory of social reality upon which research programs should be based. This would be the starting point for the quasi-Bayesian research process that Goldstone outlines. But Cruickshank notes that (critical) realists tend to avoid claims to metaphysically certain knowledge, and argue instead that social theory "ought to be derived from within current scientific knowledge about reality."[33] But then, if this knowledge of social reality is as fragmented as the contemporary human sciences are, how is one to figure out which ontology is the correct starting point?[34]

To fully understand this key aspect of the realist epistemic mode, we must return to the original arguments made for realism—and in opposition to positivism and relativism—by Roy Bhaskar in the 1970s. For contained therein are explicit arguments for two fundamental premises of the mode as it was practiced both before Bhaskar wrote his texts and as it is practiced today.

In *A Realist Theory of Science*, Bhaskar argued that, since natural science exists and is successful, one can argue retroductively to the existence of a world of natural mechanisms separate from the experiments that manipulate or trigger these mechanisms—otherwise scientific experiment would be an unintelligible human activity. There must be a world of forces and structures underneath phenomena as they are presented to the senses; otherwise, the elaborate setups of scientific experimentation—designed to isolate the powers of these forces and structures—would be both arbitrary and unnecessary. The

---

"synonymous with ontology" while the transitive dimension is synonymous with "the epistemological *process*." Marvin Hartwig, ed. *Dictionary of Critical Realism* (New York: Routledge, 2007). (The entry for "intransitive dimension" contains a lengthier discussion of the origins and uses of the terms.)

33. Cruickshank, "A Tale of Two Ontologies," 568.

34. John R. Hall points out that while the overriding conviction of realism is that social reality is definable or has a nature that transcends this or that historical case, there is very little agreement as to what this fundamental social reality *is*. This gives certain discussions around social scientific realism an "abstract and unreal air," for "when we move from philosophical positions to trying to analyze the sociohistorical world, the 'things' and 'relations' that are awkwardly characterized as acts, norms, processes and so forth all elude any straightforward realistic conceptualization . . . realists do not agree with each other about the reality (e.g., of 'intelligence,' 'class conflict,' 'kinship') that supposedly is knowable . . . In short, accepting realism metaphysically cannot entail reducing the character of reality to any particular realist description (e.g., of 'gender'). Thus, practically speaking, metaphysical realism is hard put to offer the social ontology that it would claim to warrant." John R. Hall, *Cultures of Inquiry: From Epistemology to Discourse in Sociohistorical Research* (Cambridge: Cambridge University Press, 1999), 48.

experiment, then, functions as a pragmatic point of communication between the "transitive" domain of fallible human knowledge and the "intransitive" domain of nature (the latter exists and functions regardless of whether there are humans who comprehend it scientifically). As a result, a form of judgmental rationality prevails in natural science, which moves theories—part of the transitive domain—closer and closer to a direct description of the intransitive domain. In this way, Bhaskar proposed to both account for the fact that scientific knowledge is manifestly the creation of humans and is always revising itself—it is never finished, and always flawed—and argue that science is ultimately a rational and effective way of comprehending nature.

In his next major text, *The Possibility of Naturalism*, Bhaskar proposed what was, in effect, a set of analogies that—if taken to be accurate and well worked through—would amount to a justification of a certain kind of naturalism for social research. Of particular interest are the following:

> —That the "social world," though different than the "natural world," can also be thought of as an "intransitive" realm, to which the "transitive" theories produced by social research attempt to correspond.[35]

35. Thus the whole question hinges on what can be included in the realm of "intransitive" *social* objects. Fundamentally, Bhaskar makes a categorical distinction between transitive and intransitive so as to argue that "knowledge is a social product, produced by means of antecedent social products; but that the objects of which, in the social activity of science, knowledge comes to be produced, exist and act quite independently of men" (Roy Bhaskar, *A Realist Theory of Science* [New York: Verso, 2008], 5–6). In simpler terms, the intransitive domain is that which is, and the transitive domain is human beings' various attempts to comprehend it. As one might anticipate, the existence of human conceptualization as part of "that which is"—the concept-dependency of social life—becomes, then, a major area of theoretical focus for the realist philosophy of *social* science.

Many who have carefully considered this issue in the realist philosophy of social science—including Margaret Archer, Bhaskar, and William Outhwaite—have concluded that the "constructs" of meaning, belief, etc. can be considered to be part of this "intransitive" social realm. But the problem with this is that then the transitive/intransitive distinction that founded Bhaskar's realist theory of (natural) science breaks down, since that distinction was designed *precisely* to separate the *transitive* conceptions and beliefs of certain acting human beings (scientists) from the *intransitive* structures of nature that the scientists were interacting with through experiments (and whose existence and workings are quite independent, at the ontological level, from what humans do or do not know about them). In Bhaskar's original philosophy of science, this distinction is of utmost importance, because it provides the basis for his synthesis of "epistemic relativism" and "ontological realism," the realist *aufhebung* of the Kuhnian critique of positivist philosophies of science.

Here the critiques developed by Anthony King are absolutely essential. King's central point in his critique not only of realism, but also of the structure/agency dichotomy

—That though societies are "open systems" and thus subject to unpredictable historical changes, they can still be studied scientifically, despite the lack of experimental conditions for studying these systems. The reason for this is that societies already contain—as a part of themselves—a *proto*scientific conceptual account of themselves.[36]

As a result, argued Bhaskar, social research should function as research on nature does, via ontological theory, which is to say theory that definitively points to the structures of social reality. Notoriously, however, Bhaskar termed his account of social science a combination of "critical naturalism" and "transcendental realism," which, when combined, yielded "critical realism." This meant that social scientific naturalism should not be an unthinking or direct importation of natural scientific methods and theories into the social sciences. Rather, a critical reflexivity was necessary—particularly since social structures are, according to Bhaskar, "concept-dependent" and also "emergent" realities dependent upon agents and their actions for their existence. What Bhaskar's complex oeuvre represents, then, is an extended argument that the differences between the social and natural worlds can be taken on board in a consideration of what makes social research feasible and justifiable, but that the basis for explanations—in natural science *and* in social research—is the general, coherent, and referential signification of reality by theory.

Furthermore, Bhaskar proposes, in an appealingly counterintuitive way, that the role of concepts in social life is in fact an *asset* to naturalistic approaches to social research.[37] He argues that, while the open systems of societies cannot be experimented upon, the concepts that exist as part of those societies provide a compensator for the lack of experiment. Instead of experimenting, social researchers can, through "retroduction," move from an understanding of the concepts

---

in social theory as a whole, is that to map the intransitive/transitive distinction onto the society/agency distinction, or to treat social structures as intransitive in the same way natural structures are, leads to tremendous confusion. Anthony King, *The Structure of Social Theory* (London: Routledge, 2004).

36. Roy Bhaskar, *The Possibility of Naturalism: A Philosophical Critique of the Contemporary Human Sciences* (New York: Routledge, 1998), 48.

37. Many—and most notoriously Peter Winch, whom Bhaskar spends many pages of his classic work arguing with—have argued that the role of concepts in society strictly *disables* social scientific naturalism. See Peter Winch, *The Idea of Social Science and Its Relation to Philosophy* (New York: Humanities Press, 1958), and Berel Dov Lerner, *Rules, Magic, and Instrumental Reason: A Critical Interpretation of Peter Winch's Philosophy of the Social Sciences* (New York: Routledge, 2002).

used by lay actors to understand their social reality to an understanding of that social reality itself.[38] In other words, all societies already contain within themselves a protoscience of themselves, which the investigator converts into a real science of society. This retroduction is analogous to the previously mentioned retroduction that moved from the success of experiments in natural science to the ontological status of theoretical entities, which is to say, to the affirmation of the existence of a world of intransitive powers and mechanisms that experiments access and manipulate.

Bhaskar's example of such retroduction in the human sciences is indeed one of the greatest arguments ever made in social research:

> [Marx's] *Capital* may most plausibly be viewed as an attempt to establish what must be the case for the experiences grasped by the phenomenal forms of capitalist life to be possible; setting out, as it were, a pure schema for the understanding of economic phenomena under capitalism, specifying the categories that must be employed in any concrete investigation . . . for Marx to understand the essence of some particular social phenomenon is to understand the social relations that make that phenomenon possible.[39]

With reference to the process of retroduction, Bhaskar claims that "Marx's analysis in *Capital* illustrates the substantive use of a transcendental procedure."[40]

But note that there is some mud in the water here. In Marx's critique of the consciousness of the bourgeoisie (and especially of the bourgeois economists), he posits that their understanding of capitalism is *incorrect* and also posits the social reality that produced that incorrect understanding. This is *not* analogous to the transcendental derivation whereby it is argued that natural science could only be intelligible and successful if it were the case that its theoretical terms

38. Jason Glynos and David Howarth place retroduction in intellectual-historical context in the first chapter of their book *Logics of Critical Explanation in Social and Political Theory* (New York: Routledge, 2007). In particular, they connect it to Peirce's work on Aristotelean reasoning, translated as "abductive" or "retroductive" (24–48). The direction they take this illuminating intervention is, however, significantly different than the argument of this book, in particular in so far as they tend to view hermeneutic interpretation as normative interpretation, and ultimately affirm an "ontological negativity or radical contingency," which is to say an instability to social life, as the conceptual source of their framework for critical explanation.

39. Bhaskar, *The Possibility of Naturalism*, 51.

40. Bhaskar, *The Possibility of Naturalism*, 51.

have reference to an underlying reality. The latter, transcendental-realist argument is: that which science conceptualizes and manipulates in experiments must, if the experiments work, exist. Prima facie, it seems to be manifestly the case that a direct analogy to research on the social world cannot be drawn. For, if it were, then one could say, for example: in Salem, Massachusetts, in 1692, there was a social conceptualization of "the witch," which led to a set of practical actions that were highly successful: witches were found and killed. Thus it must be the case that the category "witch," and more broadly the theory of what witches do elaborated in witch-hunting manuals of the time, must refer to a general social reality; there were (and are?) witches. (Beyond the obvious, there is a more general problem here, indicated in this case by the rather horrific irony of "successful witch trials": what social practices are equivalent to the success of scientific experiment?)

But of course Marx's argument does not run in this manner, indeed quite the opposite—he is arguing that the conceptualization of capitalism available phenomenologically to everyday actors in capitalist society is ***wrong***—it belies, and therefore helps reproduce, the real social structure, which is referred to directly by the theory of modes of production. And indeed, Bhaskar suggests that the theories of society that exist within a given society are prototheories (really, we should say pseudotheories), which have to be transformed into real theories. But how is this transformation done? And there is the rub: to do it, one has to ***already know*** Marx's theory of social reality.[41] In other words, the argument about the use of concepts-in-society to es-

41. Thus Justin Cruickshank has moved away from the realist position that he articulated in his earlier work, and toward a new interpretation of Karl Popper's philosophy of science, which emphasizes the pragmatic dimensions of Popper's work, and Popper's antiontological mode of thinking. In particular he is developing a theory of social scientific knowledge that avoids starting investigation with strict ontological definitions. Cruickshank is thus in the process of carving out a position that is neither positivist, realist, postmodern, or hermeneutic. The best name I can think of for this emerging project is "sociological pragmatism," since Cruickshank seems both more in touch with actual social research than were the neopragmatist philosophers, and to have moved beyond some of the primary concerns of Donald Davidson and Richard Rorty. See in particular Cruickshank, "A Tale of Two Ontologies: An Immanent Critique of Critical Realism," and Justin Cruickshank, "The Usefulness of Fallibilism: A Popperian Critique of Critical Realism," ***Philosophy of the Social Sciences*** 37, no. 3 (2007). For Cruickshank's earlier, realist work see Justin Cruickshank, ***Critical Realism: The Difference It Makes*** (London: Routledge, 2003); Justin Cruickshank, ***Realism and Sociology: Anti-Foundationalism, Ontology, and Social Research*** (New York: Routledge, 2003).

tablish a theory of social reality begs the question of what theoretical knowledge enables the transformation of prototheory into scientific theory; the analogy to transcendental retroduction does not hold.[42]

IV

The problem, ultimately, for the naturalist analogy is that social life may not be "intransitive." In realist philosophy of social science, a key elision is made so as to put social investigation into the box of a modified naturalism. That social reality exists outside the head of the investigator, and indeed outside the heads of any subset of individual humans engaged in it, is taken as evidence for the "intransitivity" of society, social structure, etc.[43] But—and Marx's critiques of Feuerbach are indeed the original reference here[44]—the dynamism of social life, its historicity, belies the philosophical anthropology of "man" or "society."[45] One presumes that gravity was the same for Henry II as it is for Barack Obama; the semiotic sources of legitimate domination are not. This is of course a trivial example, and there are indeed natural

42. I have, here, focused on the work of Roy Bhaskar, but many of the same arguments for realism, and against hermeneutics, postmodernism, positivism, etc. can be found in the oeuvre of Mario Bunge. For a comparison of the two philosophers' approach to explanation in social science, see Chares Demetriou, "The Realist Approach to Explanatory Mechanisms in Social Science: More than a Heuristic?" *Philosophy of the Social Sciences* 39, no. 3 (2009).

43. Anthony King writes that Bhaskar "appeals to the concept of structure because he takes a peculiar and inadequate view of it. Institutions are assumed to be autonomous by Bhaskar only because he analyses these 'structures' from the perspective of a single individual . . . From the individual's point of view, social reality is objective; it manifestly exists independently of what an individual thinks or does. From individual experience, structure is prior, it is independent and it does have causal powers. Yet, although compelling for the individual, this view is a solipsism. It takes the individual perspective as the basis of sociological analysis." King, *The Structure of Social Theory*, 79.

44. For an account of social theory that sets the "realist" Marx against the "hermeneutic" Marx, using Marx's early writings on praxis as the basis for the latter, see King, *The Structure of Social Theory*, 107–21.

45. The project of philosophical anthropology also takes as a reference point Marx and Feuerbach. See Axel Honneth and Hans Joas, *Social Action and Human Nature* (New York: Cambridge University Press, 1988). Some of the attempts to develop a critical philosophy that have emerged from realism include work that takes quite seriously the idea that specifying human nature is an essential first step to an ethics. So, Caroline New argues that critical realism can "offer philosophical grounding for ethical naturalism" and thus help save feminism from the linguistic (wrong) turn. Caroline New, "Feminism, Critical Realism and the Linguistic Turn," in *Critical Realism: The Difference It Makes*, ed. Justin Cruickshank (New York: Routledge, 2003), 57–75.

sciences that seem to have a historical element (such as evolutionary biology). But the force of the contrast remains, particularly when it comes to the "ontological status of theoretical entities." In what way, really, is "society" or "social structure," *intransitive*? Can we really ascribe to the signifiers of social theory "ontological status," if what we mean by this is the sort of permanence that, say, the natural kind "gold" has?[46] Or is the continuation of scientistic epistemology in the human studies both fetish and illusion?

The principle of realist signification is that unity in theory can bring together disparate cases under the same general scheme; theory has direct referents in social reality, and these referents are what enable evidence to be sorted and causal claims to be made. If, however, the social object is unstable or "transitive," then it is also possible that cases could be incommensurable in the sense that they do not have, underneath them, different arrangements of the same basic social forces, or mechanisms, or relational entities. This throws into doubt the premise of the realist epistemic mode—that at its core, the theoretical meaning-system is grounded in much the same way the factual meaning-system is: by reference to a reality that can be reported on. Theory, according to realism, reports upon a deeper social reality.

In the end, it is precisely the supposed compensator for the lack of experiment in social research that undermines this orderly understanding of theory and fact. Meaning and subjectivity in social life—or, in Bhaskar's terms, the concept-dependence of social structure—provide a great deal of dynamism to the social object, particularly in so far as they are *unrealistic*. Subjectivity, understood literally as that element of the world that continually exceeds its objective constraints,[47] gives to the social object of study a distinct historical dynamism and cultural difference.[48]

46. The reference here is to Hilary Putnam's work on pragmatism, realism, and natural kinds. The classic articles in this regard are Hilary Putnam, "Meaning and Reference," *Journal of Philosophy* 70, no. 19 (1973), and Hilary Putnam, "The Meaning of Meaning," in *Minnesota Studies in the Philosophy of Science*, vol. 7 (Minneapolis: University of Minnesota Press, 1975). He then revised these views in Hilary Putnam, "Why There Isn't a Ready Made World," *Synthese* 51, no. 2 (1982).

47. The original reference in this regard is Hegel's discourse on lordship and bondage. See paragraphs 178–96 in Georg Wilhelm Friedrich Hegel, *Phenomenology of Spirit*, trans. A. V. Miller (New York: Oxford University Press, 1977).

48. This emphasis on the effects of subjectivity, history, and culture on the human being, and the resultant problems with realism and, more broadly, naturalism, is one way to interpret Clifford Geertz's epigrammatic statement that "If anthropology is obsessed with anything it is with how much difference difference makes." Clifford

That subjectivity and history render the naturalist approach to social knowledge problematic has been the refrain of antiscientism arguments for over a century in academic social studies in the West. It was perhaps never more eloquently articulated than in H. Stuart Hughes's account of the revolt of European intellectuals against positivism in the 1890s. These men—Weber and Freud among them—Hughes writes, "displaced the axis of social thought from the apparent and objectively verifiable to the only partially conscious area of unexplained motivation." They thus arrived at the conclusion that "it was no longer what actually existed that seemed most important: it was what men thought existed. And what they felt on the unconscious level had become rather more important than what they had consciously rationalized."[49] But what are the true implications of this intellectual maneuver, this antinaturalism?

V

No matter how much we criticize naturalism, it is a mistake to take away from this argument the implication that effective, empirically responsible social research is impossible. The contradictions of realism emerge in the attempt to apply the naturalist metaphor to the process of using theory to build explanations. Thus to argue against realism is not to deny the existence of facts, or even the possibility of constructing social explanations. The core ambition of realism is to take the risk of depth interpretation, or in the terms developed here, to construct maximal interpretations that use theory to go beyond the facts, but remain responsible to those facts. This was also the ambition of Freud and Weber, even if they ventured outside of "science," as it was understood in their time, to achieve it. Perhaps we should consider our position, vis-à-vis realism, to be somewhat similar to that which Weber faced vis-à-vis nineteenth- and early twentieth-century positivism.

It is unfortunately the case that many of the most cogent reflections on realism participate in the strange gambit of science or nothing at all, expecting somehow the human studies to function as

---

Geertz, *Available Light: Anthropological Reflections on Philosophical Topics* (Princeton: Princeton University Press, 2000), 197.

49. H. Stuart Hughes, *Consciousness and Society: The Reorientation of European Social Thought, 1890–1930* (New York: Vintage Books, 1961), 66.

effective natural sciences without experiment and with an object—humankind—which is really a subject, and a notoriously plastic and elusive subject at that. This is the naturalist error. However, social life does, across certain swaths of time and space, work in patterned, or even systematic, ways. There are aspects of social life here and there, and perhaps especially in modern social organizations, that function mechanistically. When we consider realism's growing effect upon truth claims made in social research, we do, then, find a quite clear contribution, namely that the theorization and identification of mechanisms provides causal torque to historical argument. Yet the problem is that in realism, identifying some mechanistic aspects of social life brings with it an entire framework for investigation, wherein the basic mechanisms of the social are defined in a general social theory, and then the investigator tests for their presence or absence, strength or weakness.

Thus we could perhaps say that, alongside its naturalist ambition, there is a related, but more impressionistic, problem with realism. This is a discursive effect: realism's constant use of ontological language makes it hard to keep in mind that mechanism is a metaphor, derived originally from the mechanical clocks that surrounded the men who launched the scientific revolution in the West. Those men concluded that the processes they were uncovering in nature could (often) be adequately conceptualized as working as an elaborate clock does—producing regularities via hidden machinery that it was the job of the scientist to discover. Since that time, the language of mechanism has—all the way up through the foundational writings of Bhaskar and Bunge for the realist philosophy of social science—provided a ready counterpoint to the Humean critique of causality as a concept of the mind imposed upon constant conjunctions. Causal theories refer, in this language, to *real mechanisms*. And so one finds oneself importing into social inquiry a whole set of expectations about the cross-cultural and cross-historical efficacy of mechanisms, and a whole set of procedures for grounding a wide variety of evidence in one's theoretical articulations of social ontology. Mechanisms are expected to be found in all sorts of times and places, and, when one identifies mechanisms, one expects to use theory to resignify evidence in a realist manner. But the recognition that social life in some times and some places evidences a regularity that can be likened to a mechanism does not necessitate a commitment to the realist mode for building maximal interpretations. For the mere fact that social life has regularity does not mean that we have to model our understanding of social life on the sciences that have attended to the regularities of nature.

Rather, we should look for a way to integrate the core ambition of scientific realism (causal explanation) and its core insights into social life (that social life does proceed, some of the time, with a rather frightening regularity) into a different epistemic mode. There might be other ways to go about using theory to interpret evidence; other ways to comprehend the varying contexts of social action; other ways to elaborate and utilize the exceedingly strange meaning-system that is social theory.

If there are, it should not surprise us that the interpretation of consciousness would be central to these other modes. For, if the social is denaturalized, then the question of the institutionalization and maintenance of social realities becomes connected to the question of how the social life is normatively imagined. Another way of saying this is: if, contra Bhaskar's reading of Marx, one *cannot* identify a single social theory of reality that both debunks ideology and explains why some people would believe it, then both social criticism, and eventually the understanding of social reality itself, must reconsider themselves. Here, I begin with a consideration of the normative epistemic mode, which, leaving realism behind, retains the engagement with facts, but builds maximal interpretations in a very different way.

Chapter Three

Utopia

Mythical is that which never changes, ultimately diluted to a formal legality of thought. To want substance in cognition is to want a utopia.
—Theodor Adorno, *Negative Dialectics*

I

We can recognize easily in contemporary social and political theory an extended terrain of normative argument. Debates about modernity and postmodernity, democracy and multiculturalism, ethics and gender, and myriad other concerns form a whole layer of disputation and theorization that—to a greater or lesser degree—orients how social researchers choose their projects, publish their results, and regulate themselves in their own lifeworlds. Political theory is part of the theoretical meaning-system that, in a variety of ways, informs the practice of social research. It is not difficult, furthermore, to see that this kind of normative argument is absolutely necessary. For, if social actors orient themselves, at least some of the time, to ideals, then, since social researchers and social theorists are social actors, they too must orient their actions to ideals in some sense, some of the time. In addition, there is a loose way in which social theorists and researchers themselves constitute—discursively at least—a community of actors. Thus it would be surprising—and indeed evidence of almost willful ignorance—if such actors did not use their specific tools (intellectual argument and elaboration) to reflect upon and dispute the validity of their norms, their understanding of the good society, their theories of what, in fact, is a democratic decision, and so on.

But at stake, in this book at least, is not just the mere existence or necessity of political philosophy or political theory. It is, rather, to a specific way theory is used in the thick of investigation that I intend the term "normativism" to refer. For what normativism is, as an epistemic mode anyway, is a way of producing maximal interpretations that speak to the debates of political theory, but that speak to these debates with an intellectual authority derived from both theory and fact.

At the core of normativism as an epistemic mode is the understanding that knowledge itself has a politics. From this premise, normativism draws the following implication: that when an investigator researches other people—even others long since dead—she constructs a dialogue between herself and her subjects. This recognition of social research as communication between subjects destabilizes the human sciences: history, culture, and agency are not problems that must be overcome or got around; they are the constitutive problematics of knowledge that addresses itself to life animated by consciousness. In classical social theory, the effect of expansion this has on what is to be considered by the theorist or investigator of the social is most visible in the work of W. E. B. DuBois. His work relegated the generalized analytics of Durkheim (and perhaps even Marx) to one small piece of a larger project of social knowledge. This project, moreover, was, in DuBois' case, deeply intertwined with the political project and social movements of black Americans. Thus DuBois' arguments tend to contain layers of the dialogic, speak consistently to the need to carefully make practical judgments, as well as articulate the fullness of human life and suffering. They are thus full of connotations and resonances of a type quite uncommon in the work of Durkheim or Weber:

> But back of this still broods silently the deep religious feeling of the real Negro heart, the stirring, unguided might of powerful human souls who have lost the guiding star of the past and are seeking in the great night a new religious ideal. Some say the Awakening will come, when the pent-up vigor of ten million souls shall sweep irresistibly toward the goal, out of the Valley of the Shadow of Death, where all that makes

> life worth living—Liberty, Justice, and Right—is marked "For White People Only."[1]

The implications of DuBois' magisterial oeuvre extend far beyond the concerns of this text. But one of the implications surely is this: in theorizing consciousness in society, one must resist the reduction of consciousness to the cognitive—both in the sense that the subjects of investigation are not, merely, cognitive beings, and in the sense that investigators themselves, in trying to comprehend others, act more than just cognitively. They may act ethically and politically. They may pass judgment. This requires antinaturalism in the human sciences (though certainly not—as DuBois' work makes clear—the abandonment of empirical responsibility, or of quantitative measurement).

Which is to say that, in the process of comprehending action, investigators can and perhaps should attempt a judgment of those actions in a way that is entirely unrecognizable to the physical sciences (no one passes judgment on the behavior of H_2O). The interpretive skillfulness of the scientist is directed at the phenomena of nature and their laws; but the social investigator is ultimately interested in laws in the normative sense. This perspective reflects something about the social worlds we investigate: social movements are driven, in part, by their utopian imaginations. Moral judgments made in a court of law or in a psychiatric hospital can arbitrate life or death. Generally speaking, if social life depends, to some degree, on the judgments, ethical imperatives, and utopian ideals of the people who live it, then a deep comprehension of the workings of such judgments, imperatives, and ideals is called for. The normative epistemic mode has at its core a conceptual method for achieving this goal, a process of theoretical resignification wherein the judgments of the investigator are formed by the intersection of rigorous utopian theory and sociohistorical fact. It is an epistemic mode that can produce what David Thacher has called a normative case study.[2]

1. W. E. B. DuBois, *The Souls of Black Folk* (New York: W. W. Norton & Company, 1999), 29.

2. David Thacher, "The Normative Case Study," *American Journal of Sociology* 111, no. 6 (2006).

II

The focus on the subjective, on consciousness and on consciousness-in-society, was a recurrent theme of twentieth-century Western philosophy on both sides of the Atlantic. The philosophies of consciousness are wide ranging, but one of their recurring concerns is the ways in which human beings appear to follow rules; to judge each other's actions for their appropriateness, rationality, or morality; and to regulate themselves in groups, via norms. In other words, there is, in some sense of the term, a *normative* dimension of social life. What are the implications of this for the human sciences? The implications are developed, in the abstract at least, in a classic argument of contemporary social theory.

In a key early section of *The Theory of Communicative Action*, Jürgen Habermas makes a startling theoretical move. He has, at this point, established (to his own satisfaction at least) that there are such things as "normatively regulated actions." This appropriates a good deal of analytic philosophy on the matter, for what Habermas is relying upon is the idea that some descriptions of actions are in terms of whether they "appropriately" follow a rule, or whether they violate it. Habermas also accepts (perhaps surprisingly) that the social researcher can produce an "objectivist" account of the prevalence of a norm in a given time and place. However, says Habermas, in this kind of description "the question of a rational interpretation does not arise." And, he argues, an interpreter satisfied with this sort of description of norms will eventually have to admit that the whole idea of normatively regulated action is "theoretically unsuitable" and will ultimately resort to explanations given in "causal-behavioristic terms."[3] In other words, for Habermas, objectivist accounts of norm-regulated behavior do not understand consciousness-in-society. These accounts do not engage the problem of subjectivity that gives realism such trouble.

What comes next is important. Habermas then argues that the acceptance of the idea that actions are norm-guided, and the ensuing effort on the part of the social researcher to comprehend these norms, leads to a quite different approach to the human sciences. "[I]f," Habermas writes, "the interpreter is convinced of the theoretical

3. Jürgen Habermas, *The Theory of Communicative Action* (Boston: Beacon Press, 1984), 104.

fruitfulness of the normative model of action, he has to get involved in the suppositions of commonality that are accepted with the formal concept of the social world and allow for the possibility of testing the *worthiness* to be recognized of a norm held by an actor to be right."[4] In other words, the "moral-practical appraisal of norms of action" *is* the process of "understanding" norms, in so far as this interpretive process goes beyond objectivism. The interpretation of consciousness (or, as Habermas sometimes calls it, the practice of the "historical-hermeneutical sciences")[5] involves getting caught up in whether the norms that regulate actors' behavior are right or valid *qua normative statements.*

As a result, a parallel is set up that carries through all of Habermas's subsequent epistemological writings, in which there are (at least) two different versions of "rational interpretation." The first—connected to the human interest in controlling and predicting nature—is the process by which speakers make claims about the "objective" or physical world, and the validity of these claims is checked by other speakers in terms of their correspondence to the state of that world. The second—vital for Habermas's theory of deliberative democracy—is the process by which speakers make a claim to regulate their own and/or others' action in terms of a collective norm, and the validity of these claims is checked by others in terms of the *rightness* of the norm—its moral worth, its fairness, etc. Habermas considers any attempt to approach norms from the first of these perspectives to be an impoverished social science, which has succumbed to an ontologically incorrect account of human action as cognition-based and instrumental. A historical-hermeneutic perspective supersedes this, according to Habermas, and in so doing engages with the validity of the norms themselves. This hermeneutics, then, cannot be reduced to an account of how norms that exist at a certain time and place do or do not have certain effects or consequences. Rather, when it comes to interpretation, questions of meaning and questions of validity cannot be strictly separated.[6]

It is tempting to just take on this argument from the perspective of analytic philosophy, and argue that there is simply a slippage, in

4. Habermas, *The Theory of Communicative Action*, 104.

5. See in particular, Jürgen Habermas, *Knowledge and Human Interests* (Boston: Beacon Press, 1971), 301–17.

6. Habermas, *The Theory of Communicative Action*, 106.

Habermas, between understanding and agreement—and thus to object that to understand the existence of a norm and to agree with a norm are different operations of the mind. From a strictly analytic point of view, this is, I think, true,[7] but it massively misunderstands the Habermasian project. The philosophical problem of "what is a norm" is not what is at stake for Habermas in his extended contributions to social knowledge. Rather, what Habermas articulates in these passages from *The Theory of Communicative Action* is a philosophical description of an epistemic mode for producing maximal interpretations—a mode whereby the investigator involves herself in a dialogue with her subjects that has as its subject normative validity. Habermas's work, however, is but one exemplary instance of this epistemic mode, which in its fullness offers possibilities for social research that extend far beyond his specific concerns. But to see how it works, to understand the semiotic circuits of normativism, we have to analyze actual examples of normativist social knowledge claims. One might as well begin with a claim made by Habermas himself.

III

Consider the following quotation from Habermas's *The Structural Transformation of the Public Sphere.*

> However much the *Tischgesellschaften*, *salons*, and coffee houses may have differed . . . they all organized discussion among private people that tended to be ongoing; hence they had a number of institutional criteria in common. *First*, they preserved a kind of social intercourse that, far from presupposing the equality of status, disregarded status altogether. The tendency replaced the celebration of rank with a tact befitting equals. The parity on whose basis alone the authority of the better argument could assert itself against that of social hierarchy and in the end can carry the day meant, in the thought of the day, the parity

7. The philosopher of social science David Henderson has ferreted out the many ways in which philosophers and sociologists use the normative evaluation of rationality to do explanatory work. He has then proceeded to criticize these tendencies extensively. For his general philosophical position, see David K. Henderson, *Interpretation and Explanation in the Human Sciences*, Suny Series in the Philosophy of the Social Sciences (Albany: State University of New York Press, 1993). For this particular issue, see his exchange with Mark Risjord in the journal *Philosophy of the Social Sciences*, and especially his extended article on precisely this matter: David Henderson, "Norms, Normative Principles, and Explanation: On Not Getting Is from Ought," *Philosophy of the Social Sciences* 32, no. 3 (2002).

> of "common humanity" . . . *Secondly*, discussion within such a public presupposed the problematization of areas that until then had not been questioned . . . *Thirdly*, the same process that converted culture into a commodity (and in this fashion constituted it as a culture that could become an object of discussion to begin with) established the public as in principle inclusive. However exclusive the public might be in any given instance, it could never close itself off entirely and become consolidated as a clique: for it always understood and found itself immersed within a more inclusive public of all private people, persons who—insofar as they were propertied and educated—as readers, listeners, and spectators could avail themselves via the market of the objects that were subject to discussion. The issues discussed became "general" not merely in their significance, but also in their accessibility . . .[8]

Herein, we see again the proliferation of fact-signs. The coffee houses of Europe in the eighteenth century "organized discussion among private people that tended to be ongoing"; in the coffee houses status was disregarded; in the coffee houses, people questioned and argued about aspects of life that they had not questioned and argued about before. All of these are statements in the language of fact. They can be disputed (and have been), but such disputation also occurs in the language of fact.[9]

But these facts do not become significant, for Habermas, until they are interpreted by theory. Theoretical terms related to the normative concerns that have animated Habermas's career infuse this paragraph with a second layer of meaning. Perhaps the key theoretical signs are "the authority of the better argument" and "the public as in principle inclusive." With these terms, we start to get a maximal interpretation of the coffee house, Habermas's discovery of a "kernel" of reason and

8. Jürgen Habermas, *The Structural Transformation of the Public Sphere: An Inquiry into a Category of Bourgeois Society* (Cambridge, MA: MIT Press, 1989), 36–37.

9. Perhaps of particular relevance here are three excellent critiques of Habermas's work by Michael Schudson, Geoff Eley, and Mary Ryan, which, though they reach into the realm of maximal interpretation in their theoretical work, also do tremendous work in disputing the minimal interpretation upon which Habermas's normative conclusions rely. See Michael Schudson, "Was There Ever a Public Sphere? If So, When? Reflections on the American Case," in *Habermas and the Public Sphere*, ed. Craig Calhoun (Cambridge, MA: MIT Press, 1992); Mary P. Ryan, "Gender and Public Access: Women's Politics in Nineteenth Century America," in *Habermas and the Public Sphere*, ed. Craig Calhoun (Cambridge, MA: MIT Press, 1992); Goeff Eley, "Nations, Publics, and Political Cultures: Placing Habermas in the Nineteenth Century," in *Habermas and the Public Sphere*, ed. Craig Calhoun (Cambridge, MA: MIT Press, 1992).

deliberative democracy immanent to (in this case Western) history and society. The discussions of the coffee houses offer us a vision of democratic politics that is all the more powerful since these discussions *actually existed*. The principles implicit in these discussions are also the principles of deliberative democracy as Habermas understands it; the best argument carries the day regardless of who makes it, and, in principle, anyone who can make such an argument is welcome to do so.

It is, of course, this "in principle" that signals the modality we are dealing with, and the specific logic of Habermas's argument. For he recognizes that, in fact, only propertied white men of certain distinction and with a certain access to leisure and capital could participate in these coffee house discussions, and that the very functioning of the public sphere was thus dependent on a fictitious equation of "property owners" with "human beings."[10] But the maximal interpretation worked out in *The Structural Transformation of the Public Sphere* is not only about the facts. Rather, it is precisely the tension between the "principle" of an inclusive public and the actually existing public of the eighteenth century that is essential to Habermas's work. For his goal is to elaborate an ideal, a notion of democracy and the good society, in conversation with the normative debates of Habermas's own time. This elaboration, however, is done via the interpretation of actual societies and actual history. It travels through and reconstructs a historically located piece of social life on its way to normative argumentation.

The second half of Habermas's case study of the public sphere participates in a more familiar form of critique and negation, directly descended from Adorno and Horkheimer. Therein, Habermas contrasts the immanent ideals or principles of the coffee house to their disappearance:

> Along the path from a public critically reflecting on its culture to one that merely consumes it, the public sphere in the world of letters, which at one point could still be distinguished from that in the political realm, has lost its specific character. For the "culture" propagated by the mass media is a culture of integration. It not only integrates information with critical debate and the journalistic format with the literary forms of the psychological novel into a combination of entertainment and

10. Habermas, *The Structural Transformation of the Public Sphere*, 56.

> "advice" governed by the principle of "human interest"; at the same time it is flexible enough to assimilate elements of advertising, indeed, to serve itself as a kind of super slogan that, if it did not already exist, could have been invented for the purpose of public relations serving the cause of the status quo. The public sphere assumes advertising functions. The more it can be deployed as a vehicle for political and economic propaganda, the more it becomes unpolitical as a whole and pseudo-privatized.[11]

Here again, however, we see the same logic of normative resignification. The empirical trends in newspapers and journalism—the inclusion of advertising, the turn to "human interest" stories, and so on—are resignified as the transition from "critical reflection" to "consumption" and "pseudo-privatization."[12] And as such, an evaluation is implied, and an imperative to reawaken public deliberation. So, in the second half of Habermas's text, the normative resignification is a negation, an attempt to upset the taken-for-granted everyday life of late modern capitalist societies, and to upset, also, the liberal notion of progress that ideologically informs the people acting within them.

IV

In considering the epistemological basis for this sort of maximal interpretation, we can start by noting that Habermas's theory has a clear utopian referent—rational deliberation, or, as he would later elaborate, the ideal speech situation. In addition, the language of fact is taken to be relatively unproblematic. The real action is in the dialogue that is set up between fact and theory, with the clear implication that this dialogue, itself, has, in the end, the same utopian referent. Thus we have a hermeneutic circle in which the attempt to theorize the good, in the abstract, is completed by the discovery of the good in history and society. The formal representation of this is similar to the representation of the semiotics of realism, but note that in this case the "referent" or "ground" of signification does not exist. Rather, the ultimate ground of signification is the ideal that is held in common by

11. Habermas, *The Structural Transformation of the Public Sphere*, 175.

12. While one could define "consumption" at the level of fact or empirical trend, this is not its meaning in Habermas, given that the text is written, as he himself admitted, in the genre of Marxist ideology-critique. Consumption here takes on its meaning in relation to other theoretical terms in the Marxist lexicon, e.g., production, surplus value, and Habermas's own "systematically distorted communication."

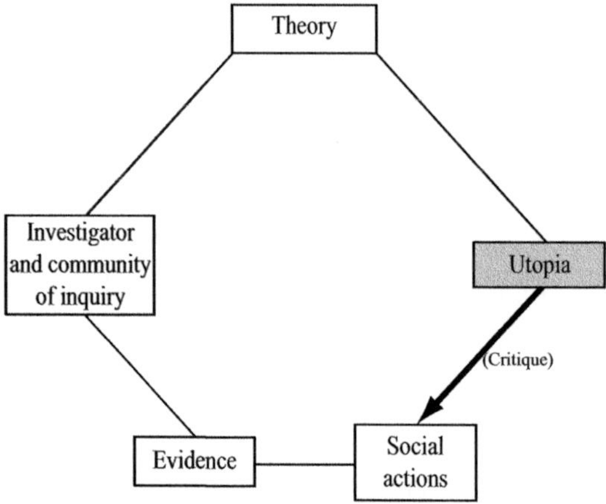

Figure 4: Normative maximal interpretation—critique as social knowledge

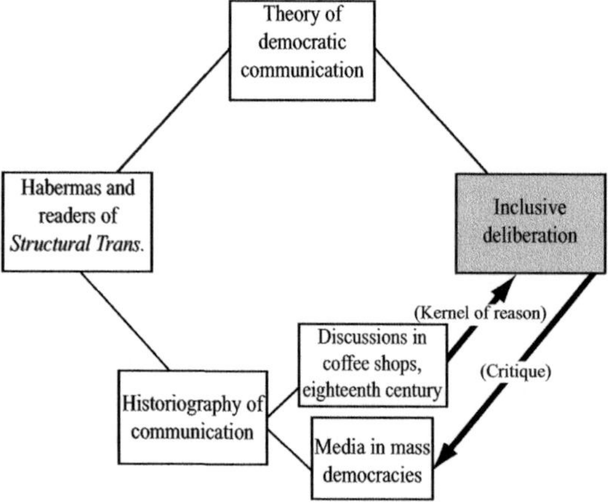

Figure 5: Jürgen Habermas's maximal interpretation in *The Structural Transformation of the Public Sphere*

the signifying consciousnesses of investigated and investigator. The utopian referent links history to critique (see figs. 4 and 5).

By following the semiotic circuit of Habermas's argument, our knowledge of "democratic deliberation" or "the ideal speech situation" is made deeper because both his theoretical terms and the social actions that happened refer back to these utopian ideals. This is not only normative argument about democracy, but also normative research on democracy. It is important, however, to understand that this epistemic mode is not limited to, nor made possible by, the particularities of Habermas's position. For this reason, I want to examine the semiotic workings of another, more recent exemplar of normative signification. This will allow the ensuing discussion of the premises and possibilities of the normative epistemic mode to be broader and better informed.

V

Leela Gandhi's position in the ongoing normative arguments of social and political theory is quite different from, and indeed antagonistic to, Habermas's position. Her search for a radically democratic politics begins from the problematics of postcolonial theory, and in particular the need to move beyond the "imperial manicheanism" that pits an anticolonial (and often elitist) nationalism against the logic of empire. This binary reproduces, inside postcolonial, anti-imperialist thinking, a reliance on Western categories and politics.[13] Previous attempts to move beyond this binary trouble her as well, however, for she finds problematic the determinism inherent in a certain version of hybridity theory, according to which the West's colonial project was always already impossible in some philosophical and/or social sense, and thus destined—eventually—to be overthrown. As she writes,

> Faced with an ultimately unsatisfactory theoretical choice between the oppositional but repetitive forms of cultural nationalism on the one hand and the subversive but quietist discourse of hybridity or

13. Gandhi writes that "close cultural readings reveal in place of anticolonial nationalism's confident claim to edenic premodern antiquity a fictive and orientalist-inspired 'invention of tradition,' in place of its bombastic assertions of radical difference and originality a 'derivative discourse,' contingent upon the oppressive forms of imperial nationalism." Leela Gandhi, *Affective Communities: Anticolonial Thought, Fin-De-Siecle Radicalism, and the Politics of Friendship* (Durham: Duke University Press, 2006), 5.

> contrapuntality on the other, some postcolonial scholarship over the last decade or so has begun the task of reengaging the colonial archive for more selfconsciously creative forms of anti-imperialism, especially in its western or metropolitan articulation.[14]

So, Gandhi wants to return to the archive to understand how agency may or may not have played a role in the dissolution of empire. The semiotics of her truth claims work in a manner quite similar to those of *Structural Transformation*, since her work of normative maximal interpretation is also two-pronged: engaging both the "colonial archive" (the language of fact) and the possibility of an "anti-communitarian communitarianism" premised on the "politics of friendship" (the language of theory). Much as was the case with Habermas's text, I cannot attempt to represent the entirety of Gandhi's argument here, but that is not my purpose. Rather, I will attempt to understand a bit more about the way theory and fact can become fused together by examining how Gandhi uses both.

First, let us consider Gandhi's language of fact. The investigated subjects of her study are late Victorian Englishmen and women who formed a variety of affect-laden affiliations with members of colonized populations, while taking up in their writing and life-practice explicitly anti-imperial politics. So, for example, the homosexual writer Edward Carpenter not only challenged the heteronormativity of Darwin-inspired sexology, he also traveled extensively to India, developed a "lifelong friendship with the Sri Lankan P. Arunachalam," and, in his book *Civilisation: Its Cause and Cure*, asserted that British civilization was a disease that could only be cured with a "fresh influx of savagery." This text was cited approvingly by M. K. Gandhi in *Hind Swaraj*.[15] She considers other cases like this, wherein the exclusion of certain whites from British civilization led to the possibility of "negative community with the nonwestern savage."[16]

Gandhi brings to her engagement with the archive a significant plurality of theoretical language. Included among these are (1) a critique of the Kantian project of linking morality and judgment to the radical autonomy of a unified subject and, in an effort to provide a positive alternative to this, (2) a theorization of the forms of sociality—with particular attention to emotional solidarities—that found polities

14. Gandhi, *Affective Communities*, 6.
15. Gandhi, *Affective Communities*, 62–63.
16. Gandhi, *Affective Communities*, 61.

and collective decision making. Kant's morality excludes the distractions of desire and the dogmatism of worship as outside the limits of reason alone. Gandhi relies on the work of Michel Foucault, Jacques Derrida, and especially Judith Butler to point out that the Kantian moral subject is asocial, and thus that, without the transcendental guarantees imagined by Kant to unify white male Europeans, the subject so imagined is a quite specious source of good action. In response, Gandhi articulates a theoretical language in which aspects of desire and divination become the basis for good communities and good action. She thus reinvents the moral actor via a "politics of friendship" that leads to "affective communities."

Thus we have in this study interesting evidence drawn from the colonial archive that points to social actions that happened; and we have an important theoretical problem: how to reimagine the critique of imperialism and the basis for the good society outside of the Manichean drama of East v. West, and with a less individuated political subject? The real fireworks of Gandhi's study, however, come not from her adept theorization of anti-Kantian ethics, nor from her historical narrative of certain late-nineteenth-century and early-twentieth-century Brits and Indians.[17] It is rather at the intersection of these two languages that the crux of her study lies. For example, concerning Edward Carpenter:

> Inverting the judgments of evolutionary psychology, Carpenter thus reclaims the homosexual's gender ambiguity as proof of his exceptionality. And with similar consequences, he extends this privilege to the sexually undifferentiated "savage," also relegated, as we have seen, to the bottom of Darwin's phyletic ladder . . . linking the homosexual and the "primitive" in a double encomium . . . the "savage" and the "invert" are named as natural allies and collaborators in a shared battle against (western) categories of sex: bound to a common cause through uncommon gifts.[18]

Gandhi details Carpenter's travels to the East and his various friendships and correspondences with Indians that he developed throughout his life. In doing so, she resignifies Carpenter's life and work in a way that strengthens and expands the normative argument for hybridity.

17. Included in her study are compelling histories of the lives of Edward Carpenter, Mirra Alfassa, Sri Aurobindo, Manmohan Ghose, and Oscar Wilde, among others.

18. Gandhi, *Affective Communities*, 59.

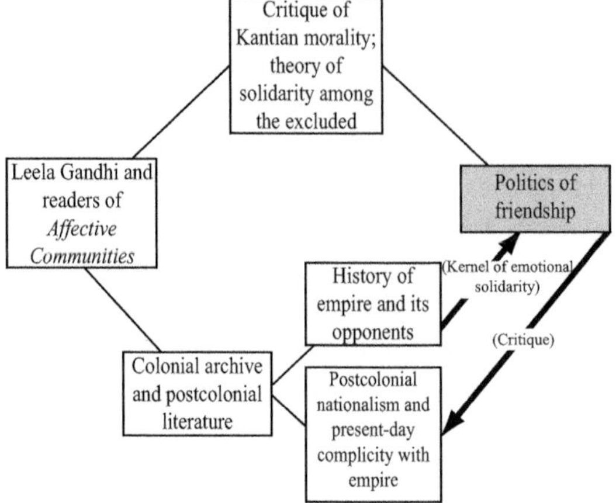

Figure 6: Leela Gandhi's maximal interpretation in *Affective Communities*

In the context of oppressive Western civilization, Carpenter found in the "invert" an exceptional subject position; Gandhi agrees and develops the implications:

> Liberated from the dull monochrome of sexual dimorphism, this constitutively doubled and hybrid intermediary was endowed with variegated sympathies and desires. His asceticism likewise equipped him for the complex affiliative demands of friendship. Here, in a nutshell, we have the raw materials for Carpenter's critique of western civilization and congruent affinities with Europe's subject races.[19]

Undoubtedly, one could construct a philosophical argument about the politics of friendship, and one could retell stories about aberrant Victorians. But that Gandhi's study is neither of these precisely, though it has elements of both, should help us understand what sort of maximal interpretations are being constructed in the normative epistemic mode. Her text shows how the transition from minimal to maximal interpretations can create political possibility, and in particular a new basis for the critique of empire (see fig. 6).

19. Gandhi, *Affective Communities*, 62. I do not have space here to go into the full extent of Gandhi's argument, but I should mention one more important normative implication of her study: an extended critique of the destruction of affective ties in scientific socialism. See Gandhi, *Affective Communities*, 177–89.

VI

The communication of utopia via semiotic circuit in these two texts also shares a narrative structure. In both cases, the author delves into relatively recent history to excavate a form of consciousness or a set of political principles that are useful for addressing a political question of present, past, and ongoing concern (for example, how do you criticize an empire when you inhabit it and benefit from its exploitations of its—and your— others?). Narrative tension results, in part, from the fact that in between the then that is being recovered and the exigencies of critique now, there is a certain sort of displacement: the rational kernel of the public sphere—deliberation of equals—is lost in the twinned process of democratization-via-commercialization; the utopian-anarchic imagination whereby one makes allies with those radically different than oneself—"affective cosmopolitanism" as a "politics of friendship"—is dissolved in the advent of "scientific" socialism, the development of Freud's science of sex, and the triumph of nationalism in the original postcolonial moment. Though I do not believe that this narrative structure obtains in all instances of normative maximal interpretation, it does provide a nice segue into a discussion of the premises of the normative epistemic mode. For we can begin by asking, what is being recovered (if not discovered) when a normativist maximal interpretation is constructed?

Presumably, it is bits and pieces of consciousness and action, moral imperatives and utopian imaginings, that can inform our current understandings of the good society. The existence of these bits and pieces lies ultimately in the meaningful lifeworlds of those under investigation, though the way in which they are drawn together is the explicit intellectual labor of the investigator. In doing this drawing together, the investigator accomplishes the resignification of consciousness via theory, and thus proposes to tell a historical story that is true, evidentially, but whose major focus is not on underlying social causes, but on political questions and problematics.

Maximal interpretations in the normative epistemic mode, then, are the empirical articulation of utopian possibility, with carefully used theory serving as the bridge from the latter to the former.

This research could be called critical sociohistory. But this raises the issue of what it means to write "critical history," and in particular raises a question that has perhaps occurred to the reader: all these utopias are well and good, but what of dystopia? Is it not a central lesson of social and political theory since "the sixties" that so many of the normative projects articulated in political philosophy and actualized in social life—from rationalized production to the talking cure—turned out to be formats of domination or exclusion? One already finds this sensibility in Gandhi's critique of Kantian morality. But to address the question—and the doubts it raises about the production of truth in the human sciences, we should go straight to the source.

VII

Consider the following passage from an essay by Michel Foucault:

> Genealogy does not pretend to go back in time to restore an unbroken continuity that operates beyond the dispersion of forgotten things; its duty is not to demonstrate that the past actively exists in the present, that it continues secretly to animate the present, having imposed a predetermined form on all its vicissitudes. Genealogy does not resemble the evolution of a species and does not map the destiny of a people. On the contrary, to follow the complex course of descent is to maintain passing events in their proper dispersion; it is to identify the accidents, the minute deviations—or conversely, the complete reversals—the errors, the false appraisals, and the faulty calculations that gave birth to those things that continue to exist and have value for us; it is to discover that truth or being does not lie at the root of what we know and what we are, but the exteriority of accidents.[20]

A short while later in the same essay Foucault unveils his famous epigram: "knowledge is not made for understanding; it is made for cutting."[21]

Is this quote evidence that Foucault insisted on writing history outside of the bounds of empirical responsibility, and thus outside the bounds of truth itself (in some sense of the word "truth")?[22] A

20. Michel Foucault, "Nietzsche, Genealogy, History," in *The Foucault Reader*, ed. Paul Rabinow (New York: Pantheon Books, 1984), 81.

21. Foucault, "Nietzsche, Genealogy, History," 88.

22. In his work on Foucault's historical sociology, Mitchell Dean writes that Foucault's reflections in the *Archeaology of Knowledge* and the essay on Nietzsche "suggest a form of critical historical study that leaves behind the methods and objectives of conventional, empiricist historiography without recourse to sterile theoretical schemas . . . [Foucault's] statements are united by a fundamental rejection of the naïve empiricist account of historiography as a reconstruction of the past, and an approach to the use of historical sources to discover the reality of which these sources

careful reading of the first quotation would suggest that the answer is no—Foucault is arguing that previous approaches to writing history have substituted metaphysics for careful minimal interpretation. But what of the epigram—what is wrong with understanding?

To understand the implications of Foucauldian genealogy and the critical histories that have been inspired by it, one must be very careful to differentiate minimal from maximal interpretations. If we do this, it becomes clear that Foucault, in his reflexive essays at least, disowned the use of theory to discover the underlying social *causes* of actions in the past. Theory, if it is to serve any use beyond obfuscation, can only be in and of the present, directed at present problems. In this view, we can compile facts from the past, and argue about minimal interpretations, but when it comes to maximal interpretation, we have to perform genealogy and mobilize the past for political purposes in the present. Foucault's distrust was directed at the sorts of knowledge that reach beyond the facts to construct *explanations* that express verisimilitude with deep structures. While I believe that this epistemological argument is at odds with what some of Foucault's own research accomplishes (as I will discuss in chapter 5), it is not, as his critics often complain, a performative contradiction.[23] For Foucault does not reject the possibility of truth in minimal interpretation. What he rejects is the realist program for producing deeper truths about history, via a general, coherent, and referential theory of society. Epistemologically speaking, Foucault's opponent was not Habermas, it was Bhaskar.

---

are traces . . . Positively, these approaches to method are united by the insight that history is above all a practice, a practice undertaken in a particular present and for particular reasons linked to that present." I suspect there are two ways to read such arguments, frequently found in the secondary literature on Foucault: (1) as opposing both empiric*ism* and the use of theory to *explain* the past causally, and thus aiming at a form of normative maximal interpretation—which is the reading I work toward below; or (2) as rejecting *empirical responsibility* as it is normatively defined within the academy, and within the discipline of history in particular. I suspect that the ambiguity of some of Foucault's more radical statements about history and truth—on the basis of which either of these two readings could be argued for—is one of the causes of the extensive interpretive controversy that has always attended Foucault's impact on the human sciences. Mitchell Dean, *Critical and Effective Histories: Foucault's Methods and Historical Sociology* (New York: Routledge, 1994), 13–14.

23. Jürgen Habermas, *The Philosophical Discourse of Modernity: Twelve Lectures* (Cambridge, MA: MIT Press, 1987). For a discussion, see Martin Jay, "The Debate over the Performative Contradiction: Habermas versus the Poststructuralists," in *Philosophical Interventions in the Unfinished Project of Enlightenment*, ed. Axel Honneth et al. (Cambridge, MA: MIT Press), 261–79.

So, consider the possibility that the Foucauldian mode of writing history—at least as it has been interpreted by "critical historians"—is a specific articulation of a more general normative epistemic mode. The "history of the present" is not the history of the determination of the present, but rather history mobilized to address present problems. What remains as a source of confusion is the way that, in many of Foucault's most well-known writings, the referent for the theoretical sign in normative maximal interpretation is *dystopian* instead of utopian. Foucault's politics around modernity and modern societies are frustratingly evasive, and for some even evidence of a hidden conservative distaste for liberal democracy.[24] This gets conflated with Foucault's supposed distaste for truth. Let us examine these arguments for a moment.

Borrowing a term from Habermas, Andrew Sayer calls Foucault's position "crypto-normative."[25] By this he means that Foucault's theorization of knowledge/power not only upends more standard philosophical accounts of an individual knower who possesses fallible beliefs, but also undermines the attempt in normative argumentation to articulate utopian possibility. Hence, echoing this argument, Justin Cruickshank writes that "whilst it is implied [in Foucault's writing] that a described state of events is objectionable, no explicit argument is put forward as to why this is the case, because the notion of making truth claims about the world has been abandoned."[26] This argument should be familiar to the reader, for the point Sayer and Cruickshank make in their work is articulated in much less precise terms in various conversations, conference presentations, graduate classes in the human sciences, and perhaps almost anywhere references to "Foucault" prevail. Informally, Foucault is always hero and villain simultaneously, destroying truth as we know it (whatever that may be), but refusing to articulate a new, deeper truth that everyone can lean on. The argument conflates two issues, however. First, the way

24. Again, Habermas is the most well-known, though by no means the only, example. Jürgen Habermas, "Modernity versus Postmodernity," *New German Critique* 22 (1981): 13. For a review of Foucault's work, and interpretations of Foucault, that focuses on different ways to read Foucault's supposed rejection of modernity and/or humanism, see Nancy Fraser, "Michel Foucault: A 'Young Conservative'?" *Ethics* 96 (1985).

25. R. Andrew Sayer, *The Moral Significance of Class* (Cambridge: Cambridge University Press, 2005).

26. Justin Cruickshank, "The Usefulness of Fallibilism: A Popperian Critique of Critical Realism," *Philosophy of the Social Sciences* 37, no. 3 (2007): 266.

in which Foucault refrains from—or perhaps rejects the possibility of—offering a positive vision as a counterpoint to his normative critique of modern social relations and discursive formations. And second, Foucault's rejection of realist and/or scientific approaches to the study of history and society, and in particular the sorts of ontological uses of theory that would theorize the causes and origins of generic social processes.

None of this denies the possibility of constructing true minimal interpretations and the responsible use of evidence that is necessary to construct them; I thus find it is specious to argue that Foucault rejects the very possibility that his evidential signifiers refer to something that happened. Foucault, in almost all of his texts, makes extended empirical truth claims, which is to say, minimal interpretations. He is quite fond of evidential signifiers and relies on the sign-system of fact frequently. What then is at stake in calling Foucault "crypto-normative"?

One issue is the substantive use of dystopia as a theoretical anchor. One can indeed argue—and argue reasonably, based on evidence from his texts—that the master referents for Foucault's normative maximal interpretations are not utopias, but dystopias: the surveillance society, the extension of sovereignty to the very production of life and subjectivity, etc. And if this argument is extended a bit, Foucault can be charged with lacking a progressive vision for social change, and thus as evidencing some sort of failure of nerve or evasiveness, I suppose. But this is an argument against Foucault made on the terms of the normative epistemic mode. It amounts to a critique of the potential practical effectiveness of Foucault's maximal interpretations, and of whether his texts can indeed produce something akin to emancipation or progress. This is not an argument I wish to resolve here, though it is worth noting how much Foucault's writing has influenced progressive thinking in such fields as queer studies.

The issue, however, that speaks directly to the problem of epistemic modes is this: can one successfully write normative maximal interpretations that do not, at least implicitly, attempt a deep and true rendering of the social reality that sits underneath that which is minimally interpreted? Do the interpretations of social life that point to utopia require, to retain effectiveness, some sort of strong interpretation of social reality—perhaps even an *explanation* of social life? Perhaps because of Michel Foucault's disavowals of the search for historical origins and, in his early work, his unwillingness to explain how one discursive formation came to replace another, his name has become a synecdoche for this issue in the human sciences. But in truth the problem concerns the entire normative epistemic mode.

Investigations that augment critical theory do so by stoking the utopian and dystopian imagination of the reader. But to use theory normatively without at least implicitly having a deeper sense of the workings of social life in a given time and place leaves the investigator in an awkward position. In fact, in most texts written primarily in the normative epistemic mode, a causal story about the social actions under study is implied. In Habermas, during his Marxist days at least, there was a causal account of the ideological formations subject to criticism. "Systematically distorted communication" was caused by objective power relations and economic system imperatives.[27] Frederic Jameson's extended meditations on and critiques of postmodern culture also assume an explanatory, causal story about capitalism's development on a global scale.[28] Amitai Etzioni's vision of the good society depends upon his theory of what communities are and how they work.[29]

But so much of this is implicit, and we recall with nostalgia an era when normativism and realism complemented each other perfectly as different expressions of the same intellectual worldview. What is to be done if this is no longer the case, if the connection between the real and the good no longer obtains the philosophical clarity that it did for Marx or Plato?

VIII

In normative maximal interpretation, the purpose of resignification is to work out and work through knowledge of the good society and of human emancipation via empirical investigation. The master referent for such interpretations is utopia, and the question is not so much what *is* the good as *how*, *when*, *and where* the good can be or was made actual, in actors' minds or in social institutions. The narratives

27. Jürgen Habermas, *Legitimation Crisis* (Boston: Beacon Press, 1975).

28. Frederic Jameson, *Postmodernism; or, the Cultural Logic of Late Capitalism*, Post-Contemporary Interventions (Durham: Duke University Press, 1991); Fredric Jameson, *The Geopolitical Aesthetic: Cinema and Space in the World System* (Bloomington: Indiana University Press and the British Film Institute, 1992).

29. Amitai Etzioni, "Creating Good Communities and Good Societies," *Contemporary Sociology* 29, no. 1 (2000).

of history are resignified with attention to the tension between a set of social ideals and their empirical manifestation or lack thereof. This organization of knowledge can be inverted, as dystopia can anchor critique within the normative episteme mode. For, normative resignification can show how supposedly utopian consciousness contributes, via its elaboration, to social power and domination. But what does one need to know about social reality to make such a claim?

Hence the dilemma referred to above: normative work requires some sort of deeper knowledge about how social life works. The discovery of utopian possibility would be stronger if it was informed not only by fact, but also by some sort of explanation. And yet, in much of what we recognize as normative social research, the contours of utopian resignification are not directly guided and controlled by a general, coherent, referential theory of social reality—functionalist, historical materialist, rational-choice, etc. Normativist work that has rejected realism—perhaps for reasons not that different than the reasons articulated in chapter 2—appears, then, to be unmoored. But this dilemma's appearance of intractability is a result of conflating the possibility of knowing something about social reality with the necessity of the realist epistemic mode as it has so far been articulated. There might be other possibilities.

Many social investigators—and especially ethnographers—value dialogue with their subjects not only because of its normative dimension, but also because investigators do not expect their theories to set out how the social works tout court. Normative maximal interpretations rely upon subject-to-subject dialogue so as to recover utopian and dystopian consciousness, and ultimately construct compelling social criticism. But there is another purpose for dialogue between investigator and investigated—to get into the meaning of social life in certain time and space.[30] This very simple idea—that the investigator must somehow "get to know" her subjects and produce an interpretation of the meanings that infuse their lives—will serve as the basis for the third epistemic mode I will examine. But an examination of this epistemic mode will require us to consider the possibility that theory was not quite what we thought it was.

30. For the philosophical articulation and defense of this idea, with specific reference to the debate between Gadamer and Habermas, see Paul Ricoeur, "Hermeneutics and the Critique of Ideology," in *Hermeneutics and the Human Sciences: Essays on Language, Action and Interpretation* (New York: Cambridge University Press, 1981), 61–100.

For, there is a formal similarity to the manner in which realism and normativism square the hermeneutic circle—a similarity masked by the supposed opposition, in scholarly discourse, between "facts" and "values." (As we have seen, normative resignification not only makes a place for facts but draws tremendous authority from them, since to argue without facts would move a truth claim from the space of social research to the space of political philosophy.) Both realism and normativism use theory to produce ultimate and organizing referents for the research text. Theory relocates the facts in a second conceptual space, a larger world unknown to the facts themselves: a world of the fundamental structures of the social (realism) or a world of the fundamental problems and possibilities of critique (normativism). The result of this resignification can be precise and elegant.

But with normativism—and in particular, in the doubts cast upon the rationalist utopias of Western political philosophy by thinkers like Michel Foucault and Leela Gandhi—we begin to see how at least some of this precision and elegance, perhaps most available in certain strictly realist explanations, comes at a great intellectual cost. There is, in the realist epistemic mode, and in the rationalist normativism of Habermas as well, a disavowal of the meaningfulness of social life as DuBois recognized it—seething with emotion, bound up in history and culture, and organized by human beings whose "natures" are so varied, so different, that the effort of the human sciences is perhaps confounded more than it is aided by concepts like "human nature." For, in engaging the consciousness of others, normative maximal interpretation opens up to the investigator the sheer variety of ways in which human beings make their social worlds more or less coherent, in ways more or less compelling to each other.

There is a dialectical process at work—or at least there was for this author—in traveling from realism to normativism and finally to interpretivism. To leave theories of social reality for theories of social good has the effect of unleashing knowledge of human subjectivity that, like Ulysses, had been tightly bound to its ship, and could only hear the siren songs of sensuality, meaning, and emotion from far away. Thus when one returns to social reality—which, as a social researcher, one must—it does not look the same anymore. Gone is the certainty that general theory, unmediated, can pick out the central entities and relations in a society. In its place is the realization that social life—and not just the production of knowledge about it—is subject to the vagaries of meaning.

Chapter Four

Meaning

The central place of discourse—of the arts of communication and decision making—in the treatment of problems today gives it the force of a new architectonic art which transforms the methods of inquiry and discussion in all fields.
—Richard McKeon, "Discourse, Demonstration, Verification, and Justification"

I

What was the texture of social life for a French Revolutionary? What was it like to attend a Jacobin meeting or to barricade the streets of Paris? What sorts of meaningful gestures and social risks were involved in attempting to convince the peasants in your village to give up their allegiance to the pope? Such questions spur a different mode of resignification in social research. To answer these questions, the investigator must spiral out through the layers of meaning that construe human experience.[1] Her goal is understanding.

1. Though there are many reference points for the "what was it like" question and the focus on human experience as a category of understanding for social research, my specific ones, beyond the obvious reference to Joan Scott's "The Evidence of Experience," are two. First, W. G. Runciman divides understanding into primary, secondary, and tertiary levels, with the first being reportage (what happened), the second being explanation (why what happened happened), and the third being the more interpretation-heavy, aesthetic, and emotional exploration of "what it was like" to be the actors that were part of what happened. Runciman's primary concern is the second of these, and it for this reason, I believe, that he ultimately parts ways with Max Weber, and with interpretive sociology, to affirm mechanisms of selection as the

By interpreting layers of social meaning, she may indeed address questions familiar from realism and normativism. She may answer the explanatory question of "Why did the French Revolution happen when and where it did?" or the political question of "How can we restructure radical social critcism by examining the sansculottes of Paris?" But, in the interpretive epistemic mode, the investigator mediates attempts to answer these questions with questions about the meanings swirling through the experiences of social actors. She does not begin with a general, coherent, and referential set of theorized mechanisms, or by attempting to describe the fundamental social kind referred to by the term "state," or, for that matter, by defining what radical politics is, has been, or could be. This is not to say that she is not interested in ancien régime states, what caused the collapse of the French ancient régime state, or the possibility of a more democratic France. It is rather to say that she does not expect the answers to such questions as "What is a state?" or "What is radical criticism?" to provide the kind of direct intellectual leverage that is needed to do the work of the social analysis of evidence. Rather, these questions have to be approached indirectly, mediated through the interpretation of social meaning. She directs her efforts, then, to reconstructing the

---

explanatory reference point for social research, and the interpretation of meaning as an issue of description.

In contrast, Andrew Abbott has recently championed the cause of "lyrical sociology," which he describes as relying upon figurational language to communicate a concrete, emotional connection between the investigator and social life as experienced. Abbott explains that this sort of sociological writing, often found in urban ethnographies (a good example from historical writing being E. P. Thompson's *The Making of the English Working Class*), is opposed to "narrative" writing in sociology. The latter includes both positivist, variable-based explanations, but also explanations of the particularized sort, often found in narrative history—or, as Abbott explains, a variety of work ranging from "oral histories of individuals to grand chronicles of classes and ethnic groups." Abbott insists that lyrical sociology offers a way to connect to social life that sociologists should not sacrifice at the altar of explanation.

In this chapter, I take up a position in clear opposition to Runciman, but slightly different than that expressed in Abbott's paper. Although Abbott articulates quite well a core aspect of hermeneutic sociology—the willingness to openly engage the social actions of interest in all their strangeness and concreteness—I am of the view that interpretive analysis can have a lyrical moment that is then elaborated into an explanation—an explanation that attends to causes excluded by, and uses schemas foreign to, the more standard explanatory projects of social science (see chapter 5). Joan W. Scott, "The Evidence of Experience," *Critical Inquiry* 17, no. 4 (1991). W. G. Runciman, *A Critique of Max Weber's Philosophy of Social Science* (New York: Cambridge University Press, 1972), and W. G. Runciman, *A Treatise on Social Theory*, 3 vols. (New York: Cambridge University Press, 1983). Andrew Abbott, "Against Narrative: A Preface to Lyrical Sociology," *Sociological Theory* 25, no. 1 (2007): 69.

textures of human subjectivity, and to the meaningful worlds of social life in which subjects act in a certain place and a certain time.

This effort at reconstruction is also an attempt to build maximal interpretations. All three of the epistemic modes examined in this book take as their project the development of a deeper comprehension of social life, a reading of the evidence that goes beyond the evidence and yet remains responsible to it. In realism and normativism this is done by counterbalancing the meaning-system of facts by positing, via the meaning-system of theory, something *other than* the social meanings that attend the social actions under scrutiny. In going beyond the facts with theory, realism also goes beyond meaning—to structures of the social as such.[2] In this epistemic mode, then, maximal interpretations are constructed via the use of a (general, coherent, and referential) theoretical scheme to order and explain the facts. In a similar way, though with a different purpose, normativism also uses theory as a sort of window unto the meanings of facts, reframing them as evidence for utopian possibility. In both cases, theory provides the means to a resignification of social action that is also a displacement, moving the "social actions that happened" into a brand new conceptual space. In realism this conceptual space (supposedly) corresponds to a social reality that exists and has clear causal power; in normativism this conceptual space is specifically nonexistent and for that very reason the fount of critique. But both epistemic modes share a certain aspect of the operation of resignification—theory, by referencing a new world, enables us to comprehend the evidence as the expression of something both deeper and more general.

The third epistemic mode under consideration works with a different notion of what theory is and can do. For, the aim of this mode is to resignify the evidence by recontextualizing it into a set of

2. This locution raises the issue of whether there is such a thing as a "cultural realism." This phrase could mean different things. In the terms of this text, a single, general, coherent, and referential theory of the social that focused on the fundamental nature of culture "as such" would qualify as "realist." Examples might include the work of Talcott Parsons and Claude Levi-Strauss. But this is slightly misleading, because the point of interpretivism is not only the focus on meaning and signification in social life, but also *how the investigator uses theory to interpret meaning and signification in social life*. I hope this will become clear as the text proceeds. If "realism" were to mean simply the making of truth claims about certain social actions via the use of theory as I outline it in this chapter, then I suppose the rather oxymoronic "interpretive realism" could apply to the perspective developed here. But as I argued in chapter 2, in terms of the use of theory in the human sciences, "realism," or the realist epistemic mode, means something more specific than that.

deeper meanings that are *also* historically and socially limited. The resignification moves from one set of social meanings to another set of social meanings: from the "surface" meanings easily inferred from the evidence to the "deep" meanings that require much more interpretive work to access. In the interpretive epistemic mode the work of maximal interpretation makes claims about the symbolic order and makes these claims in a way that remains within the orbit of the social actions under scrutiny. The investigator moves from one set of meanings that she finds in the evidential signifiers of her case to another set of meanings that, she claims, are also existent in that case. It is because of this meaning-to-meaning relationship that I call this mode of resignification *interpretive*, and refer to it as *interpretivism*.

Interpretivism also carries with it certain ontological commitments. But these commitments sanction a very different use of theory in research, and undermine the realist preference for a general, coherent, and referential social theory, as well as undermining the tendency, in certain sociological realisms, to get underneath meaning entirely, to the hard structures of the social that are theorized ontologically. In interpretivism, there is no social as such—at least not in the way there is for realism. Instead, the social (and the possibility of criticizing it) emerge on what I will call landscapes of meaning.* These landscapes are historically particular (and often peculiar), and yet can, in some cases, extend through large swaths of time and space, thus making them discursive formations with tremendous inertia and power. In this chapter, I look at the process by which theory is used by investigators to reconstruct these landscapes of meaning. In chapter 5, I argue that this interpretation of meaning can in fact form the basis for the investigator to reach the goals central to both normativism (critique) and realism (explanation), with a special focus on how precisely the interpretation of meaning can contribute to the causal explanation of social action.

But first things first: invoking "interpretive" social research tends to bring to mind a series of problems and skepticisms rather than a positive program for knowledge. Winch's impossibility arguments concerning social science qua science, Rorty's ironic antiessentialist epistemology, and myriad other arguments for the impossibility or even the sheer irrationality of social knowledge are often associated

*After this text went into production, I discovered that William Sewell Jr. uses this phrase on the last page of his essay "The Concept(s) of Culture," in *Logics of History: Social Theory and Social Transformation* (Chicago: University of Chicago Press, 2005), 174. For Sewell's account of interpretive social science and history, see *Logics of History*, 318–72.

with any discussion of interpretation or hermeneutics. But this is not necessary. To understand that interpretive social research makes strong knowledge claims, one only has to look at some of its iconic texts. Then, we will be able to understand the epistemic premises and workings of such knowledge claims without the interferences of a postmodern skepticism that merely rewrites in reverse the overconfidence of a scientistic sociology.

II

That Clifford Geertz's "Deep Play: Notes on the Balinese Cockfight" is—despite the author's occasional comments to the contrary—what I am herein calling a maximal interpretation is easily gleaned from the cries of his critics, whose objections to Geertz's ability to provide a deep interpretation of Balinese culture are many and well known.[3] But let us set aside, for the moment, the extended debates about the politics, epistemology, and philosophical implications of this rather infamous essay and ask—as Geertz himself might have done were the essay not his but a "note in a bottle"—what actually takes place in this text? Undoubtedly, Geertz's text is full of ethnographic detail, or, in the terms being used here, evidential signifiers. However, it also makes extensive use of theory. Consider an example:

> Bentham's concept of "deep play" is found in his *The Theory of Legislation*. By it he means play in which the stakes are so high that it is, from his utilitarian standpoint, irrational for men to engage in it at all. If a man whose fortune is a thousand pounds (or ringgits) wages five hundred of it on an even bet, the marginal utility of the pound he stands to win is clearly less than the marginal disutility of the one he stands to lose. In genuine deep play, this is the case for both parties. They are both in over their heads.[4]

This theoretical signifier is plucked from its original intellectual context, and is used to illuminate a phenomenon far from Bentham's concern—and indeed, far from his utilitarian social theory. Consider

3. See, in particular, Vincent Crapanzano, *Hermes' Dilemma and Hamlet's Desire: On the Epistemology of Interpretation* (Cambridge, MA: Harvard University Press, 1992); Michael Burawoy, *Ethnography Unbound: Power and Resistance in the Modern Metropolis* (Berkeley: University of California Press, 1991), 278–83; Ann Swidler, *Talk of Love: How Culture Matters* (Chicago: University of Chicago Press, 2001), 19–23.

4. Clifford Geertz, "Deep Play: Notes on the Balinese Cockfight," in *The Interpretation of Cultures* (New York: Basic Books, 2000), 432–33.

first some of the evidential signification pointing to the social actions under study:

> the general pattern is for the betting to move a shorter or longer distance up the scale towards the, for the sidebets, nonexistent pole of even money.[5]

> (1) the higher the center bet is, the greater the pull on the side betting toward the short odds end of the wagering system, and vice versa; (2) the higher the center bet is, the greater the volume of side betting, and vice versa.[6]

In other words, in cockfights, the big fights are the ones in which much money is wagered by the owners of the birds, indeed, *too* much money. Here, then, is Geertz's analysis of "what the Balinese are up to," in which theory and evidence are brought together:

> despite the logical force of Bentham's analysis men do engage in such [deep] play, both passionately and often, and even in the face of law's revenge . . . for the Balinese, though naturally they do not formulate it in so many words, the explanation lies in the fact that in such play, money is less a measure of utility, had or expected, than it is a symbol of moral import, perceived or imposed . . . in deep [games] where the amounts of money are great, much more is at stake than material gain: namely, esteem, honor, dignity, respect—in a word . . . status.[7]

Geertz uses a piece of theory to illuminate a piece of meaning that underlies the actions of the men who engage in cockfighting in Bali. Already, we can see that this is not realist resignification, because the term "deep play" is not expected to point to some entity that underlies and explains men who gamble in all sorts of places. Rather, it is used to "ferret out hidden meanings" and thus illuminate the meaningful context of Balinese gambling.

However, before jumping to a consideration of the semiotic workings and epistemological premises of this text—and the many texts of cultural history and cultural sociology that followed it—we need to notice something else. Geertz *repeats* this exercise of using a theoretical concept to illuminate social context. And the theories he uses to do this are quite different from each other. Consider another instance:

5. Geertz, "Deep Play," 428.
6. Geertz, "Deep Play," 430.
7. Geertz, "Deep Play," 433.

> the deep psychological identification of Balinese men with their cocks is unmistakable. The double entendre here is deliberate . . . Bateson and Mead have even suggested that, in line with the Balinese conception of the body as a set of separately animated parts, cocks are viewed as detachable, self-operating penises, ambulant genitals with a life of their own. And while I do not have the kind of unconscious material either to confirm of disconfirm this intriguing notion, the fact that they are masculine symbols par excellence is about as indubitable, and to the Balinese about as evident, as the fact that water runs downhill.[8]

Geertz here puts the (Freudian-anthropological) theory before the evidence, following this paragraph with an extended catalogue of the variety of ways in which *Sabung* (the word for "cock") is used in everyday speech. It is, Geertz shows, a signifier of extended and varied metaphorical use.[9] So, at stake in cockfights is not just status but a certain sort of masculine status (this would not be as surprising to anthropologists informed by feminist theory as it is to Geertz).

Then, after finishing his analysis of the cock metaphor with a quote from his landlord that "we are all cock crazy," Geertz moves to a third meaningful dimension of the cockfight. He writes:

> The madness has some less visible dimensions, however, because although it is true that cocks are symbolic expressions or magnifications of their owner's self, the narcissistic male ego writ out in Aesopian terms, they are also expressions—and rather more immediate ones—of what the Balinese regard as the direct inversion, aesthetically, morally, and metaphysically, of human status: animality.[10]

This illuminates another aspect of his data, which is a binary that runs throughout Balinese culture between human (sacred) and animal (profane). Geertz again interprets a whole series of evidential signifiers with this (Durkheimian) theoretical idea.[11] In addition, he argues that this binary is exquisitely produced, represented and transgressed by the cockfight itself: "In the cockfight, man and beast, good and evil, ego and id, the creative power of aroused masculinity and the destructive power of loosened animality fuse in a bloody drama of hatred, cruelty, violence, and death."[12]

8. Geertz, "Deep Play," 417–18.
9. Geertz, "Deep Play," 418–19.
10. Geertz, "Deep Play," 419.
11. Geertz, "Deep Play," 419–20.
12. Geertz, "Deep Play," 420–21.

Thus, contra the myriad commentaries on Geertz that refer in one way or another to his writing style, his extraordinary rhetorical abilities, or to his supposedly idiosyncratic academic personality, there is in fact a structure to this analysis that cannot be written off as "Geertz being Geertz."[13] That structure is this: different theories are brought to bear on the evidence, in an attempt to comprehend what begins as a relatively undefined and un-understood meaningful context. As each theory illuminates an aspect of this context, a fuller comprehension of the context as a whole is developed. By the end of the cockfight essay, Balinese cockfighting "makes sense" to the reader, because it has been adequately contextualized—in this case, by the comprehension of the meanings of masculinity, animality, and wealth/status in Balinese culture. The social actions of cockfight are situated within a larger context, and thus resignified as an expression of that context (see fig. 7).

13. Comments on his "literary flair"—as the *New York Times* obituary for Geertz put it—are common, and generally tend to be complimentary. And yet, there is a way in which the repeated insistence on Geertz's academic *style* has combined with his own reticence to participate in theoretical disputation to suggest subtly that his work, while deeply influential in many different disciplines, cannot be assimilated into the core logic(s) of social science. The most recent iteration of this argument—compelling and complimentary of some of Geertz's unique abilities, to be sure, but ultimately problematic in its conclusions—can be found in Fred Inglis's editor's introduction to a collection of Geertz's essays (for the *New York Review of Books*) and recent lectures. There, Inglis, citing Geertz as a "great writer," argues that "it is, however, precisely Geertz's concern to refuse and, if possible, paralyze the assumptions which direct [courses in social-scientific methodology] and which pour concrete over the brains of those who have to take them," and thus that "the inimitability of Geertz's style makes it intractable to discourses on method."

I think to draw a connection between Geertz's genius as writer and his refusal of methodology in the way Inglis does—concluding, then, that Geertz's brilliance justifies, somehow, not reasoning about conceptual method in social research—is a mistake. There is no doubt that Geertz resisted the kinds of methodological formalization that he thought reduced interpretive sensitivities and the possibility of ethnographically achieved understanding. But does this mean that Geertz was antimethod altogether? And anti-conceptual-method in particular? This argument, oddly, has the tone of an elitist approach to the human sciences (no one except for supergeniuses like Geertz can do what Geertz did), and ultimately, I think, serves to marginalize Geertz's contribution. Why should we not scrutinize Geertz's texts for clues to the epistemic mode he was employing?

I want to avoid *writing off* Geertz's work as "pure genius." Instead, a central goal of this chapter and this book is to see the highly influential work of figures such as Geertz as manifestations of a broader articulation of the conceptual logic of the human sciences. Geertz's particular take on interpretive or symbolic anthropology should thus be taken as something of an exemplar—not the only one, and with specific flaws that should be addressed and remedied—of the interpretive epistemic mode.

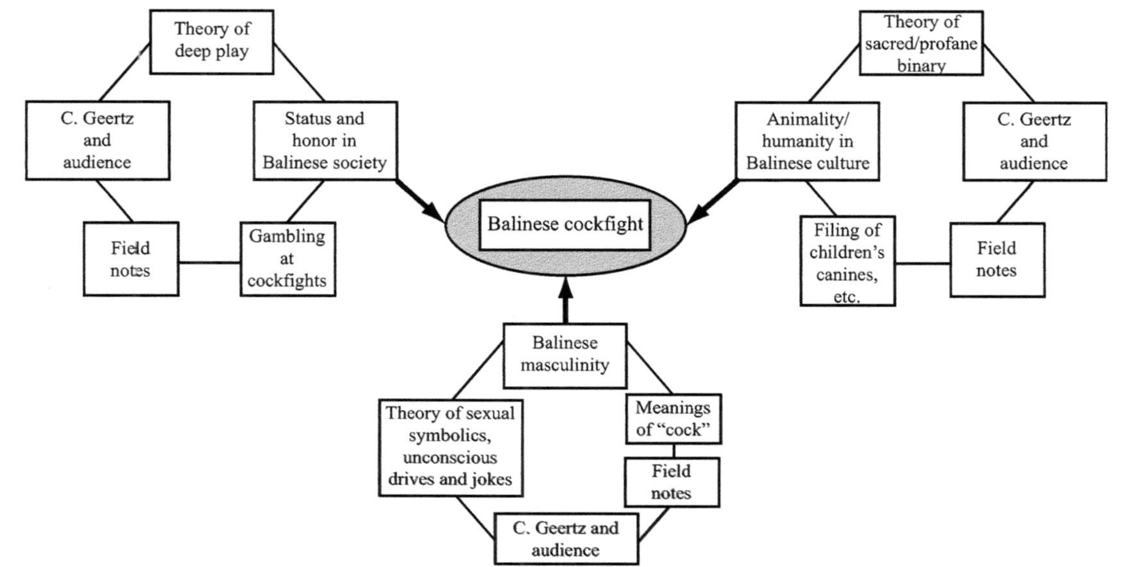

Figure 7: Clifford Geertz's maximal interpretation in "Deep Play"

So, Geertz is indeed in search of depth in interpretation. The point of such resignification is manifestly to resituate cockfighting as an expression of a set of larger tensions and themes within Balinese culture. This differentiates Geertz radically from Peter Winch; Geertz does not stay "close to the ground," nor does he just produce an interpretation of the rules attending the cockfight. He does reconstruct these rules, of course: the betting system surrounding cockfights in Bali, for example. But these rules are then *resignified via theory.* Reconstructing the rules of the betting system is a minimal interpretation. Resignifying these rules as involved in a masculine status game that thematizes the distance every high-status man desires from animality is a maximal interpretation.

But what is the epistemic status and knowledge-purpose of this maximal interpretation? What intellectual work does it do? Geertz was notoriously ambivalent about the answer to these sorts of questions. There is no better evidence of this frustrating ambiguity than the end of Geertz's "thick description" essay, wherein he claims that the purpose of interpretive anthropology is "not to answer our deepest questions, but to make available to us answers that others, guarding other sheep in other valleys, have given, and thus to include them in the consultable record of what man has said."[14] At best, this is evasive. At worst, it is an imperative to salvage the savage. Serious effort, then, needs to be devoted to figuring out how these sorts of interpretations work, and what their claims to knowledge really claim. Another example of such analysis—one with quite different politics and a lot less dissembling about what is at stake in taking an approach dedicated to elucidating the consequences of meaning-in-society—will be helpful in this endeavor.

III

"Anorexia," writes Susan Bordo, "appears less as the extreme expression of a character structure than as a remarkably overdetermined *symptom* of some of the multifaceted and heterogeneous distresses of our age."[15] She goes on to develop her remarkable explanation of

14. Clifford Geertz, "Thick Description: Toward an Interpretive Theory of Culture," in *The Interpretation of Cultures* (New York: Basic Books, 2000), 30.

15. Susan Bordo, "Anorexia Nervosa: Psychopathology as the Crystallization of Culture," in *Unbearable Weight: Feminism, Western Culture, and the Body* (Berkeley: University of California Press, 2003), 141.

anorexia as a behavior that results from three overlapping themes or "axes" in contemporary (1980s) American culture. She takes as her overarching premise a very interpretive, meaning-centered proposition: "cultural practices have their effect on the body as experienced," but also on the physical body itself. This sets up her argument that takes "the psychopathologies that develop within a culture, far from being anomalies or aberrations, to be characteristic expressions of that culture; to be, indeed, the crystallization of much that is wrong with it."[16] In other words, both the body and the mind are situated within culture, and what we do with our bodies and our minds is overdetermined by the "cultural currents" we all swim in.

But, as with Geertz, this general proposition does not get you very far—it is rather in the mobilization of theory for the project of recontextualizing anorexia where one finds the action of her essay. First comes the "dualist axis." A longstanding theme in Western culture, Bordo finds the division of self into mind and body, or soul and body, or even into immaterial self and body as not-self, to be written not only throughout Western philosophy beginning with Plato, but also in the diaries of anorexics. The body is alien, a confinement, and an enemy. By setting these diaries against the classics of philosophy, Bordo makes clear that "a highly conscious and articulate scheme of images and associations—virtually a metaphysics—is presented by these women."[17] Anorexic women struggle to overcome their evil appetites, as if they were philosopher kings. They are trapped in their bodies, much as Augustine's soul was trapped in his.

Second is the "control axis." Trapped these women may be. But they draw not only from the longstanding division in Western culture between mind (sacred) and body (profane). They also articulate a hypermodern desire for a realm of complete control, separate from need and practicality. Like bodybuilders, anorexics feel that while their lives may be completely out of control, at least they can master their bodies, over which they can achieve total domination. Every bodybuilder, and every anorexic, is a local Stalinist. Each plan met, each successful dietary restriction performed, goes further in denying the inevitable decline of age, the development of "baggy" body parts, and so on. As Bordo writes,

16. Bordo, "Anorexia Nervosa," 141.
17. Bordo, "Anorexia Nervosa," 147.

> The dream of immortality is, of course, nothing new. But what is unique to modernity is that the defeat of death has become a scientific fantasy rather than a philosophical or religious mythology. We no longer dream of eternal union with the gods . . . we work on keeping our bodies as smooth and muscular and elastic at forty as they were at eighteen. . . . Finally, it may be that in cultures characterized by gross excesses in consumption, the "will to conquer and subdue the body" (as Chernin calls it) expresses an aesthetic or moral rebellion.[18]

Third, Bordo introduces the coup de grace, the "gender/power axis." These women are engaged in a rejection of their mothers—their rounded bodies and the feminine mystique that went with those bodies. Anorexics also revolt against the image of the female as needy; repelled by this image the anorectic throws herself into the project of thinness. This is a doomed revolt, however, because it happens on the terms of sexist culture, and, importantly, under the male gaze. Anorectics report carrying a voice in their heads—a male voice—that objects to their eating. They thus both aspire to the traditionally male ideals of spiritual discipline, and submit themselves to men in so doing—many anorexics report going on their first diet in response to a comment from a male authority figure.

This rather terrifying analysis of cultural pathology, in which subjective motivations are shown to be a crucible of social power precisely in so far as they are formed by overlapping discursive formations, is simultaneously an exercise in specifying historically the meaningful context for a certain set of social actions. Each axis Bordo introduces reduces the time-space swath to which she is referring, until she is analyzing a specific generation of American middle-class (white) women—all subject to the same commercials, the same diets, and the same men. And, at each point, she uses different theoretical resources to illuminate the axis she is focusing on: first Western philosophy itself; then theories of science, modernity, and control; then theories of the male gaze (see fig. 8).

The mantra of interpretive analysis, then, is plurality in theory, unity in meaning. In the texts of Geertz and Bordo, there is a clear sense in which a single theory is not supposed to carry the day. And there is just as clear of a sense that, with the use of multiple theories, a structure of meaning can be disclosed that—however fragmented,

18. Bordo, "Anorexia Nervosa," 153.

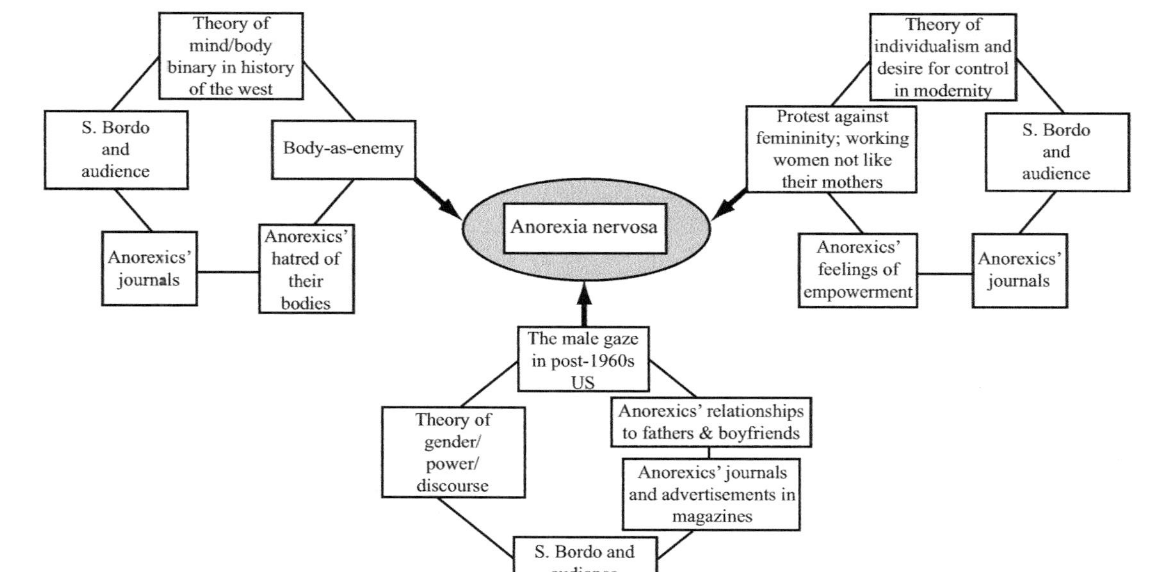

Figure 8: Susan Bordo's maximal interpretation in "Anorexia Nervosa"

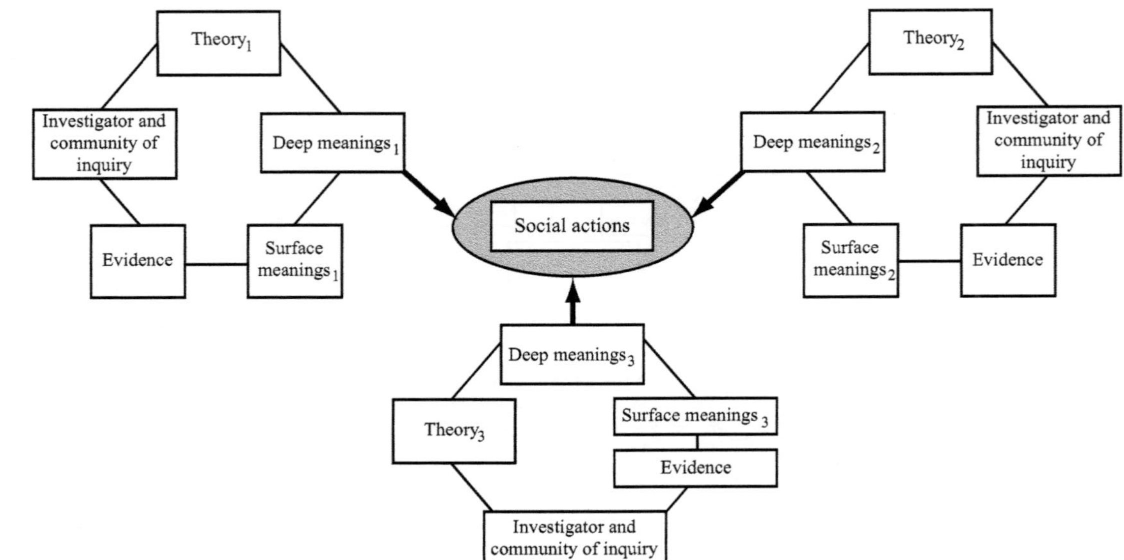

Figure 9: Maximal interpretation in the interpretive epistemic mode

contradictory, or labyrinthine—holds together into a sort of whole with deep social consequences. The criteria, so central to the realist resignifications of Skocpol and Moore, that theory be general, coherent, and referential, have been jettisoned. Instead, theories are used to illuminate aspects of a meaningful social context, regardless of whether these theories are true as descriptions of the social in some general sense, and the coherence of the maximal interpretation derives from the coherence of background meanings interpreted to be surrounding the social actions under study, and not from the coherence of the social theories mobilized to achieve this understanding. The coherence is *in the case*, not in the theorist's head.

The ontological commitment, then, is to the efficacy of social meaning. The said and the sayable, the social imaginary, the symbolic framework, the discursive formation, and so on: these terms have quite different valences and different uses, but they are all impossible to use without some notion of the social consequences of collective representation. What is not necessary, however, is the idea that these meanings always work in the same way with the same social effects—to create solidarity, for example, or to exalt a charismatic leader. Meaning has myriad, and perhaps infinite, uses—the investigations of Geertz, Bordo, and others are dedicated to tracing some of them.

Cultural sociology and cultural history, then, commit to the reality of meaning. But, in so far as they work in the interpretive epistemic mode, they dispense with the idea that a singular theory of culture can master this reality. Instead, the reality of meaning is mobilized in the service of a certain form of resignification that draws upon theories pluralistically (see fig. 9).

IV

In the time since Max Weber called for—and worked through many of the premises of—an interpretive sociology, myriad theories of meaning-and-society have sprung forth, as have myriad theories of the complex human subject, whose actions and motivations must be understood by *verstehende* sociology. If each of these theories were used in a realist way, they would be found incommensurable with each other. For example, if one takes Julia Kristeva's theory of the abject as a general, coherent, and referential theory of the social actor *as such*, then it of necessity will come into conflict with Weber-inspired theories about the historical development of a certain sort of agential rationality, wherein at least some agents, some of the time, are not motivated by the horror of death embodied in the not-me, but rather are motivated to make money via double-entry bookkeeping.[19] Each of these theories, that is, produce a very thick and detailed account of the social actor and what makes them act, and the theories are—if taken as general theories that refer directly to the reality of social actors—massively incompatible with each other. To put them together in a single general framework which references social reality would render that framework incoherent. But just because the use of a theory does not match the premises of realism does not mean that it is not useful for investigating reality.

For, these theories are not, as we have seen in Geertz and Bordo, mobilized in a realist way. Rather, the theories merge with the meanings of the evidence so as dig up the "double meaning" of the social actions under study—the hidden or tacit background within which actors act.[20] Reconstructing the meanings of social life that are not consciously intended or obviously denoted by interviewees' state-

19. Or, people are motivated to make manifest the disposition of their souls . . . which leads, eventually, to double-entry bookkeeping, which is a practice useful to those who are more instrumentally motivated. See the discussion of Weber's *Protestant Ethic* in chapter 5.

20. Harry Collins's brilliant new work, *Tacit and Explicit Knowledge*, clarifies many of the essential philosophical issues surrounding the idea of "tacit" or "background" knowledge as used by human beings. Collins divides tacit knowledge into three types: (1) weak-relational tacit knowledge, which is knowledge that could easily be made explicit but is not for logistical or strategic reasons (e.g., secrecy); (2) somatic tacit knowledge, which is knowledge linked to the specificity of the substance of human bodies; (3) strong/collective social knowledge, which is the property not of an individual but of society, and is thus available to individuals only if they become "parasitical" upon society. Though Collins, working in the philosophy of knowledge, focuses on a term, "knowledge," which is not in the end equivalent to what social researchers mean by either "meaning" or "culture," his examination of the way that collective tacit knowledge is the most powerful sort of tacit knowledge is parallel to the line of thought I pursue here. Just as the depth interpretation of meanings must go beyond the first-level rules that "knowledgeable agents" follow in interaction, so in Collins's work, the questions philosophers of tacit knowledge have asked about rule-following, game-playing, and bicycle-riding are recontextualized into the strong, collective dimension of tacit knowledge. As Collins writes: "In world championship chess there is much more going on than what happens on the board—there is all the gamesmanship that begins with the setting up of the challenges and the location of the tournament—at which Bobby Fisher seems to have been an arch-exponent. Chess played under the circumstances of the cold war does not follow the same conventions of aesthetics and gamesmanship as chess in the first half of the twentieth century, and it has probably changed again with the victory of Deep Blue." This points directly to the historicity of landscapes of meaning that I will discuss at length below. Harry Collins, *Tacit and Explicit Knowledge* (Chicago: University of Chicago Press, 2010), 120.

ments or archival documents, but that underlie, form, and structure those very statements, is the primary intellectual goal of the interpretive epistemic mode. The meanings come in various layers, with various valences, and must be reconstructed using various theories. In doing this reconstruction, the investigator will move beyond her subjects' conscious understandings of what they are doing, and beyond her evidence, into the territory of maximal interpretation. But when she does so, she must stay responsible to the depth understanding of her case, using theory to dig out the underlying meanings. This intellectual instinct toward the in-depth case study, enacted by many ethnographers, has a deeply historicizing implication for social research and social theory.

As many historians and sociologists influenced by Geertz and Bordo (and Foucault) have realized, the commitment to the reality of social meaning that orients interpretive analysis implies that all other social ontologies must be historicized.[21] The classic terms of debate in social theory—agency, structure, mechanism, solidarity, rationality, etc.—which are taken to be both general and referential, and thus to transcend historical particularity in their ontological status, now have to be analyzed relative to shared meanings, which are historically variable. Geertz made as much clear in his classic essay on "Person, Time and Conduct in Bali," and historians such as Robert Darnton have taken up this implication, in the sense that they articulate how certain social forces (e.g., workers' solidarity) emerge within and through certain meaning-formations, informed by certain mythological themes (e.g., the evilness and femininity of cats, the imaginative possibilities of carnival).[22] What we need, then, is a metaphor for the

21. This point, more than anything else, differentiates the interpretive epistemic mode from attempts, in critical realism, to include meaning, concept-dependence, conscious actors, etc. into the realist scheme. The historicizing implications of interpretive sociohistorical inquiry, in my view, cannot be squared with the ontological ambitions of realist social theory, wherein real mechanisms and structures are present and *interact with* meanings or concepts in some way. As I argue in chapter 5, the meaning-mechanism relation is not one of different social forces interacting, but rather one in which meaning gives concrete form to the social forces that, in realism, are the touchstones of social explanation. Without the form given by meaning, the theorization of social forces remains a useful abstraction at best and a nonexistent illusion of the analyst at worst. See chapter 5 for further discussion of the former possibility, and for an account of how interpretive historicism constructs explanatory truth claims.

22. Clifford Geertz, "Person, Time, and Conduct in Bali," in *The Interpretation of Cultures* (New York: Basic Books, 2000), 360–411. Robert Darnton, *The Great Cat Massacre and Other Episodes in French Cultural History* (New York: Basic Books, 1984).

interpretive goal of understanding the meanings within which social processes take place, a metaphor that can capture the way in which meaning is the ground upon which social life proceeds. One metaphor has suggested itself in a particularly powerful way in the last thirty years of social theory—the metaphor of field.

V

The imperative for the investigator working in the interpretive epistemic mode is to grasp a world of communicated sociality: the meanings that make up relations, script rituals and performances, inflect messages and gestures, and give weight to social ties; the meanings that constitute the "space" upon which social action proceeds. That is what all of this talk of layers of meaning, historical location, and cultural difference ultimately references. Social life, rather than being reducible to the will and intentions of its members and the mechanisms that emerge from their interactions to constrain and enable them, is instead infused with and formed by the concrete, available symbols through which actors move, as they get on with their strategies and manipulations, their rebellions and reproductions, their struggles and jubilations.

In a good deal of sociological and anthropological literature, the metaphor that has been used to take social research beyond individuals, interactions, and social mechanisms has been that of *field*.[23] Associated not only with Pierre Bourdieu's *champ* but also with a variety of work in social psychology and institutional analysis, the

23. John Levi Martin explains that "field theory . . . emphatically does not attempt to give an explanatory account in terms of mechanisms" and thus points toward a realm of explanation that addresses neither "lower level" mechanisms nor "higher level" functions. "Somewhat formulaically, we may say that field theories, like mechanistic theories (and unlike functionalist theories), reach toward the concrete and propose only local action, but like functionalist theories (and unlike mechanistic theories), they insist that any case must be understood in terms of the global pattern." Levi Martin also hazards that field theories are proposed when there appear to be no good mechanistic explanations of a phenomenon on the horizon. However, while admitting the provisional nature of field theories, he also suggests that sociological theories need to "refrain from privileging automatically a theory that can be linked to mechanisms." I agree with the latter argument, but I think field is not the right metaphor to get at the nonmechanistic, nonindividual, nonfunctionalist format of explanation that Levi Martin is clearly interested in. John Levi Martin, "What Is Field Theory?" *American Journal of Sociology* 109, no. 1 (1): 10, 12, 13.

idea is that there are certain social fields upon which action takes place, and moreover—as the multiple meanings of the metaphor would dictate—these fields make social life somewhat like a battle, and somewhat like a game. The field metaphor attempts to capture the tacit dimension of social life, and in particular the way that the habits of body and mind upon which actors rely end up aligning with, and quite often reproducing, the social worlds they have to navigate. There is argument here of tremendous theoretical intensity—over whether Bourdieu's development of the concept of *habitus* in relation to *field* is a fundamental key for sociological theory and explanation,[24] or whether it is entirely ill defined,[25] or whether in its definition it is contradictory because it relies upon an unsustainable idea of unconscious strategy.[26]

Whether or not *habitus* is a sustainable sociological concept, however, the metaphor of field does other important work. First, it construes the social world as a set of realms of struggle—from academic careers to artistic recognition to politics and economics. A field embodies a set of rules according to which struggle takes place, as well as struggles over the rules and regulations of the field itself. Here again theoretical argument over the utility of the metaphor is intense. Does field theory hide, underneath its account of different overlapping fields, with different rules, a universal theory of the actor as cynical and power-seeking? If so, it would appear that field theory does not live up to its claim to account for the way in which subjective dispositions emerge from socialization into various ways of being, and into the rules of certain fields—rather it has a universal theory of the actor not entirely unlike rational choice theory.[27] But to this critique there is an answer: actors who struggle for position in a field almost always simultaneously evidence some sort of orientation to the core values of the field in so far as they struggle to embody

24. David Swartz, *Culture and Power: The Sociology of Pierre Bourdieu* (Chicago: University of Chicago Press, 1997), 95–142.

25. Peter Hedström, *Dissecting the Social: On the Principles of Analytical Sociology* (Cambridge: Cambridge University Press, 2005), 4.

26. Jeffrey C. Alexander, *Fin De Siècle Social Theory: Relativism, Reduction, and the Problem of Reason* (New York: Verso, 1995), 152–55.

27. Craig Calhoun, "Habitus, Field, and Capital: The Question of Historical Specificity," in *Bourdieu: Critical Perspectives*, ed. Craig Calhoun, Edward LiPuma, and Moishe Postone (Chicago: University of Chicago Press, 1993), 70–72.

them, approach sacrality, etc.[28] So actors are both value oriented and instrumental, simultaneously.[29]

But ultimately the theoretical torque of the metaphor of "field" comes neither from its implied ontology of the actor, nor from its conception of social life as a struggle. It comes, rather, from the way in which field theory enables the investigator to grasp the tenor of social life beyond and *in between* subjective perception, on the one hand, and the relatively map-able ("objective") social environment on the other. Field theory grasps the tacit and the intersubjective as the core medium in social life, and this, it seems to me, is why field theory represents such a tremendous theoretical advance over various ontological dualisms in social theory. But the way field theory does this is by setting up a topology of social life in the specific meaning of the term 'topology'—the idea being that fields, if bent or stretched, would look very similar to each other.

For, in attempting to grasp the tacit rules that make social order possible, navigable, and reproducible, field theory suggests that different fields are, ultimately, isomorphic. The "relational theory" of the social implied by field theory suggests that fields are graspable in terms of the reality of relationships that obtain between winners and losers, orthodoxy and heterodoxy, and so on. And because fields are isomorphic, actors can move between them by converting their field-specific capital. If you diagram a basketball court on a piece of malleable rubber, with enough stretching you can make it resemble a soccer pitch; the struggle for territorial gain on an American football field can, from a bird's eye view, look like the reenactment of a Civil War battle. This isomorphism, furthermore, is what enables the close connection between field theory and a conception of social life as what Sherry Ortner has called "serious games."[30]

28. In this way, Bourdieu's sociology, in particular, attempts to synthesize the classical traditions stemming from Emile Durkheim, Karl Marx, and Max Weber, a point made clear by the interpretations of Bourdieu that have emerged in American sociology.

29. A point made by Talcott Parsons. See, in particular, Talcott Parsons, *The Structure of Social Action: A Study in Social Theory with Special Reference to a Group of Recent European Writers* (New York: McGraw-Hill Book Company, 1937; and Talcott Parsons, Edward Shils, and Neil J. Smelser, *Toward a General Theory of Action: Theoretical Foundations for the Social Sciences*, abridged ed. (New Brunswick, NJ: Transaction Publishers, 2001).

30. Sherry B. Ortner, *Making Gender: The Politics and Erotics of Culture* (Boston: Beacon Press, 1996).

It is this element of field theory—and not the elements of unconscious strategy, or the emphasis on social power and domination in Bourdieu's writings—that I find to be the most problematic. For, in my view, the isomorphism of fields, and the conversions that, according to the theory, actors make in moving from one field to another, belie the sorts of *translations of meaning* that are actually required of actors when they navigate different spaces of social life. The overlapping meaningful worlds of ritual, gesture, bodily comportment, writing, speech, and deep mythological meaning that give social life its texture cannot so easily be made commensurable. Is it not in fact with a great deal of meaning-work that translations from one social context to another are made?

To understand this meaning-work, the formalistic advantages of the field metaphor have to be sacrificed so that the content and contours of meanings, and the phenomenology of the subjects who use these meanings, can be reconstructed with more attention to their peculiarities, their strange myths, their specific semiotic singularities, their unusual regimes of signification. The concrete effectiveness of meaning upon social action requires a different metaphor if the epistemics of the operation of interpreting it are to be fully understood.[31]

VI

So, try this instead: what interpretive analysis does is reconstruct landscapes of meaning. The analogy for social investigation, then, is not the opening up of a mechanical clock (and thus looking for a mechanism), nor is it the observation of a chess game or the diagramming of the action on a football field (and thus identifying the

31. This, then, is where one must depart from John Levi Martin's quite brilliant articulation of field theory, and go down the hermeneutic rabbit hole, in which the formal structures of social life, be they mechanisms or fields, are in fact given concrete effectiveness by the meanings that, in many sociological perspectives, they are supposed to produce. This problematic could also be expressed as a debate about how to interpret and apply Bourdieu's theories, and in particular as to how meaning-full, and how historically specific, "fields" really are. For an example of an analysis of fields that evidences this sort of historical sensitivity (and shows much less fondness for formalized theory), see George Steinmetz, *The Devil's Handwriting: Precoloniality and the German Colonial State in Qingdao, Samoa, and Southwest Africa*, Chicago Studies in Practices of Meaning (Chicago: University of Chicago Press, 2007).

field and its rules),[32] but rather the painting of a landscape. When an investigator reconstructs the layers of meaning in which the social actions under scrutiny are embedded, what she does is paint a picture of the meanings—historically located, fabricated by the human imagination—upon which social life proceeds.

In other words, the core truth claim of maximal interpretations in this epistemic mode is the disclosure of a landscape or landscapes of meaning. Consider a classic Brueghel painting, such as *The Harvesters*. On this vast and varied landscape, there are a variety of human actors, which we can infer are motivated to do a variety of activities. Examining the landscape further, we see that various hard "institutions" can arise—trees, houses and a church, a city in the distance—and various soft ones—the fields of wheat that have certain paths cut through them, for example. The actors have certain capacities to interact effectively with the landscape—tools with which to reap the fields and repair buildings, etc. In these interactions, they activate certain larger processes and mechanisms. However, ultimately the actors and their related social processes are painted with the same paint, and painted in the same style, as the landscape upon which they move. This landscape is the concrete instantiation of meanings made by humans, to which humans become subject, and through which humans must act and interact. As actors position themselves in different places on a given landscape, they take up different (subject) positions, and thus have different views of it. The world looks different from the bell tower than it does from the fields, takes on different meanings from within the schoolhouse than from within the factory, and so on. Thus the landscape metaphor captures the variety of ways in which meaning and processes of communication provide the basis for, and give form to, actors' subjectivities and strategies.

The landscapes that surround certain actions are not necessarily similar to, or easily transformable into, other landscapes that surround other actions—or even landscapes that overlap and thus provide certain actions with more than one meaningful context. A joke made in one landscape makes no sense in another; a certain performance finds an avid audience here, but not there; the technology of printing is

32. In Bourdieu's field theory, finding the investigator's place on the field is important for understanding what can and cannot be seen, much as, for Niklas Luhmann, observation of a social system or subsystem can be conceptualized as a function of the system or subsystem itself. Niklas Luhmann, *Social Systems* (Stanford: Stanford University Press, 1995).

useful for spreading the oral authority of ministers in one landscape of meaning, and for spreading democratic demands for transparency in another.[33] And finally: the transformation of landscapes of meaning takes *work*; it is precisely this that captures how social actors can only do so much—even in tandem—to change underlying meanings. And it is for this reason that actors who act at the intersection of more than one landscape of meaning tend to invent clever ways of switching between them rather than trying to overhaul one of them.

It must immediately be said that the social researcher's metaphor of landscape is in direct opposition to what landscape painting did ideologically during the formation of the British empire. There, landscape was supposed to naturalize and objectify a given relationship between classes, and between human beings and nature.[34] But the point is quite different for the social researcher. The researcher reconstructs a landscape that is ultimately fabricated by human minds and human bodies. She reconstructs meaning as a landscape so as to capture the way in which meaning is made by groups of humans, and yet exceeds the grasp and manipulation of any subset of them.

Thus, in participating in landscape reconstruction—something that, literally speaking, happens in the investigator's text—the investigator cannot reduce different social landscapes to isomorphic fields. She has many theoretical tools to enable good painting. But no master brush will reduce jokes about killing cats, religious demonstrations about gay marriage, and the meaning of soul music to a fundamental set of social antagonisms, cleanly set out in the master (theoretical) painting of which all others are derivative. There is no master painting—only scenes to reconstruct using different brushes.

What does this mean for social investigation? Many have concluded that it means that theory is useless, or even that achieving verisimilitude between the truth claims of social knowledge and what actually proceeds in social life is impossible. But instead, consider this: on the one hand, the interpretive investigator still does what social investigators do: she must give an account of actors and the situations they are in, the institutions they participate in, the mechanisms they trigger. And yet, before this makes any sense, she will have to get the

33. Michael Warner, *The Letters of the Republic: Publication and the Public Sphere in Eighteenth-Century America* (Cambridge, MA: Harvard University Press, 1990).

34. Denis Cosgrove, *Social Formation and Symbolic Landscape* (Madison: University of Wisconsin Press, 1998 [1984]).

landscape right. She will have to identify the contours and colors of the fields, hills, and mountains upon which everyone has to move. Actors and the occasional institution or historically located, highly specific social mechanism may be the more proximate and singular causes of this or that event, but none of this will make the remotest bit of sense if the landscape upon which it all takes place is not reconstructed. In Puritan America, a printing press enabled ministers to bring their authority into the homes of those who did not hear their sermons. In the Early Republic, it allowed pamphleteers to create a protodemocratic public. Without understanding the concrete landscape of social meaning, the investigator will only comprehend a printing press without form or content (a machine with no purpose), and distribution through a social network that is real but mute (a mechanism without meaning).

But how, in the interpretive epistemic mode, does the investigator use theory and evidence together to disclose these landscapes?

VII

Let us first note that there is one way in which a given landscape of meaning is "general." It is general for the social actors that move upon it. And, for this reason, in disclosing it, the investigator necessarily generalizes from her evidence to posit a meaning-system or discursive formation. Presumably, Geertz's insights about Balinese masculinity, the Balinese status system, and the repulsiveness of animality to the Balinese are meanings that do not only hold for the actual cockfights he witnessed. And presumably, in addition to being on display at other cockfights that he did not attend, these meanings hold during other concrete activities as well—not just during cockfights. (Though perhaps they are never so clearly expressed as they are during cockfights.)

But this is not what social researchers usually mean when they refer to the generality of their concepts. Rather, as we saw in the realist mode of resignification, what "generality" means—particularly when sociology and political science are contrasted with history and anthropology—is that certain concepts are part of a general, coherent, and referential theory of social life, which has wide applicability. In the realist mode, of course, not all mechanisms are present in all cases—if so, there would be no basis for comparison. But in principle, the theoretical conceptualization of a causal mechanism could apply anywhere, anytime. That is what makes them general, and, in the realist epistemic mode, useful.[35] In realism, the articulation of a causal mechanism in abstract theory is what creates the intellectual conditions for "testing" for its existence. So, maximal interpretations are founded on a general, complex theory of the social world that works itself out in the analysis of comparable and ultimately commensurable cases.

In interpretive social research, however, the relationship of general concepts to the production of maximal interpretations works differently. The maximal interpretations emerge from the disclosure of a landscape for action, but this particular landscape is not a general feature of the social. It is historically located and culturally specific. Thus in interpretive research a sort of hybrid sign tends to emerge repeatedly, a sign whose denotations and connotations seem to exceed the sum of what is indicated by the theoretical and evidential signifiers that make it up: 'deep play in the Balinese cockfight'; 'the male gaze internalized by the anorexic girl.' These compound signs mark out a certain dimension of the meaningful context for a set of social actions. In them, abstract theoretical terms are brought to bear on the evidence, and, mediated by the evidence, they help to disclose a landscape of meaning that is effective for a certain swath of time and space. The precise time-space extension of the landscape is itself a case-based question.

In using theory and evidence in this way, we are a long way from the testing of hypotheses.[36] So what are the constraints upon interpretation? It appears—from our examples at least—that there

35. An exemplary version of this approach has been developed by the philosopher of social science and comparative social researcher Daniel Little, whose early work in analytic Marxism was followed by his account of social science as concerned with causal mechanisms at the mesolevel. See Daniel Little, *The Scientific Marx* (Minneapolis: University of Minnesota Press, 1986); Daniel Little, *Understanding Peasant China: Case Studies in the Philosophy of Social Science* (New Haven: Yale University Press, 1989); Daniel Little, *Microfoundations, Method, and Causation: On the Philosophy of the Social Sciences* (New Brunswick, NJ: Transaction Publishers, 1998); Daniel Little, "Explaining Large-Scale Historical Change," *Philosophy of the Social Sciences* 30, no. 1 (2000).

36. Indeed in what follows I depart from the long tradition of fitting so-called qualitative analysis into a frame imported from natural science or from realist social science. My point, in the following discussion, is to try to imagine (1) how theory is used in the reconstruction of deep meanings, and (2) how the practice of "ferreting out" these meanings is still one that seeks validity and verisimilitude. My conclusions about how social analysis should be executed thus differ considerably from, for example, Gary King, Robert O. Keohane, and Sidney Verba, *Designing Social Inquiry: Scientific Inference in Qualitative Research* (Princeton: Princeton University Press, 1994).

are two constraints operating on this process wherein investigators "ferret out hidden meanings" and disclose the landscape upon which action proceeds, two regulators of interpretation that hold epistemic relativism at bay.

The first is localized verificationism: a piece of theory (a subset of the theoretical signs used in a given maximal interpretation) must adequately and reasonably comprehend the surface meanings indicated by a subgroup of evidential signs. Theory moves beyond data toward deeper meaning, but in doing so the surface meanings still have to *make sense* to the researcher and her audience as the deeper interpretation develops. For example, the theoretical term "deep play" allows Geertz to move beyond a surface understanding of Balinese gambling as action guided by a specific set of rules and conducted—as gambling generally is—in the hopes of making money. Yet, even as "deep play" risks a deeper interpretation of Balinese cockfight gambling, it remains nonetheless a concept *appropriate to* the practice of gambling. Implicit in the idea of deep play—that some bets are for so much money that it is beyond rationality to make them—is the more mundane meaning of gambling (to take risks and make money). Indeed, this is perhaps precisely why Geertz takes the concept from Bentham. And: when Bordo goes beyond her evidence to conceptualize the role of the male gaze as an aspect of post-1960s American middle-class culture, it is nonetheless the case that her theory of the "gender-power axis" fits a certain bundle of evidence: the diaries of anorexic women that attest to feeling spurred on in their diets by an imagined male voice, or to have started a diet at the urging of a father, brother, or boyfriend. Thus, in this aspect of building maximal interpretations, interpretations are tethered to the meanings of the evidence, but still underdetermined by them.[37] Thus a nonvicious

37. Thus this moment in interpretive analysis parallels, though it does not replicate precisely, the possibilities and problems of the Duhem-Quine thesis. To use Quine's terms, theories form a "web of belief" that changes when confronted by facts, but not via a process of rejecting a clearly testable hypothesis. The analytic philosophy of science has worked through a variety of types of underdetermination and what their consequences are for the rationality of the scientific endeavor. And, as Daniel Little points out, these appear to be exacerbated in social science: "It would seem that social science claims are even more subject to underdetermination than the claims of mechanics and physics. In addition to the problem of unidentified interfering causes and the need for auxiliary hypotheses, we have the problems of vagueness and specification. We commonly find that social science theories offer general statements about social causes and conditions that need to be further specified before they can be applied to a given set of circumstances. And there are almost always alternative and equally plausible ways

hermeneutic circle ensues: having used a piece of theory to guess at these deep meanings, the investigator then sets out to gather more evidence for or against them.[38]

Localized verificationism is thus one constraint on interpretation. It is a constraint "from below," in which theoretical concepts must be appropriate or adequate to the evidence. But there is pluralism here, since different theories can be brought to bear on different bundles of evidence within a case. There is, however, another constraint to the interpretive reconstruction of landscapes of meaning, a constraint "from above."

For, in building a maximal interpretation, the hidden, depth meanings posited by each theory-evidence interaction must be themselves brought together in an overarching reconstruction of the meaningful landscape. There must be some coherence to the reconstruction of the case. Thus, as the investigator attempts to build a maximal interpretation of a set of social actions, her localized theory-fact interpretations must be brought together in some way that makes sense. From this constraint, several of the most recognizable maneuvers of interpretive analysis result. An investigator returns to a certain, problematic bundle of theory-and-evidence and reexamines it in terms of her

of specifying the concept in a particular setting." Daniel Little, *Understanding Society*, 879. Published electronically at http://understandingsociety.blogspot.com.

Here, I am suggesting that the reason why the problem of the specification in explanation is different (or "worse") in the human sciences is the arbitrary and conventional nature of signification, and thus the idiosyncrasy of the impact of meaning on social life. Ultimately, then, this underdetermination to interpretation is countered by the second constraint on interpretation—holism or "making sense" of a case—discussed below. See Sandra Harding, ed., *Can Theories Be Refuted? Essays on the Duhem-Quine Thesis* (Hingham, MA: D. Reidel, 1976), especially Pierre Duhem, "Physical Theory and Experiment," 1–40, and W. V. O. Quine, "Two Dogmas of Empiricism," 41–64. For an account of how the problem of underdetermination relates to current controversies in the philosophy and sociology of natural science, see Helen Longino, *The Fate of Knowledge* (Princeton: Princeton University Press, 2002), 59–67, 124–28.

38. This is, I believe, Richard Biernacki's interpretation of how the investigator is to construct and use ideal types in research. Biernacki writes that the search for truth in social science involves an "ethics of interpretation," and thus that "the inconvenience of evidentiary findings for our ideal types and the pressure these findings put on the value positions anchoring those types comprise the truth process as it is available to Weber." And he writes in a particularly provocative passage, "if we insist our conceptual models originate in and remain in some sense creative fancies, explanation in sociology does not consist of propositions about the interactions among these dreamt concepts." Richard Biernacki, "After Quantitative Cultural Sociology," in *Meaning and Method: The Cultural Approach to Sociology*, ed. Isaac Reed and Jeffrey C. Alexander (Boulder: Paradigm Publishers, 2009), 119–207, 178, 179.

emerging overall interpretation. Or, confronted with contradictory deep meanings posited by different theory-and-evidence pairs, she looks to her evidence for an indication of how the actors under study manage such a contradiction *or* the way the contradiction is merely apparent and in fact masks a deeper unity *or* whether there are, in fact, different sets of actors in her case, with different meanings operating for each of them.

The constraints on interpretation, then, are coherence from above and adequacy from below. It is both of these constraints, working in tandem, that make the pluralistic use of theory remain empirically responsible to the case. Thus, in the interpretive epistemic mode, although the investigator does not demand coherence of all her theories taken in the abstract, she does work with the imperative that there must be at least a minimal coherence to the case. Landscapes change, and terrains can have hills, meadows, and even deserts. They have cities, towns, and army barracks. But landscapes cannot be radically incoherent. Neither can the hidden meanings of a case. Or at least we must know: if, on the landscape of meaning, the church is across the road from the liquor store, how do the agents who frequent both manage this apparent contradiction?

If this account of how the disclosure of landscapes functions is correct (and I believe that it fits well the interpretations of both Geertz and Bordo reconstructed earlier), then some important consequences for social analysis follow. First, the sort of interpretive perspicuity and selectiveness that makes for a compelling maximal interpretation of the social actions under study should not be mistaken for *theoretical* parsimony. The maximal interpretation may indeed present a parsimonious or elegant reconstruction of a case, creating analytical leverage with which to better comprehend certain social actions. But the interpreter may use many theoretical terms or schemas to accomplish this, and thus theoretical parsimony should not be a governing criterion for what makes a good maximal interpretation. The task is, first and foremost, to make the meaningful landscape intelligible to the reader, to render its contours clearly, and show its fault lines with care. The actions under study must come to make sense, even if one must use multiple theories to reconstruct the landscape of meaning that enables our maximal interpretation to achieve this.

Secondly, a well-disclosed landscape may or may not give hints as to what another landscape, from another time and another place, will be like. A landscape, once disclosed, is not immediately generalizable. For this reason, theories come to prominence not because they are shown to explain directly many different instances or cases, but because they have been repeatedly useful as part of many different investigations into many different meaningful landscapes, each one using a plurality of such theories. Maximal interpretations are better or worse, in so far as they responsibly use evidence and conform to the case at hand; theories are more or less useful, in so far as they allow the interpretive investigator to do this reconstruction.

VIII

What does the pluralistic use of theory to reconstruct a meaningful landscape *do*? What sorts of knowledge claims are these reconstructions of the meanings of a case? In the next chapter, I will argue that maximal interpretations of this sort are explanations. But I would like to set up this question by returning to our beloved French Revolution, and to the debate between William Sewell Jr. and Theda Skocpol about ideology and the French Revolution, which took place in the *Journal of Modern History* in the 1980s. This intellectual exchange has become a reference point for debates about the relationship of the "cultural turn" to comparative-historical sociology and to social research more generally. But what it also reveals is an epistemological question about causality and interpretation.

Sewell and Skocpol argued about the role that ideology played in the run up to, and during, the momentous events that took place in France—and especially in Paris and Versailles—between 1789 and 1799. Originally Skocpol admitted that "revolutionary ideologies and people committed to them were undoubtedly necessary ingredients in the great social revolutions," but nonetheless found these ideologies wanting in terms of their generalizability into her scientific scheme. She thus wrote that "it cannot be argued . . . that the cognitive content of the ideologies in any sense provides a predictive key to either the outcomes of the Revolutions or the activities of the revolutionaries who built the state organizations that consolidated the Revolutions."[39] Ideologies, for Skocpol, were relegated to the

39. Theda Skocpol, *States and Social Revolutions: A Comparative Analysis of France, Russia, and China* (Cambridge: Cambridge University of Chicago Press, 1979), 170.

unstructural, and thus unscientific, theories of revolution, alongside "the purposive image of how revolutions develop."[40]

Sewell, on the other hand, was part of a larger move in the American historiography of the French Revolution toward a fuller engagement with the symbolic in social life. He insisted in his critique of ***States and Social Revolutions*** that Skocpol "has not made her causation multiple enough—she has not recognized the autonomous power of ideology in the revolutionary process."[41] A structural theory of ideology, Sewell argued, could add explanatory power to Skocpol's framework. Empirically speaking, Sewell was interested in the existence of monarchial, corporatist, and Enlightenment ideologies among elite political groups in the years leading up to the revolution.[42] So, in his critique, Sewell suggested that Skocpol needed to include ideology in her multifactor approach to revolutions.[43] But Sewell also suggested a different, and somewhat contradictory, implication of bringing a structural theory of ideology to bear in the analysis of the French Revolution. He wrote that "doing this [i.e., bringing ideology in] . . . does more than add one more 'factor' that can account for some portion of the change that took place. It also leads to a fundamentally different conceptualization of the process of revolution."[44] This is because, according to Sewell, "ideology must also, as most recent theorists have insisted, be understood as constitutive of the social order . . . It is not enough to treat ideology as a possible causal factor explaining some portion of the change wrought by revolution. If society is understood as ideologically constituted, then adding ideology to the account will also mean rethinking the nature, the interrelations, and the effects on the revolution of state, class, international and other structures."[45] This is a much stronger statement, and there is an important epistemic incongruity between

40. Skocpol, ***States and Social Revolutions***, 17.

41. William H. Sewell Jr., "Ideologies and Social Revolutions: Reflections on the French Case," ***Journal of Modern History*** 57, no. 1 (1985): 58.

42. Sewell, "Ideologies and Social Revolutions," 62–66.

43. I am glossing here key issues of the difference between "culture" and "ideology" in their ***many*** uses (see William H. Sewell Jr., "The Concept(s) of Culture," in ***Beyond the Cultural Turn***, ed. Lynn Hunt and Victoria E. Bonnell. Berkeley: University of California Press, 1999). I want to emphasize instead the difference between the inclusion of some notion of "culture" in a realist explanatory framework, on the one hand, and the development of an interpretive approach to social explanation, on the other.

44. Sewell, "Ideologies and Social Revolutions," 58.

45. Sewell, "Ideologies and Social Revolutions," 61.

Sewell's two suggestions. It is precisely this incongruity that Skocpol exploited in her reply to Sewell, with particular attention to the extreme-sounding claim that ideology is "constitutive of the social order." She wrote that Sewell had an "unrealistically totalistic and synchronous" understanding of ideology. She thus considered his "anthropological" perspective as unable to comprehend the "complex, changing, highly stratified sociopolitical orders" that are at issue in comparative historical sociology and, presumably, in social research generally.[46] Instead, Skocpol suggested, we should follow a "more historically grounded approach."[47] She thus wrote that "Historians, sociologists, and political scientists are not well served by supposing that sets of ideas—whether intellectual productions or cultural frameworks of a more informally reasoned sort—are 'constitutive of social order.' Rather, multiple cultural idioms coexist, and they arise, decline, and intermingle in tempos that need to be explored by intellectual and sociocultural historians."[48] If we examine Sewell's own work, however, we find that he by no means assumes a totalistic or synchronous understanding of "cultural frameworks." For example, in *Work and Revolution in France*, he describes how workers drew on the corporate language of the ancien régime to articulate their claims in the context of, and in opposition to, the liberal, individualist language that formed the meaningful background for many postrevolutionary institutions, especially the law.[49]

What to make of this now iconic exchange? The trouble was, and is, with the verb "constitute." Sewell argued that Skocpol needs an

46. Theda Skocpol, "Cultural Idioms and Political Ideologies in the Revolutionary Reconstruction of State Power: A Rejoinder to Sewell," *Journal of Modern History* 57, no. 1 (1985): 89–90.

47. Skocpol, "Cultural Idioms and Political Ideologies in the Revolutionary Reconstruction of State Power," 90. Given the reception of Skocpol's *States and Social Revolutions* by some historians, I am inclined to view the use of "historical grounding" as a discursive maneuver, one that perhaps covers real differences in epistemic mode by operating in the language of empiricism.

48. Skocpol, "Cultural Idioms and Political Ideologies in the Revolutionary Reconstruction of State Power," 91.

49. William H. Sewell Jr., *Work and Revolution in France: The Language of Labor from the Old Regime to 1848* (Cambridge: Cambridge University Press, 1980). For a further exploration of how this work exemplifies interpretive social research, see Isaac Ariail Reed, "Justifying Sociological Knowledge: From Realism to Interpretation," *Sociological Theory* 26, no. 2 (2008): 101–29. For Sewell's own theoretical reflections on the epistemological contours of his work, see William H. Sewell Jr., *Logics of History: Social Theory and Social Transformation*, Chicago Studies in Practices of Meaning (Chicago: University of Chicago Press, 2005).

understanding of ideology as "anonymous, collective, and as constitutive of social order."[50] The third term in this description of ideology allowed Skocpol to criticize Sewell's emphasis on the symbolic as both simplifying and reductive. But the problem with Skocpol's response was not, or not only, that it did not correctly comprehend or evaluate Sewell's own work. Rather, in hindsight, it appears questions about how one should build a social explanation were somewhat distorted in so far as they were translated into a debate about "material" and "ideal" factors. After all, in the end, neither Sewell nor Skocpol deny the importance of either "material" or "ideal" factors in bringing about the Revolution—though there is a lot of criticism back and forth concerning how focus on one type tends to lead to an underestimation of the role of the other.[51] So what was really at stake in all of this talk about ideology, and the "constitution" of the social order?

Sublimated into the battle between "cultural" and "material" factors were unacknowledged differences between Sewell and Skocpol in epistemic mode. This was perhaps hidden by the way in which Sewell and Skocpol both sought an "explanation" of the French Revolution. But what is an explanation? The two scholars construct maximal interpretations of the French Revolution in fundamentally different ways. Indeed it is the case that for Sewell ideology is not just one more factor. But this is *not* because he views ideology as the *only* factor. It is, rather, that his interpretive work on ideology also changed his fundamental approach to what makes for a good explanation, and how to achieve it.[52]

Sewell's critique of Skocpol, then, contains in pristine, historically grounded form an ambiguity that runs through the entire cultural turn: is meaning "one more cause" in a general model of the social, or does the importance of meaning to social life imply an entirely

50. Sewell, "Ideologies and Social Revolutions," 61.

51. Jeff Goodwin has pointed to chapter 4 of *States and Social Revolutions* in an effort to argue that, while perhaps not attending to "cultural idioms," Skocpol does include an analysis of "political ideologies" in her explanation. See Jeff Goodwin, "How to Become a Dominant American Social Scientist: The Case of Theda Skocpol," *Contemporary Sociology* 25, no. 3 (1996): 294. Reciprocally, Sewell himself admits that ideology is not the only thing that matters—the exigencies of political situation and access to resources contribute to determining the course of social action. So we are left with the question of what, exactly, is the argument between these two researchers?

52. William Sewell Jr., *Logics of History; Social Theory and Social Transformation* (Chicago: University of Chicago Press, 2005).

different mode of social analysis? If the latter is true, then one is faced with the question of how to comprehend causality in the shifting historical world to which the human sciences must, according to interpretivism, address themselves. How, that is, can we reconceptualize causality once we have moved from robust correlations and/or mechanism identification into the interpretive epistemic mode, where we reconstruct meaningful landscapes?

Consider, then, a fact that Skocpol makes a point of—that the Russian revolutionaries knew about the French Revolution, and the Chinese revolutionaries knew about the French and Russian revolutions. What is the significance of this? For Sewell, and for interpretivism, the significance would be great, because the landscape of meaning upon which the Russian Revolution proceeded *included the outcome and subsequent interpretation of the French Revolution.* And the outcome and subsequent interpretation of the Russian Revolution makes up part of the meaningful landscape upon which the Chinese Revolution occurred. Different meanings, for different revolutions, in different valleys . . . But how should we think of these landscapes of meaning as effective?

Chapter Five

Explanation

A symbol whose interpretation does not reach into the production of physical effects, bring its reasonableness into the universe, is a failure as a symbol.
—C. S. Peirce, unpublished manuscript 417, 41[1]

I

The compelling fusion of theory and evidence creates a maximal interpretation that, by power of intellect, reconstructs the critical reader's understanding of the social actions under scrutiny. How this fusion happens can differ according to what I have called epistemic mode. So, different notions of what theory is for, and how theory does what it does, emerge: realist, normative, interpretive.

If one is inclined to the position developed in the last chapter—that the human sciences are in some deep way interpretive, and that this is reflected in how researchers use both evidence and theory—then a key philosophical move awaits the interpretivist. It is sophisticated and informed by developments in both Anglophone and Continental philosophy, and it is draws upon a pluralism and liberal universalism that feels familiar to many academics in the West. The move is this: to argue that what realists call explanation is in fact redescription,

1. Cited in John R. Lyne, "Rhetoric and Semiotic in C. S. Peirce," *Quarterly Journal of Speech* 66, no. 2 (1980), 163. Lyne's recasting of the issue is: "Because it calls out a habit of interpretation, the sign has a capacity for excercising a regulative force, and for making things happen" (162).

which is to say, the resituating of known facts and actions in a new intellectual context. And what normativists call critique is, likewise, redescription from a new perspective, according to which previously acceptable actions become intolerable, old ways of being and acting are revealed as domineering, and visions of what can and should be acquire new life. Inquiry generally—perhaps even natural scientific inquiry—can be understood as recontextualization.[2]

In this view, the earnestness of realism and of normativism—to try to know what is really there, on the one hand, and to demand and hope for what might be possible, on the other—are perhaps necessary for our knowledge practices to proceed. But ultimately, we have to recognize that the pretentions to superior and long-lasting rationality that are implied by the knowledge claims of realists and normativists are a bit much. The knowledgeable interpretivist may indeed agree with many of the substantive claims made when social knowledge is constructed by investigators working in the realist or normativist mode. But he resists the frameworks that secure such knowledge claims, for not only does he find these frameworks indelibly flawed, but he also finds fault with the very idea that one needs a sustainable framework to prop up social knowledge. In the end, then, he is a metatheoretical ironist. As an expert philosopher and epistemological insider, he upholds only a (neo-)pragmatic attitude, inflected by postmodern hermeneutics. After all, most knowledge claims are *just* interpretations.

This philosophical move is a terrible idea and should be resisted at all costs.

The political problems of overdone irony and proliferating skepticism have been much discussed and should by now be relatively clear—it is an intellectual mood that can rend not only the possibility of deep, and deeply held, truth in social research, but also the ways that such truths might be brought to consequence, thus undermin-

2. The generality with which this thesis is sometimes stated can be startling. In "Inquiry as Recontextualization," for example, Richard Rorty suggests that his neo-pragmatist, antiessentialist account of inquiry would understand the development of a "new context" to accommodate new beliefs to cover, among other things, "a new explanatory theory, a new comparison class, a new descriptive vocabulary, a new private or political purpose, the latest book one has read, the last person one has talked to; the possibilities are endless." Richard Rorty, "Inquiry as Recontextualization: An Anti-Dualist Account of Interpretation," in *The Interpretive Turn: Philosophy, Science, and Culture*, ed. David R. Hiley, James Bohman, and Richard Schusterman (Ithaca: Cornell University Press, 1991), 59–80, 61.

ing the pragmatist ambition that supposedly supports it.[3] But there is another problem to this line of thought. If all sorts of knowledge claims are, in the end, "just interpretation," then the victory won over scientistic philosophy and naturalist social research is a pyrrhic one. We will have criticized the philosophical pretentions of positivist or realist explanations, or the transcendental ambitions of normative critique, but we will not have attempted to alter the mode by which they produce their maximal interpretations. We will have left intact the process that produces the actual, substantive knowledge claims. The in-house goings-on of these maximal interpretations are left unchanged if the interpretivist, stepping back from the study of social action, resigns himself to philosophy as ill-fated commentary.

In contrast to this, one of the greatest intellectual contributions of realism—especially clear in the writings of Rom Harré, Roy Bhaskar, and Mario Bunge—is that social researchers can and should attempt to construct causal claims about the social world.[4] I have tried to show how the realist mode of making such claims draws upon a metaphor that connects social scientific theory to natural scientific theory, and consequently that, because this metaphor breaks down, realism for the human sciences has to be critiqued, reformed, and resituated. To this argument I would now propose an addition: to throw away the possibility of knowing social causes with the possibility of naturalism is to conflate the goals of social research with its means.[5]

3. Perhaps the most cogent of these critiques is Thomas McCarthy, "Private Irony and Public Decency: Richard Rorty's New Pragmatism," *Critical Inquiry* 16, no. 2 (1990): 355–70.

4. Bhaskar and Bunge still find naturalism a useful frame for this project, while Harré has rejected the ontological approach to social structure taken up by Bhaskar, and has turned toward the analysis of narrative and symbol as ways to understand the mind's construction of the world instead. Rom Harré and Grant Gillett, *The Discursive Mind* (Thousand Oaks, CA: Sage Publications, 1994); Rom Harré, "Social Reality and the Myth of Social Structure," *European Journal of Social Theory* 5 (2002).

5. It is tempting to use Rorty's critique of representational theories of truth as a weapon against realism and naturalism in social research, but I think this is a mistake and a conflation. One can maintain that to make truth claims involves making representations of the world, but argue that the way that this works in the human sciences involves the pluralistic use of theories to build better concrete, historically located maximal interpretations of events, and thus that the naturalistic inheritance of realism is highly problematic as a conceptual method for social research. This critical view towards Rorty's antirepresentationalism emerged in conversations with Neil Gross and Benjamin Lamb-Books. For an account of the development of Rorty's philosophy as a case study in the new sociology of knowledge, see Neil Gross, *Richard Rorty: The Making of an American Philosopher* (Chicago: University of Chicago Press, 2008).

A similar point can be made when it comes to interpretation and social criticism. If we must deeply engage the meaningful life experiences of people in various social groups, variously defined, when developing social critique, should we not emerge from this process of interpretation with a much firmer sense of commitment, as opposed to a distanced irony about different ways of being? It is by no means a logical finality that recognizing the ambiguities of interpretation that attend to social criticism implies a dismissal of the use of theory in producing it. Perhaps we must give up the system-building, false universalisms of an earlier era and engage the spheres of justice and different logics of justification that are available to both actors and philosopher-critics, and perhaps not.[6] But either way, surely the shedding of false universalism is a means to a more effective politics of knowledge?

The position of the earnest, committed interpretivist is well known and relatively well established in political theory, with clear and distinct articulations made in explicitly hermeneutic registers by Georgia Warnke, Charles Taylor, Alastair MacIntyre, and Michael Walzer.[7] Through their work the argument for the interpretive basis of social critique has shed the connection between the intellectual project of hermeneutics and the conservative reliance on tradition and authority as the source of morality. In their view, it is not the authority of meaningful tradition but the possibilities granted by close interpretation and thick description that allow the development of critique. And so, the idea that the interpretation of social meaning can ground normative social research is a synthesis well on its way for the human sciences. And yet, there is something missing in the movement toward meaning, experience, and discourse in political theory. For if the engagement with meaning is going to found critique, it must be the case that interpretation and reinterpretation are expected to have an *effect* on social life. And it is the social effect of meanings that is really the problem.

6. Michael Walzer, *Spheres of Justice: A Defense of Pluralism and Equality* (New York: Basic Books, 1983). Luc Boltanski and Laurent Thévenot, *On Justification: Economies of Worth*, Princeton Studies in Cultural Sociology (Princeton: Princeton University Press, 2006).

7. Of particular interest in relation to the concerns of this text: Michael Walzer, *Interpretation and Social Criticism* (Cambridge, MA: Harvard University Press, 1993), and Georgia Warnke, *Justice and Interpretation* (Cambridge, MA: MIT Press, 1994).

II

Certainly interpretive sociology appears to answer the sorts of why-questions that call forth explanation.[8] For example: why was a certain volunteer church group in the American Midwest successful in building bridges to other communities, and thus able to combat the deleterious social effects of welfare retrenchment, while other groups with the same goals and the same sort of motivated, anxious-to-help volunteers failed? In his answer to this question, Paul Lichterman

8. I do not, in the space of this chapter, address directly contemporary work in the philosophy of explanation, the beginning of which could be approximated by the publication of Van Fraassen's *The Scientific Image.* In that text, he proposed an "erotetic" approach to explanation, wherein an explanation is understood as answer to a why-question. Wesley Salmon, in turn, distinguished between modal explanations, ontic explanations, and erotetic explanations, and much of the ensuing debate focused on the difference between the last two. For Salmon, ontic explanation takes place when an event is situated inside a network of patterned occurrences and causal processes in the world, whereas erotetic explanation puts the emphasis on the interests and linguistic context of the investigator.

Even if many philosophers feel that the success of an explanation must ultimately hinge on its ability to say something true about what is in the world, the central insights of the erotetic approach seem undeniable. In particular, a why-question about a given event or occurrence has a topic (that which must be explained), a contrast class or "foil" (often consisting of the counterfactuals that inform the why-question), and a set of relevance criteria (which limit what sorts of true statements can be used in the explanation). The contrast class is a useful tool in dictating how a social researcher might go about constructing her explanation—so, for example, "Why did the French Revolution happen (in 1789, as opposed to before 1780 or after 1800)?" would require a different approach than "Why did the French Revolution happen (as opposed to a late-eighteenth-century revolution in Prussia, England, Spain, or the Austro-Hungarian Empire)?" Likewise, the relevance criteria can suggest which aspects of the necessarily infinite number of causes of an event or an occurrence are of interest to a particular community of inquiry—indeed Mark Risjord has argued that the sorts of relevance criteria and contrast classes that determine a specific why-question for investigation are, to some degree, determined by what he calls the "constitutive interests" of a discipline or community of inquiry. Mark Day argues that the synthesis of erotetic and ontic explanation involves using the erotetic approach to distinguish different sorts of why-questions from each other, and then, when two why-questions are identified as essentially the same erotetically, ontic explanation would kick in, with disputes focusing on which real processes best account for the event in question. But what makes for the "best account in answer to a well-defined why-question" involves a series of questions about how theory is used in the building of explanations. Or at least that is the argument of this book.

See Bas C. Van Fraassen, *The Scientific Image* (New York: Oxford University Press, 1980); Mark W. Risjord, *Woodcutters and Witchcraft: Rationality and Interpretive Change in the Social Sciences* (Albany: State University of New York Press, 2000), 83; Mark Day, "Explanatory Exclusion, History, and Social Science," *Philosophy of the Social Sciences* 34, no. 1 (2004).

points to the different meanings that molded the actions of each group, accessed in his ethnography by reconstructing the "customs" of each set of volunteers.[9] His provocative conclusion is that it is the development of a specific set of customs of *social reflexivity*—customs that lead to extended discussions about what the group *is* and eventually to the group's self-transformation—that in the end allows "Park Cluster" to succeed where other groups fail. What it means to be a member of the volunteer group—and in particular the idea that to be a member means extended discussions and deliberations with actual members of disadvantaged communities—is deeply consequential for what gets done, and how. Hence Lichterman has made a clear explanatory claim and a claim with practical, political relevance for those interested in changing American society (and in particular for those who want to differentiate between the good and bad social effects of religion in a way grounded in strong sociology). Lichterman's interpretive explanation grounds his social critique.

Interpretive explanation: Lichterman shows how the meanings that define the social context of action in a specific way are tremendously important in determining what, when, and where certain actions happen, certain social relationships emerge, and certain sorts of community arise as a result of these relationships. In particular, what Lichterman's explanation accomplishes is to show why some social ties last and lead to much-needed public goods (such as provision for a neighborhood nurse) and some do not. His interpretation of meaning, that is, gives him leverage on the question why "Park Cluster" created a vibrant slice of civil society and other volunteer groups, also drawing on and constructing social ties, did not. This is leverage that the Putnam-led social capital format of analysis, which examines networks, norms, and trust without interpreting meanings, cannot attain. Indeed, in some cases, the meanings attached to certain social ties actually *cut off* the possibility of mobilizing action for the common good. For Lichterman, network ties without meanings are empty, and thus network analysis without interpretation remains blind.

Surely this is a causal argument. And yet, if one examines monographs in the philosophy of social science and the pages of sociol-

9. Lichterman breaks down customs analytically into how a group marks itself off from the wider world (*boundaries*), how group members define obligations within the group (*bonds*), and the *speech genres* that define what is and is not appropriate talk within the group. Paul Lichterman, *Elusive Togetherness: Church Groups Trying to Bridge America's Divisions* (Princeton: Princeton University Press, 2005), 52–54.

ogy research journals, one will find that the specifically interpretive approach that Lichterman and many other ethnographers espouse is often contrasted directly to explanation, to the point that the dichotomy of understanding (through interpretation) and explanation (through causal analysis) is taken to be foundational for the social sciences.[10] Thus, despite Max Weber's imperatives in the opening pages of *Economy and Society*,[11] such contemporary Weberian interventions as Richard Swedberg's outline for an interpretive economic sociology,[12] and Jack Katz's reflexive discussions of how ethnographies can move from "how" to "why,"[13] various theoretical obstacles have been erected over the last century to understanding the social knowledge gained through careful interpretation as consisting of, among many things, social explanations.[14]

10. So, for example, Gurpeet Mahajan writes that "hermeneutic understanding is a way of *understanding*, rather than *explaining*, a given occurrence. The advocates of this view argue that causal explanation (Erklarer) is a mode of investigation that is suitable to the *Naturwissenschaften* (natural sciences) where we try to apprehend objects as they are given to us externally through sensory perception." In contrast to this Paul Roth has argued that psychoanalytic interpretation, at least, is explanation—though this raises this issue of the ontological ambitions of Freudian theory. Gurpeet Mahajan, *Explanation and Understanding in the Human Sciences* (Delhi: Oxford University Press, 1997), 51; Paul Roth, "Interpretation as Explanation," in *The Interpretive Turn: Philosophy, Science, Culture*, ed. David R. Hiley, James Bohman, and Richard Schusterman (Ithaca: Cornell University Press, 1991). I discuss unconscious motives and their relationship to interpretation and explanation below.

11. It is worth noting that Weber developed his vision of the intersection between interpretation and explanation when the available models of explanation and philosophies of causality derived almost entirely from nineteenth-century positivism. See Susan J. Hekman, "Weber's Concept of Causality and the Modern Critique" *Sociological Inquiry* 4, no. 4 (2007). The one exception is conceptions of causality and responsibility developed in legal theory, which Weber did draw on extensively. I discuss these in the footnote on Fritz Ringer and Weberian methodology, in section VI below.

12. Richard Swedberg, "Max Weber's Interpretive Economic Sociology," *American Behavioral Scientist* 50, no. 8 (2007).

13. Jack Katz, "From How to Why: On Luminous Description and Causal Inference in Ethnography (Part I)" *Ethnography* 2, no. 4 (2001): 443–73; and Jack Katz, "From How to Why: On Luminous Description and Causal Inference in Ethnography (Part 2)," *Ethnography* 3, no. 1 (2002): 63–90.

14. In what follows, I draw inspiration from the classics of hermeneutic theory from the 1960s forward, and in particular from Charles Taylor and Paul Ricoeur whose work in hermeneutic philosophy defies summary. See in particular Charles Taylor, "Interpretation and the Sciences of Man," in *Philosophy and the Human Sciences: Philosophical Papers*, vol. 2 (New York: Cambridge University Press, 1985), and Paul Ricoeur, "What Is a Text? Explanation and Understanding," in *Hermeneutics and the Human Sciences: Essays on Language, Action, and Interpretation* (New York: Cambridge University Press, 1981). For a narrative about how the hermeneutic tradition of social thought has, and has not, engaged the problem of social explanation, see Isaac Ariail Reed and

For, investigation that moves through the hermeneutic circle has not only been relegated to the less "scientific" side of the divide between the humanities and the social sciences, it has been explicitly theorized in a variety of nonexplanatory ways. "Interpretation" can mean a philosophical exercise that reveals the existential conditions of life for all humans. Or, it can be a literary exercise in which the interpreter critically and creatively reinterprets the traditions handed down via texts, and comes to understand herself "before the text." Or, it can be a psychoanalytic process by which the investigator, with the help of an interlocutor, obtains a sort of self-knowledge. In this way, two frequent hermeneutic arguments get tethered together: (1) the healthy hermeneutic objection to the effacement, by certain scientistic epistemologies, of the role of the investigator from the process of investigation, and (2) a refusal of the possibility that the hermeneutic social investigator's interpretations could grasp something causal about the world.

Is it really better to defend the hermeneutic citadel against naturalism than to risk a counterattack? It seems an oddly Spartan position for an intellectual tradition dedicated to the possibility (and, admittedly, the difficulty) of mutual understanding. But then, even in Clifford Geertz's work, the distinction is confidently announced in what is perhaps the iconic sentence of the cultural turn: "Believing, with Max Weber, that man is an animal suspended in webs of significance he himself has spun, I take culture to be those webs, and the analysis of it to be therefore not an experimental science in search of law but an interpretive one in search of meaning."[15] When we contrast this comment to the *opening sentence* of Max Weber's *Economy and Society*, in which sociology "is a science concerning itself with the interpretive understanding of social action and thereby with a causal explanation of its course and consequences," we come to the crux of the issue. Causality, and the social explanations that causal claims help produce, have to be reconsidered, not rejected, from within the interpretive epistemic mode.[16]

Benjamin Lamb-Books, "Hermeneutics and Sociology: Deepening the Interpretive Perspective," in *New Directions in Sociology: Essays on Theory and Methodology in the 21st Century*, ed. Ieva Zake and Michael DeCesare (Jefferson, NC: McFarland, 2011).

15. Clifford Geertz, "Thick Description: Toward an Interpretive Theory of Culture," in *The Interpretation of Cultures* (New York: Basic Books, 2000), 5.

16. The opposite operation, whereby the insights of hermeneutics or discourse analysis is brought into the critical naturalism of the realist mode, is quite common.

III

Of course, Geertz had social scientific positivism (and perhaps Parsons's excessively abstract and general theoretical schemas) in mind when he rejected the search for laws in social research. And the search for laws was, in the middle of the twentieth century at least, essential to the construction of social explanations. The point of explanation was to subsume a particular set of social behaviors under a more generalized schema. To use semiotic terminology, the goal was to show that certain actions were tokens of a well-known type[17]—if they could be understood as such, then the universal hypotheses that apply to that type of behavior would do the work of explanation.[18] Explanation thus required the development, in social science theory, of covering laws, which would then be combined with particular conditions to deduce the actions that need explaining. According to Carl Hempel and others, the social and natural sciences were united by this structure of scientific explanation. In the terms developed in this book, the semiotic circuit of positivist explanation was defined by the intersection of laws and general propositions (theoretical language) with quantitative data gathered by methods transposable from one setting to another, such as surveys (factual language).

The critiques of this model are extensive, and indeed postpositivism can be understood, from one point of view, as a set of frustrations with the Hempelian philosophy of science and with the various attempts to modify and amend this philosophy to better fit sociology

---

In the terms of the philosophy of social science, the classic in this regard is William Outhwaite's *New Philosophies of Social Science: Realism, Hermeneutics, and Critical Theory* (New York: St. Martin's Press, 1987). In terms of research programs, the examination of mechanisms of *semiosis* in the program of Critical Discourse Analysis also resituates hermeneutics inside critical realism. See Norman Fairclough, *Discourse and Social Change* (Cambridge: Polity Press, 1992).

17. Umberto Eco, *A Theory of Semiotics* (Bloomington: Indiana University Press, 1976).

18. William Dray argues that, for Carl Hempel, how, what, and why questions all had their answers in universal hypotheses and covering laws. In other words, for Hempel and for many other logical empiricists, any process of conceptual interpretation in the human sciences that involved an "empirically respectable concept" was ultimately understandable as the application of a covering law to a particular situation or series of events. See William H. Dray, "'Explaining What' in History," in *Readings in the Philosophy of the Social Sciences*, ed. May Broadbeck (New York: Macmillan, 1968). Hempel's classic essay on the human sciences, "The Function of General Laws in History," is reprinted in *Theories of History*, ed. Patrick Gardiner (New York: Free Press, 1959).

and political science.[19] What is worth noting for our present purposes, however, is how, at its core, the covering-law model of explanation was agnostic about causality. Take the ubiquitous example given to show the symmetry problem that attends this approach: from the general proposition that light travels in straight lines and the rules of trigonometry, one can explain the length of the shadow cast by a pole in the sun, if one knows the particular facts of the height of the pole and the angle of the sun in the sky. However, one could just as precisely "explain" the height of the pole by the length of the shadow. Hempel was well aware of this problem, but he maintained that explanation and prediction were essentially the same. This causal agnosticism should not entirely surprise us; the broad intellectual constellation of the empiricist and positivist traditions in philosophy and social thought has often been very uncomfortable with notions of causality that go too far beyond Hume's initial formulations.[20] Frustration with this philosophical unwillingness to consider the reality of basic, if unobservable, causal forces—and thus to end this symmetry problem in scientific explanation—was one of the key intellectual sources of realist philosophies of natural science.[21]

Positivist sociology suffered from an ambiguity parallel to that of philosophy: are prediction and explanation really just the same, or do sociologists need a stronger, overtly causal understanding of what constitutes an explanation? Andrew Abbott traces how the early

19. Perhaps the most impactful of these attempts is Ernest Nagel, *The Structure of Science: Problems in the Logic of Scientific Explanation* (New York: Harcourt, 1961). It is hard to underestimate the importance of Robert K. Merton's sociological theory, and his sociology of science, to this project of bridging the logical empiricist philosophy of science to the social sciences in a way that kept the core principles of the former intact, including Riechenbach's distinction between the context of discovery and the context of justification. For commentary on this connection, see Alan Richardson, "Robert K. Merton and Philosophy of Science," *Social Studies of Science* 34, no. 6 (2004). For Merton's reliance on the distinction between the context of discovery and the context of justification, see his chapter "The Sociology of Knowledge," in Robert Merton, *Social Theory and Social Structure*, enl. ed. (New York: Free Press, 1968), and especially his critique of Sorokin on 529–30.

20. For an elaboration and critique of the dominance of the Humean approach to causality in Anglophone philosophy, see Rom Harré and E. H. Madden, *Causal Powers: A Theory of Natural Necessity* (Oxford: B. Blackwell, 1975).

21. It is interesting, in this regard, that the most recent challenge to positivism made in the terms of rigorous mathematics—Charles Ragin's development of set theory and fuzzy-set methods for social science—also emphasizes asymmetric relations in sociological explanations over the symmetries implied by studies of correlation. See Charles C. Ragin, *Redesigning Social Inquiry: Fuzzy Sets and Beyond*. (Chicago: University of Chicago Press, 2008), 15.

twentieth century saw many American sociologists eschew causal talk—rejecting, perhaps, certain crude causal notions inherited from nineteenth-century social Darwinism. Starting in the middle of the twentieth century, however, quantitative research brought causality back in, occasionally through explicit epistemological reflections, but more often through a sort of commonsense causal realism about variables. In this view, certain social factors, understood as independent variables, *force* changes in other social factors, understood as dependent variables. The evidence for this variable-forcing form of causality was developed by showing correlations to be robust—to hold with controls for other variables. Such an approach—still hegemonic in American sociology—tends to go by the name of positivism because of its reliance on quantitative methods and its often quite explicit commitment to the idea that the unity of the sciences derives from the unity of their methods. But in contradistinction to Hempel and others, it is quite liberal in its use of causal language and causal modeling—and has developed a variety of highly sophisticated philosophies of probabilistic causation.[22]

IV

It is this law-based and hypergeneralized model of explanation that so many of the interpretivist reactions to positivism steel themselves against. But then, it is not just interpretivists, but postpositivists in general who seek modes of explanation that reach outside covering laws and/or variable correlations. In social theory and the philosophy of social science since the 1960s, there developed a widespread tendency to, first, draw a distinction between *social* explanations and explanations that focus on the *subjective* motivations of individuals,

22. Andrew Abbott, *Time Matters: On Theory and Method* (Chicago: University of Chicago Press, 2001), 97–125. For a discussion of probabilistic causation in relation to other formats of causation in the social sciences, see Julian Reiss, "Causation in the Social Sciences: Evidence, Inference, and Purpose," *Philosophy of the Social Sciences* 39, no. 1 (2009). For an extended discussion of the different sorts of causal claims that tend to appear in the major journals of American sociology, see Brandon Vaidyanathan, Michael Strand, Austin Choi-Fitzpatrick, and Thomas Bushman, "Causality in Contemporary American Sociology: An Empirical Assessment," unpublished manuscript. For a realist critique of empiricist sociology that focuses directly on the issue of causality, see Douglas Porpora, "Sociology's Causal Confusion," in *Revitalizing Causality: Realism About Causality in Philosophy and Social Science*, ed. Ruth Groff (London: Routledge, 2007).

and, second, to seek some sort of postpositivist synthesis in the reconciliation of these two sorts of explanation. This is, perhaps, what all the fuss over agency and structure comes to in the end. As Margaret Archer writes, "The 'problem of structure and agency' has a great deal in common with the 'problem of objectivity and subjectivity.' Both raise the same issue about the relationship between their component terms, which entails questioning their respective causal powers. Once we have started talking about causal powers, it is impossible to avoid talking about the ontological status of those things to which causal powers are attributed or from which they are withheld."[23] According to this view—perhaps the quintessence of reflexive, well-constructed realism—what happens in the world is explained as the result of a combination of agentic projects for action, the unintended consequences of these actions, and the social patterns in which agents are embedded. Agents are creative and motivated, and structures are real abstractions[24] that envelop human beings and causally influence social action

23. Margaret S. Archer, "The Trajectory of the Morphogenetic Approach: An Account in the First-Person," *Sociologia: Problemas e Práticas* 54 (2007): 41. Archer's critique of Anthony Giddens leads her to a structure/agency schema with much more traction; others are even more skeptical of the utility of the language. John Levi Martin argues that discussion of structure and agency tends to be a way to negotiate a détente between warring micro and macro camps without necessarily introducing any theoretical advances, and Anthony King argues that the opposition between agency and structure sublimates into social theory the experience of the individual with the modern state in the West. John Levi Martin, "What Is Field Theory?" *American Journal of Sociology* (2003): 2. Anthony King, *The Structure of Social Theory* (London: Routledge, 2004), 13–18.

24. The concept is traceable to Marx's *Grundrisse*, and has been the subject of much interpretive dispute for over a hundred years in various theoretical circles. In his discussion of labor and of Adam Smith's concept of "labor in general," Marx writes that "with the abstract universality of wealth-creating activity we now have the universality of the object defined as wealth, the product as such or again labour as such, but labour as past, objectified labor." He then writes that this move, if interpreted as the discovery of "the abstract expression of the simplest and most ancient relation in which human beings—in whatever form of society—play the role of producers," is "correct in one respect," but "not in another." Marx hereby introduces a central problematic for social theory, iterated today in the debates that take place in and around critical realism. That is: how historical are the real abstractions that structure societies? And how are we to approach these real abstractions? For Marx, the example of labor reveals "how even the most abstract categories, despite their validity—precisely because of their abstractness—for all epochs, are nevertheless, in the specific character of this abstraction, themselves likewise a product of historic relations, and possess their full validity only for and within these relations." Karl Marx, *Grundrisse* (New York: Penguin, 1973), 104–5. The question is what this historicity of abstraction amounts to, and whether "abstraction," as an increasingly prominent feature of socioeconomic reality *and* thought about that reality, is itself a product of modern capitalism. The answer of

in a variety of ways, whether or not the actors doing the actions know of, or want, that influence. Thus to synthesize agency and structure is to recognize the interdependence of agentic projects and the social configurations that exceed them. And so, maximal interpretations must reference the causal force of both the interiority of social actors and the broader patterns or mechanisms of social structure.

But let us examine more closely the rationale for thinking of actors' interior states, on the one hand, and social processes, on the other, as essential causal components of any social explanation. Doing so will lead to a quite different conclusion than the usual "détente" between structure and agency.[25] My argument will be that meaning intersects these two causal realities by giving their *force* concrete *form*, and thus that the interpretation of meaning is central to constructing causal explanations in the human sciences.

V

The philosophical basis for thinking about actors' interior states causally can be found in Donald Davidson's essays on reasons and causality.[26] Davidson argued against a keystone of the logical positivist philosophical architecture: the idea that reasons have a *logical* relationship to the actions for which they are the reasons. According to this argument, because the relation of reasons to actions is "internal," reasons cannot be causes. The cause of an action must be something else, something "external" to the action. Davidson argued that this approach was misconceived, and that reasons are indeed distinct from the actions for which they are the reasons,[27] and thus that actions

this text, which I suppose comes from a combination of Weber and Saussure, is that the historicity of real abstractions results not from the historical trajectory of human relations contained in the dialectical-materialist philosophy of history, but rather from their embeddedness of arbitrary and conventional systems of signification.

25. Martin, "What is Field Theory?" 2

26. Donald Davidson, "Actions, Reasons, and Causes," in *The Essential Davidson* (New York: Oxford University Press, 2006); Donald Davidson, "Problems in the Explanation of Action," in *Problems of Rationality* (New York: Oxford University Press, 2004); Donald Davidson, "Causal Relations," *Journal of Philosophy* 64 (1967). For contemporary post-Davidsonian philosophy of social science, see in particular David K. Henderson, *Interpretation and Explanation in the Human Sciences*, SUNY Series in the Philosophy of the Social Sciences (Albany: State University of New York Press, 1993).

27. So, for example, the reason for turning on the light (wanting to see what is on the kitchen table) and the action of turning on the light are in fact in causal relationship

can be explained as the behavioral outcomes of reasons.[28] So, if one accepts that reasons and actions are not the same, then, there is no discernable linguistic difference between proposing 'the stove is hot' as the cause of someone moving their hand and proposing 'wanting to get to Denver' as the cause of someone turning right at a traffic light. Davidson thus simultaneously argued that mental reasons were not reducible to some physical substrate upon which they depended ***and*** that such mental reasons causally interacted with the behavioral, observable world, thus making them the basis for explanation.

But what are reasons? Conscious intentions do help drive social life, but the investigator must also grasp those "springs of action" that result from interior states that are (relatively) opaque to the actor himself. So, I would change "reasons as causes" to "motivations as causes" and expand the focus on agent's intentions to a more encompassing account of the effect upon the social world of the interior states of people. Furthermore, in thinking about motivations as causes, what we want to imagine is not thousands of unit acts, each consciously or unconsciously motivated, strung together by the investigator to produce an aggregate outcome, but rather what Mustafa Emirbayer and Anne Mische have referred to as the "temporally embedded process of social engagement" in their theorization of agency.[29] The point is that motivated actors have *projects* or lines of action-in-the-world that they pursue, and analysts who ignore these projects put the validity of their explanations in peril. For grasping the causal force of these projects, however, I believe the term 'motivation' is appropriate precisely because in its generality it refers to conscious and unconscious, and rational and irrational, sources of action. As I explain below, it is a more encompassing, inclusive concept of interiority that is needed for explanation in the interpretive epistemic mode.

In parallel to the focus on "motivation," there is reason to think that "mechanism" has inherited some of the linguistic functionality of "structure" for nonpositivist explanation. If we compare the

---

with each other, and not "logically" related, as is made clear in the event that the light has short circuited and does not go on when the switch is flipped.

28. This position involved Davidson in a series of more technical arguments about the irreducibility of the mental to the physical. For the purposes of this text, however, it is his argument about the conceptual structure of explanation that was crucial.

29. Mustafa Emirbayer and Ann Mische, "What Is Agency?" *American Journal of Sociology* 103, no. 4 (1998).

writings of the realist philosophers Roy Bhaskar and Mario Bunge, for example, it becomes clear that both terms refer to social realities whose power can be triggered, and which then bring about certain outcomes. As a way of grasping the emergent social processes that confront, constrain, and in certain cases enable the willful actor, theorists of mechanisms inherit the longstanding mantle of structural thinking that runs back to classical sociology. In addition to the argument that focusing on underlying mechanisms allows social research to move beyond the descriptive-positivist focus on correlations, I think that there is another reason that mechanism is a particularly compelling way to think about "structure."

For, specifying mechanisms is precisely what overarching explanations derived from structural-functionalism and structural Marxism often did not do. Looking to identify the mechanism, in other words, shifts the meaning of the terms 'structure' and 'agency' because doing so brings a level of concreteness and comparability to the causal narratives that are constructed in nonpositivist research. The connection between structural social theories and the current focus on mechanisms is overt and clear if one considers the intellectual lineages of realism, such as Bhaskar's reinterpretation of *Capital*, or Hedstrom and Swedberg's use of Merton's "self-fulfilling prophesy" as their primary example of a mechanism.[30] As a metaphor to think with, then, "mechanism" allows the social researcher to conceptualize structural causation shorn of teleological or functionalist reasoning.

So: motives and mechanisms push the social world forward. Yet there remains a fundamental problem with this picture of social life, with which so much postpositivist social theory is occupied: it impedes the historicization of what sorts of motivations, and what sorts of mechanisms, are effective at a given place and time. This was part of the point of chapter 4—that mechanisms and motivations have to emerge upon landscapes of meaning. But perhaps the language of poststructuralism will be useful for making this point. What Ian Hacking called "historical ontology" (an intentional oxymoron) and what

30. Roy Bhaskar, *The Possibility of Naturalism: A Philosophical Critique of the Contemporary Human Sciences* (Atlantic Highlands, NJ: Humanities Press, 1979), 56–58; Peter Hedström and Richard Swedberg, *Social Mechanisms: An Analytical Approach to Social Theory* (New York: Cambridge University Press, 1998), 18. For the relationship of the concept of mechanism to the concept of structure, also see Hedström's discussion of Parsons: Peter Hedström, *Dissecting the Social: On the Principles of Analytical Sociology* (Cambridge: Cambridge University Press, 2005), 3.

Foucault called "archeology" refers to a mode of analysis according to which the mechanics of social life are given their concrete form by the discursive formations, the meaningful spaces of possibility, upon which they take place.[31] Judith Butler articulated the antirealist philosophical implications of this:

> Clearly this project does not propose to lay out within traditional philosophical terms an *ontology* of gender whereby the meaning of *being* a woman or a man is elucidated within the terms of phenomenology. The presumption here is that the "being" of gender is *an effect*, an object of a genealogical investigation that maps out the political parameters of its construction in the mode of ontology. To claim that gender is constructed is not to assert its illusoriness or artificiality, where those terms are understood to reside within a binary that counterposes the "real" and the "authentic" as oppositional. As a genealogy of gender ontology this inquiry seeks to understand the discursive production of the plausibility of that binary relation and to suggest that certain cultural configurations of gender take the place of "the real" and consolidate and augment their hegemony through that felicitous self-naturalization.[32]

The implications for social research of arguments such as these have been massively misunderstood. Butler's philosophical meditations imply neither relativism in knowledge nor some sort of theory of the radical flexibility of everyday social life. Rather, the point is that meaning inheres in the flow and process of social life in such a way that knowledge of social life must be based in its interpretation. To see how this is the case, and thus to begin in earnest our reconstruction of social explanation within the interpretive epistemic mode, we can turn to a sociological classic.

VI

In *The Protestant Ethic and the Spirit of Capitalism*, Max Weber wrote:

> Above all, practical pastoral work, which had immediately to deal with all the suffering caused by the doctrine, could not be satisfied. It met

31. Ian Hacking, *Historical Ontology* (Cambridge, MA: Harvard University Press, 2002), 1–26. Michel Foucault, *The Order of Things: An Archaeology of the Human Sciences* (New York: Vintage Books, 1970).

32. Judith Butler, *Gender Trouble: Feminism and the Subversion of Identity* (New York: Routledge, 1999), 43.

> these difficulties in various ways. So far as predestination was not reinterpreted, toned down, or fundamentally abandoned, two principal, mutually connected, types of pastoral advice appear. On the one hand it is held to be an absolute duty to consider oneself chosen, and to combat all doubts as temptations of the devil, since lack of self-confidence is the result of insufficient faith, hence of imperfect grace . . . On the other hand, in order to attain that self-confidence intense worldly activity is recommended as the most suitable means. It and it alone disperses religious doubts and gives the certainty of grace.[33]

This passage identifies a key link in Weber's overall argument about the rise of capitalism—which is to say, rational-bourgeois capitalist activities—in the early modern West, and it is this link that I want to focus on here.[34] If we suspend disbelief a little bit, we can imagine how this paragraph could be understood in the (realist) language of motivations and mechanisms. Thus a causal pattern of behavior is triggered by a specific interest of certain actors (to be saved), and the pattern "regularly generates the type of outcome to be explained."[35] It is also the case that Weber has opened up some "black boxes," and that this passage points to some of the "cogs and wheels" that led to a new work ethic in certain parts of early modern Europe: an authority relation between pastors and their congregants, for one, and perhaps the more pernicious mechanism, gestured at elsewhere by Weber, that competition with and surveillance of one's neighbors played an important role in institutionalizing the new work ethic.

This anachronistic interpretation of Weber as a sociohistorical investigator of motivations and mechanisms is reasonable as far as it goes.[36] But one is inclined to point out that Weber's causal argu-

33. Max Weber, *The Protestant Ethic and the Spirit of Capitalism*, trans. Talcott Parsons (Mineola, NY: Dover Publications, 2003), 111–12.

34. Thus I do not directly engage here the extensive literature on the "Weber thesis" concerning Protestantism and capitalism as a whole, because, for the purposes of this discussion, it is the logic of Weber's argument that is of particular interest. However, my discussion here does fall into the line of the interpretation of Weber given by William Sewell Jr. in his criticisms of James Coleman. See William H. Sewell Jr., "Theory of Action, Dialectic, and History: Comment on Coleman," *American Journal of Sociology* 93, no. 1 (1987): 6.

35. Hedström, *Dissecting the Social*, 25.

36. Richard Swedberg argues that "Though Weber does not use this term [mechanisms] (which is common in contemporary sociology), one may nonetheless argue that he lays bare a number of interesting social mechanisms in his work, not least in his sociology of religion." Swedberg goes on to discuss a variety of moments from *The Protestant Ethic and the Spirit of Capitalism* where Weber could be said to be ar-

ment does not make any real sense—does not grasp, that is, the concrete causal effectiveness of the pastors' rather creative solutions to a problem of practical theology—if we do not know the landscape of meaning that *formed* the basic desires of actors and the mindsets of the pastors, and that *justified* the authority relationship between them. And indeed, a good part of Weber's book—and in particular the section that discusses the texts of Richard Baxter and the theology of John Calvin—is dedicated to disclosing the landscape of meaning of early modern Protestant life. It is on this landscape that the motivations of the actors involved become effective forces: people want to be saved, and pastors want to spread the Gospel. Likewise for the mechanisms: interaction with pastoral authority, and the development of both social surveillance and self-discipline about working-in-the-world are also formed by meaning. Every forceful cause that helps produce the social outcome is infused with, and formed by, meaning. The mechanisms only make sense as models for social behavior inside the meaning-system of Calvinist (and, more broadly, Protestant) Christianity. They combine with certain desires and intentions that also only make sense inside that meaning-system: to be saved/receive God's grace/know once and for all if one is elect. As a desire, this subjective state is formed by the shared religious meanings of the context. But then, the mechanism that it triggers is inflected by this landscape as well—the authority of the pastors, and thus the fact that people tended to do what the pastors told them, also makes sense within the meaningful world of Calvinism. Finally, the solutions offered by the pastors (removal of doubt/working in the world), which, because of their authority in this context, result in actual shifts in behavior, are themselves recognizable only with reference to Calvinism's this-worldly asceticism.

Thus, in Weber's explanation, meaning appears as a cause that is not a separate force in the world, over and against mechanisms and motivations, but rather appears to inhere in them, to form the shape and direction in which mechanisms work, and give meaning to the thoughts, intentions, and desires of individual agents. The landscape

---

ticulating mechanisms (and motivations) as causal processes. Richard Swedberg, *The Max Weber Dictionary: Key Words and Central Concepts* (Stanford: Stanford University Press, 2005), 250–51.

of meaning *forms* those entities that *force* social life forward. How are we to understand the epistemic basis for such a claim?[37]

VII

"Causes are forces" and "causation is forced movement" remain, in both the everyday understanding of cause and effect, and in much social research, the primary metaphors for understanding what causes are and how they work.[38] There are experiential reasons for this, as well as methodological ones. Our most fundamental experiences of cause derive from our ability to manipulate physical objects of a

37. Weber's own excursions into social scientific methodology have received a great deal of attention, to the point that Weberian methodology is a language game unto itself. Perhaps the most important hint, in the objectivity essay at least, that Weber intended a different understanding of causality and explanation in social research than that which has been set out by realism is the following: "even in the case of all so-called 'economic laws' without exception, we are concerned here not with 'laws' in the narrower exact natural science sense, but with *adequate* causal relationships expressed in rules and with the application of the category of 'objective possibility.'" Max Weber, *The Methodology of the Social Sciences* (New York: Free Press, 1949), 80. For a general discussion of adequate and objective causality in Weber's work, see Swedberg, *The Max Weber Dictionary*, 27–31.

This particular quotation is significant because the historian Fritz Ringer has taken these two concepts of adequate causation and objective possibility as the center of Weber's methodology, and thus argued that "singular causal analysis" is the keystone of Weber's contribution. Ringer's argument is that Weber, as he moved away from the neo-Kantianism of Rickert, formulated a conception of causality appropriate to the "sciences of reality" (*Wirklichkeitwissenschaft*) as opposed to "law-seeking science" (*Gesetzeswissenschaft*). He then argues, with significant textual evidence, that Weber appropriated and transformed the legal philosophy of Johannes von Kries, and in particular, the terms 'adequate causation' and 'objective possibility.' For Weber, a social process could be identified as an *adequate cause* of a later development if it could be shown, by the investigator, that the presence of the event or process increased the *objective probability* of the later development (the "effect"). In this way, argues Ringer, the investigator "is to locate the explanandum in its 'interconnection' with other singular phenomena."

Thus Ringer writes that what Weber's methodology amounts to is an "image of causal relationships—and causal analysis—that deals in *courses* of events, in counterfactuals, and in *divergences* between alternate *paths and outcomes* (italics in original). Fritz K. Ringer, *Max Weber's Methodology: The Unification of the Cultural and Social Sciences* (Cambridge, MA: Harvard University Press, 1997), 73, 77. For an account of the relationship between Weber's thinking about causality, the positivism of his time, and post-positivist discussions of causality in social science, see Susan Hekman, "Weber's Concept of Causality and the Modern Critique" *Sociological Inquiry* 49, no. 4 (1979).

38. George Lakoff and Mark Johnson, *Philosophy in the Flesh : The Embodied Mind and Its Challenge to Western Thought* (New York: Basic Books, 1999), 184–87.

certain size (not too large and not too small: moveable by the use of a human individual's muscles and nerves). So kicking a ball, putting building blocks together and knocking them over, etc., reproduce from childhood the sense that causality is inherent in humans' ability to intervene in the world. Thus our first causal metaphors probably derive from how we come to know the forces of nature via our own bodies' experiences of it.[39] And there are intellectual-historical reasons why this experience with what Aristotle would have called *efficient causes* was imported into various scientific epistemologies, in so far as interaction with nature in a controlled way was essential to the development of modern science.[40]

Simultaneously, the highly elaborated methodologies of quantitative social science that Andrew Abbott has discussed as the "general linear model" mode of social analysis have transferred this idea of causes-are-forces from the interaction of persons with the world to the interaction of variables with other variables.[41] And in the realist epistemic mode, the forcing conception of causality is affixed to the language of motives and mechanisms. Motives, within agents, "force the action," and mechanisms exert pressure on willful actors and upon other (mechanistic) social processes. This is what we would find in the strictly realist reading of Weber—certain intentions and desires, combined with certain social structures-qua-mechanisms, account for that link in a long causal chain that has, as its analytically chosen endpoint, the takeoff of capitalism in the West.

But as I have already suggested, though cause-as-force is clearly in some way essential to social research, I do not think it will get us far enough along in the task of explanation without a willingness to

39. Karl Popper argues that our initial definitions and sense of what is *real* derives from the experience of objects of a certain size or, as he writes, "material things of ordinary size—things which a baby can handle and (preferably) put into his mouth." Karl Popper and John C. Eccles, *The Self and Its Brain* (Boston: Routledge & Kegan Paul, 1977), 9.

40. Roughly speaking, the scientific revolutionaries of early modern Europe combined two of Aristotle's four causes into a conception of *material efficient* causes as the central occupation of scientific research. The history of how this happened is complex and disputed, but the overall picture of early modern science engaging in a fierce repudiation of scholasticism, and thus throwing out some of Aristotle's key ideas unnecessarily, can probably still serve as a good heuristic. For more details on the matter, see Lyn S. Joy, "Scientific Explanation from Formal Causes to Laws of Nature," in *The Cambridge History of Science: Early Modern Science*, ed. Katharine Park and Lorraine Daston (New York: Cambridge University Press, 2006), 73.

41. Abbott, *Time Matters*, 44–47.

understand how the forceful causes of social life are given concrete form by the landscapes of meaning upon which they emerge and proceed. Forcing causes cannot be understood in their effectiveness without understanding the forming causes that mould them.

What, then, are these forming causes? Simply put: forming causes are the arrangements of signification and representation that give forcing causes their concrete shape and meaningful character. This idea—that force has to be given a form—originates, in the West at least, with Aristotle.[42] I therefore return to one of his texts here, in an initial attempt to explicate the idea of forming causality and its difference from forcing causality, which I believe sets the interpretive epistemic mode apart from realism and normativism in the resignification of minimal interpretations into maximal interpretations.

Aristotle's doctrine of the four causes (material, formal, efficient, and final) is well known; what is less frequently commented upon, in the social sciences at least, is that he often explicated these causes with reference to human action, and in particular a piece of creative labor: the casting of a bronze statue.[43] The bronze, perhaps obviously, constituted the material cause or "substratum" upon which the ac-

42. For an explicit philosophical discussion of Aristotle's philosophy of science and its relationship to the erotetic theory of explanation, see Bas C. Van Fraassen, "A Re-Examination of Aristotle's Philosophy of Science," *Dialogue* 19 (1980). To see Aristotle's approach to "natures" recuperated for postpositivist philosophy of science, see Nancy Cartwright, *The Dappled World: A Study of the Boundaries of Science* (New York: Cambridge University Press, 1999). These essays are particularly important to mention because they go against my argument, which is to say they bring Aristotle's texts into the disputations of contemporary epistemology and philosophy in a different way. Both Van Fraassen and Cartwright recapture Aristotle's modal realism, which I am, admittedly, trying to avoid. Indeed, the connection between Aristotle's and Marx's realism is well known and well drawn (e.g., George E. McCarthy, ed., *Marx and Aristotle: Nineteenth Century German Social Theory and Classical Antiquity* [Savage, MD: Rowan & Littlefield Publishers, 1992], and especially Howard Engelskirchen, "The Aristotelian Marx and Scientific Realism: A Perspective on Social Kinds in Social Theory" [Ph.D. diss., State University of New York at Binghamton, 2007]).

So, I am reading Aristotle's philosophy of science against the grain to a certain degree. In doing so, I draw inspiration from the connection drawn in political philosophy between Aristotle and the hermeneutic tradition, by MacIntyre in particular, but more generally in readings of Aristotle's *Poetics* that suggest the sorts of philosophical maneuvers made by Richard McKeon in the mid-twentieth century.

43. The original idea to turn to Aristotle—and in particular to bring Aristotle to bear on the problem of interpretive explanation—is due to Lyn Spillman's excellent paper on causal reasoning in history and sociology. Lyn Spillman, "Causal Reasoning, Historical Logic, and Sociological Explanation," in *Self, Social Structure, and Beliefs: Explorations in the Sociological Thought of Neil J. Smelser*, ed. Jeffrey Alexander, Gary Marx, and Christine Williams (Berkeley: University of California Press, 2004), 216–34.

tion of statue casting works. In social explanations, material causes are recognized in so far as we understand that action proceeds within certain physical limits and biophysical conditions.

Moving beyond material causes, in *The Metaphysics*, efficient causes are defined in opposition to final causes. The efficient cause is "that from which the change or resting from change begins,"[44] while the final cause is "the end and the good of other things" and "that for the sake of which other things are." Although in certain places in his work it becomes easy to dismiss Aristotle's account of final causes,[45] in other places it is clear that he is referring to actors' intentions, and thus can be interpreted (liberally, to be sure) as referring to reasons or motivations as causes: "health is the cause of walking. For 'Why does one walk?' we say; 'that one may be healthy'; and in speaking thus we have given the cause."[46] So, final causes can be thought of as a precursor of motivations as causes.

Social mechanisms, on the other hand, can be thought of as the articulation, by social science, of efficient causes in the social realm. For, mechanisms are triggered or set into motion, and thus become "that from which the change or resting from change begins."[47] These social mechanisms, moreover, emerge from and react back upon actors' intentions and agency (final causes), which in turn would take place under certain biophysical conditions (material causes). Thus far, then, we have causes that nicely fit a reflexive, theoretical realism.[48]

Spillman's interpretation of how the four causes map onto sociological and historical analysis is different than mine, however.

44. This and the following quotations are taken from *Metaphysics*, especially book 5, chapter 2. Aristotle repeats the arguments in *Physics* book 2, chapter 3. Aristotle, *The Basic Works of Aristotle*, ed. Richard McKeon (New York: Random House, 1941), 752.

45. For a general discussion of teleology in Aristotle, see Susan Sauve Meyer, "Aristotle, Teleology, and Reduction," *Philosophical Review* 101, no. 4 (1992).

46. Aristotle, *The Basic Works of Aristotle*, 752.

47. This requires letting go of the positivist notion of an efficient cause as simply that event ("cause") that precedes another event ("effect"). But this conceptual work has been done, and the influence of Aristotle on Marx, and of Aristotle's conception of "natures" on Marx's realist epistemology, is well documented.

48. In contrast to what follows, the proponents of critical discourse analysis argue that "semiosis" should be considered one mechanistic cause among the others theorized in the realist mode, and reject the historicist and pluralist implications of interpretivism as developed in chapter 4. Thus in "seek[ing] to show that semiosis involves mechanisms that are intelligible from a critical realist point of view," Norman Fairclough, Bob Jessop, and Andrew Sayer argue that part of the critical realist account of social structuration involves an examination of "the evolutionary mechanisms of variation, selection, and retention that shape the relationships between semiosis and

And we have captured the core idea of the post-positivist debates about 'structure' and 'action' in so far as we see both final causes (motivations) and efficient causes (mechanisms) as *forcing* social life forward.[49] But what of Aristotle's fourth category: formal causes?

Aristotle describes the formal cause[50] as "the whole, the synthesis, the form." The concrete reference here is the way in which the plaster cast gives shape to the bronze poured into it. I would submit, however, that the plaster's shape itself derives from meaningful practices.[51] The plaster, which shapes the statue, takes the shape that it does in relation to the shapes of other statues, and thus takes on meaning via its relations within a system of signification. The implication of this for social theory is that, when considering social action, efficient causes cannot be adequately understood in their causal force without understanding the formal causes that give them shape. There is evidence for this idea in Aristotle, because at one point in the *Metaphysics* he actually refers to the *art of statue casting* as the efficient cause of the statue: "Both the art of sculpture and the bronze are causes of the statue not in respect of anything else but *qua* statue; not however, in the same way, but the one as matter and the other as source of movement."[52] Thus Aristotle actually considered the *art of sculpture* to be *the* efficient cause, and an individual artist casting a statue as

social structuration," and that "these mechanisms are common to natural and social evolution." Norman Fairclough, Bob Jessop, and Andrew Sayer, "Critical Realism and Semiosis," in *Realism, Discourse, and Deconstruction*, ed. Jonathan Joseph and John Michael Roberts (New York: Routledge, 2004).

49. The idea here being that while the positivist model involves variables forcing other variables, the postpositivist turn (and especially the work of Giddens, Bourdieu, and Archer) involves an account of social mechanisms of reproduction/change, and subjective dispositions/motivations, as the forces that best account for social life.

50. In what follows, in emphasizing the form as a sort of concrete shaping of causal forces, I venture toward an extremely anti-Platonist reading of Aristotle, for better or worse.

51. Aristotle thus anticipates the entire basis of hermeneutic philosophy. While Alaistair MacIntyre is the clearest representative of the scholarly line that runs from Aristotle to contemporary hermeneutics (e.g., Alasdair C. MacIntyre, *After Virtue: A Study in Moral Theory* [Notre Dame, IN: University of Notre Dame Press, 1981]; Alasdair C. MacIntyre, *Against the Self-Images of the Age: Essays on Ideology and Philosophy* [London: Duckworth, 1971]), it is also the case that Aristotle's comments on form in *The Metaphysics* adumbrate Wilhelm Dilthey's development of epistemology for the human sciences. See Wilhelm Dilthey, "The Construction of the Historical World in the Human Studies," in *Dilthey: Selected Writings*, ed. H. P. Rickman (New York: Cambridge University Press, 1976), and Wilhelm Dilthey, *Selected Works, Volume 4: Hermeneutics and the Study of History* (Princeton: Princeton University Press, 1996).

52. Aristotle, *The Basic Works of Aristotle*, 753.

a manifestation of this cause in a particular case of statue making. What does this mean?

It means that there is an intimate connection between efficient causes and formal causes, because the holistic, formal cause gives to the artist's direct actions on the statue their meaning and aesthetics.[53] Statue making is a "form of life," and as such, when an artist makes a statue, she combines a formal cause (the artistic basis for the shape of the plaster cast of the statue), an efficient cause (the direct actions of the artist in making the plaster cast and pouring the statue), a final cause (the intention of the artist to make the statue in a certain way), and a material cause (the properties of bronze).

This four-dimensional understanding of causality is metaphorical to varying degrees in so far as it has to be used as a heuristic for thinking through the problem of social explanation. The essential addition is formal causes. By thinking about the way in which a well-designed plaster cast gives form to liquid bronze, I propose to understand the way in which social life is arranged, in its concreteness, by (arbitrary and conventional) formations of meaning. Social life has an aesthetic or rhetorical dimension, and must be explained with reference to this dimension, upon which the efficient forces of interests and unconscious aggression, forces of repeated interactions and leveraged network connections, and so many other motivations and mechanisms emerge. In the interpretive epistemic mode, the forcing causes of social life—motivation and mechanism—are formed by landscapes of meaning. But how does this work?

VIII

Let us start with motives. Consider George Steinmetz's recent study of the policies and actions of the German colonial state in the late nineteenth century, *The Devil's Handwriting*. Steinmetz begins by insisting that a cultural and historical sociology also needs a psychology, and in particular an account of unconscious motivation to complement the emphasis on the strategic actor that creeps into many sociological explanations. He thus develops a Lacanian account of

53. The clearest restatement of this Aristotelean position in the language of meaningful social practices is Alasdair C. MacIntyre, "The Intelligibility of Action," in *Rationality, Relativism, and the Human Sciences*, ed. J. Margolis, M. Krausz, and R. M. Burian (Boston: Martinus Nijhoff Publishers, 1986).

the social subject[54] as unconsciously motivated toward two sorts of identifications—symbolic and imaginary. Symbolic identifications derive from the publicly sanctioned, "appropriate" sphere of law and culture and "are linked to the construction of an ego ideal."[55] In other words, these identifications reenact and reinscribe norms. Here the motivation is the desire for recognition, formed by the cultural context. Simultaneously, however, subjects are driven to an imaginary identification with a fantasy: an ideal, whole, complete self. These identifications run counter to the requirements of official, legal, or "serious" society, and are often "organized at the level of the body and bodily images."[56] Though the subject's motivations toward imaginary identification begin in infancy with the mirror stage, Steinmetz takes from Lacan the idea that "the contents of imaginary identifications later in life are provided by suggestions coming from the symbolic order."[57]

For, in Steinmetz's explanation, it is the representations of "natives" from a previous generation of anthropologists that differentially mould the motivations of German state officials, which is what leads to different colonial policies. Consider this example from the text, where Steinmetz considers the policies set in Samoa by Wilhelm Solf:

> Solf's images of the Samoans emerged as much from interactions with European discourses about the colonized as from interactions with the colonized themselves. It is notable that Solf embarked on his program of salvaging and enforcing Samoan savage nobility almost immediately after he assumed office. Solf . . . had no prior experience in Polynesia.[58]

Thus it was the specific, concrete, available version of the "European discourses about the colonized"—that is to say, the ethnographic

54. It is worth mentioning that Steinmetz's specific subjects of study—German colonial administrators—are overwhelmingly male. Needless to say, as the extended discourse of feminist criticisms and interpretations of Lacan has made clear, Steinmetz's synthesis might work differently if his subjects of study were female, or both male and female. For an overview of the relationship between Lacanian and feminist social theory, see Deborah Leupntiz, "Beyond the Phallus: Lacan and Feminism," in *The Cambridge Companion to Lacan*, ed. Jean-Michel Rabate (New York: Cambridge University Press, 2003).

55. George Steinmetz, *The Devil's Handwriting: Precoloniality and the German Colonial State in Qingdao, Samoa, and Southwest Africa*, Chicago Studies in Practices of Meaning (Chicago: University of Chicago Press, 2007), 57.

56. Steinmetz, *The Devil's Handwriting*, 61.

57. Steinmetz, *The Devil's Handwriting*, 60.

58. Steinmetz, *The Devil's Handwriting*, 347.

literature about Polynesia that Solf immersed himself in—that gave meaningful form to Solf's forceful unconscious motivations. In a key passage Steinmetz writes:

> Solf styled himself as a Samoan chief . . . One might interpret these practices as little more than a strategic bid to appropriate indigenous symbols of power . . . But it is difficult to discern a strategic rationality behind the Solfs' giving their daughter a Samoan name, Lagi ("heaven") and their son a Samoan middle name, Tupua . . . Nor is it likely that Solf expected Samoans to respect him if he inserted himself into their categories of authority, since his government was loudly declaring those categories to be inferior. Solf seems to have formed an imaginary identification with an imago of Samoan notables, of the highest chiefs and the holders of the most distinguished titles, such as Mata'afa and Lauaki.[59]

This identification, writes Steinmetz, "makes sense of Solf's strong adherence to the Samoan noble savage perspective and the associated native policies and of his equally impassioned rejection of the settlers' alternative."[60] In other words, Steinmetz uses the forming of policy makers' motivations by meaning to explain why, in Samoa, the Germans implemented a salvage colonialism that mixed intervention in power structures and exploitation with cultural preservationism.[61] The landscape of meaning upon which colonial policy takes place is the archive of anthropological representations of natives, and it is the landscape that forms the motivations that force.

In considering the anatomy of Steinmetz's truth claims about what explains the different state policies in different German colonies, it is important not to remain only at the level of arguing about whether Freudian or Lacanian accounts of the subject can be given the universality that Freud and Lacan claimed for them. Rather, the power of Steinmetz's explanatory claim is attributable to how he historicizes Lacan's terms via his reconstruction of the anthropological archive as the meanings in which the colonial officials were immersed. Desire and drive are comprehended as they emerge upon a landscape of meaning in which the savages appear differently, depending upon the archive.

59. Steinmetz, *The Devil's Handwriting*, 353–54.

60. Steinmetz, *The Devil's Handwriting*, 355.

61. Steinmetz puts this result in comparative perspective, and in particular with the German colonization of southwest Africa, where the result was the first genocide of the twentieth century. Steinmetz, *The Devil's Handwriting*, 75–239.

Hence different actions "spring from" certain psychic structures, but only in so far as they are given concrete form by discourse.

Still, the very act of reaching into the motivational realm is—as Steinmetz points out in his critique of Bourdieu's avoidance of psychology—controversial in sociology. I believe Steinmetz's text exemplifies how it can be done, since it is a *formal* cause, and not an efficient mechanistic one, that reaches in to mould motivation in his explanation. But this issue—the relationship between sociological and depth-psychological explanations—is an old one, and should perhaps be examined in its most pristine form.

IX

For thinking about how social researchers think about motives, we can contrast C. Wright Mills's essay on vocabularies of motive from the *American Sociological Review* with its intellectual counterpoints, R. M. MacIver's writing in the *American Journal of Sociology* from almost exactly the same time, concerning the imputation of motives and social causation. Mills, as is well known, advised a move away from "the inferential conception of motives as subjective 'springs' of action"[62] and toward a sociology of vocabularies of motive, which is to say, the analysis of how people talk about motives and give reasons for actions, and how these given motives and reasons are deemed appropriate or inappropriate depending upon the "societal situation." And so, "institutionally different situations have different *vocabularies of motive* appropriate to their respective behaviors."[63] Thus motives are a certain sort of words, used in conversations as justification, when questions are asked or implied. It is worth noting, however, that in taking us outside of subjectivity, Mills nonetheless retained the goal of developing causal accounts of social life: "To term [motives] justification is *not* to deny their efficacy,"[64] Mills writes, and so "the motives actually used in justifying or criticizing an act definitely link

62. C. Wright Mills, "Situated Actions and Vocabularies of Motive," *American Sociological Review* 5, no. 6 (1940): 904. See also C. Wright Mills, "Language, Logic, and Culture," *American Sociological Review* 4, no. 5 (1939): 670–80.

63. Mills, "Situated Actions and Vocabularies of Motive," 906.

64. Mills, "Situated Actions and Vocabularies of Motive," 907. This is of particular importance as the divide between actors' justification of the actions, on the one hand, and the motivations for those actions, on the other, has become a significant issue recently in cultural sociology. See Christian Smith, *Moral Believing Animals: Human Personhood and Culture* (New York: Oxford University Press, 2003), 125–45,

it to situations, integrate one man's action with another's, and line up conduct with norms."[65] Motives, then, are "common grounds for mediated behaviors."[66]

Mills's essay has become an essential reference point for integrating meaning into sociology, for it suggests a way that talk is a form of effective action, in so far as it frames and conditions other actions. However, part of the appeal of this approach, articulated by Mills himself and picked up over and over again in various subfields that have turned toward "culture" and "framing," is the idea that, in focusing on vocabularies of motive the investigator leaves behind the problem of inferring the subjective states of actors. In its consequences for research this is not unlike the implications sometimes drawn from poststructuralist theory that researchers should move away from the *why* questions (whose answers might refer to motives and to structures or mechanisms) toward *how* questions about the working of discourse in very specific locales.[67]

But it is not clear that one has to accept Mills's utter denial of the possibility and/or utility of inferring subjective "springs" of action to accept his idea that vocabularies of motive help define situations and communicate institutional power. Nor is it clear that culture, defined as the frames people use, will somehow require *less interpretation* than the subjective reasons, interests, drives, and desires that occupy an actor's mind. For if frames are effective, they are effective because their interpretation by others is efficacious—which raises the issue of how those others interpreted the frames, which brings us back to interpreting other people's interpretations. Mills wants to avoid the hermeneutic circle, to be sure, but perhaps more than anything he wanted to avoid naïve Freudianism and criticize the language of ego-psychology—common among the American elite in midcentury—as just another way to talk about other human beings. My argument is that you can avoid naïve ego-psychology but cannot avoid the

---

and Stephen Vaisey, "Motivation and Justification: A Dual-Process Model of Culture in Action," *American Journal of Sociology* 114, no. 6 (2009): 1675–715.

65. Mills, "Situated Actions and Vocabularies of Motive," 908.

66. Mills, "Situated Actions and Vocabularies of Motive," 908.

67. Leslie Salzinger, *Genders in Production: Making Workers in Mexico's Global Factories* (Berkeley: University of California Press, 2003). For a critique of Salzinger's epistemological choices, and their consequences for the study of the global economy, see Jennifer Bair, "On Difference and Capital: Gender and the Globalization of Production," *Signs* 36, no. 1 (2010): 203–36.

interpretation of subjectivity.[68] This becomes quite clear when one considers the arguments of Mills's direct opponent, who did believe that motives should be part of what sociologists investigate, but also had skepticisms about ego-psychology.

In his article "The Imputation of Motives" R. M. MacIver argues strongly that social investigators *should* attempt to grasp actors' motives as part of what generates actions. He first points out that just because imputing motives presents certain problems to the sociologist does not mean that he should dispense with the task. This tendency to dismiss the imputation of motives is usually justified by the empiricist stance that the social scientist studies that which is manifest and observable, thus leaving motives "for the novelist or the moralist."[69] MacIver thus concludes, "if this art is still rudimentary it is not because the evidences of motivation are lacking but because the scientific study of these evidences has gone so short a way."[70]

What does MacIver advocate? His critique of "the Freudians" is that they make the distinction between conscious and unconscious motives "sharp and decisive" and then claim to have the only technique that can get at unconscious motives, which, they claim, are the true and real springs of action. Instead, he prefers to think of motives as (1) ranging from opaque to apparent to the agent who possesses them, and (2) ranging in the degree to which they are apparent or hidden to other social actors, including social researchers. His point is that, for the researcher, some motives take more digging, and more interpretive work, to decipher. He favors a sociological perspective that allows a wide variety of motives to become part of a social explanation.

MacIver's focus on motivation is part of his more generalized study of social causation, and so he does not exclude the possibility that vocabularies of motive, and the various conventions that they enact, would also be of causal significance. In the terms I have developed here, then, we might say that vocabularies of motive play

68. For a similar argument, made in terms of the opposition between interactionist and Weberian perspectives, see Colin Campbell, *The Myth of Social Action* (New York: Cambridge University Press, 1996).

69. Robert M. MacIver, "The Imputation of Motives," *American Journal of Sociology* 46, no. 1 (1940): 4. See also Robert M. MacIver, *Social Causation* (Boston: Ginn and Company, 1942).

70. MacIver, "The Imputation of Motives," 9.

a deeply important part of certain landscapes of meaning, but that (1) these landscapes themselves have to be interpreted, which is to say reconstructed via the use of theory, and (2) upon such landscapes, human beings do emerge with subjective motives that force action forward. The problem for interpretive explanation, then, is to do what Steinmetz did—show carefully how the landscape gives form to the motive, which applies force in causing social action.

What we have developed within the language game of social theory, then, is a plurality of abstract accounts of how the human mind is, in one way or another, a force in the world. We would be well served to accept a spectrum of motives running from conscious to unconscious—and set about examining how these possibilities, granted by the plasticity of human nature, appear at different places and different times, molded by signification and representation. The resultant explanations—as we can see from Steinmetz's analysis—would not "exclude motivation," but they would radically historicize and contextualize it. We cannot use the motivations of actors to construct an explanation without understanding the meanings in which these motives are immersed (see fig. 10).

In delving into the problem of motivation, the interpretive epistemic mode suggests a historicized dialectic, contrasting the emergent motives, possessed by individuals, and the meanings that make these motivations concretely effective. And so, the interpretive investigator plays theater critic to her subjects' performances. On the

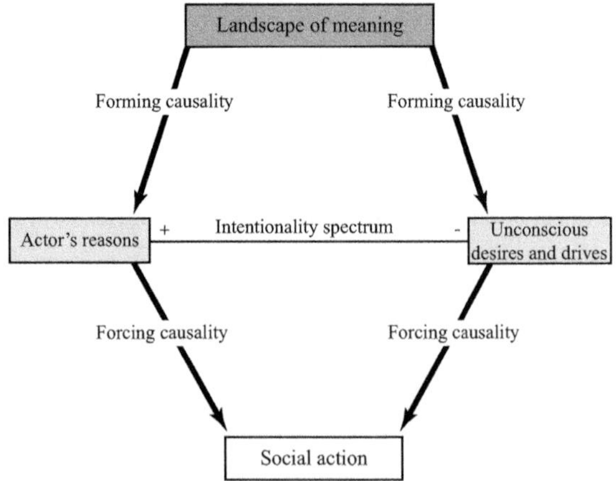

Figure 10: Meaning and motivation

stage, characters' motivations emerge in the context of a set and script, which are what give the playwright's imagination of what human beings are like, and what her characters want, the concrete immediacy that pushes the play forward. Something similar happens when we reconstruct motivation for an interpretive explanation, but set and script are written by history and culture.

This interpretive dialectic cannot only be conceived as the interaction of interiority with representation and signification, however. For there are productive forces in the social world that are not the possession, more or less controlled, of individual subjects, more or less rational. These processes or structures—and, in the end, it is best to think of them as mechanisms—must also be part of interpretive explanation.

X

After all, this talk of motivation and meaning should make not only the realist-Marxist theorist of structural power, but also the good Foucauldian uncomfortable. Is it not the case that this *language of desire* that Steinmetz uses in the process of constructing his explanation should *itself* be the topic of inquiry? Is not Steinmetz's use of psychoanalytic language complicit with the vast operation of discourses that *produce* these human subjects with deep motives? Do not motives emerge from a social process; do they not have, themselves, a social history?

They do. Sometimes the mechanism produces the subject with the motive. But this too is a process in which social force is given form by meaning. This is the insight delivered in all its brilliance in some of Michel Foucault's most well known writings. Foucault writes:

> The confession is a ritual of discourse in which the speaking subject is also the subject of the statement; it is also a ritual that unfolds within a power relationship, for one does not confess without the presence (or virtual presence) of a partner who is not simply the interlocutor but the authority who requires the confession, prescribes it and appreciates it, and intervenes in order to judge, punish, forgive, console, and reconcile; a ritual in which the truth is corroborated by the obstacles and resistances it has had to surmount in order to be formulated.[71]

71. Michel Foucault, *The History of Sexuality: An Introduction* (New York: Vintage Books, 1990), 61–62.

A ritual, a repeated set of actions embedded in a social relationship of domination: confession is a mechanism, and a mechanism that has, as its regular outcome, a certain sort of human subject. The mechanism is social; it is part of our taken-for-granted, socially produced reality; it exceeds any agent and indeed whole domains of highly reflective and sophisticated discourse. It is "so deeply ingrained in us, that we no longer perceive it as the effect of a power that constrains us; on the contrary, it seems to us that truth, lodged in our most secret nature, 'demands' only to surface." And only if we are "taken in by this internal ruse of confession" can we really believe that Freud has discovered some massive truth about human nature, covered up heretofore by Victorian censors and, before that, by pre-Enlightenment ignorance. This mechanism, moreover, is expanding its reach—it is "relayed through so many different points," and from 1215 AD to the present, procedures of confession go through "a dissemination . . . a multiple localization of their constraint, a widening of their domain."[72] And the focus, of course, was on sex, and on sex as the location of the truth of the subject, thus drawing a deep connection between sex and truth that is unique to Western civilization, and especially intense in Western modernity.

But then, it is with the issue of modernity that this whole story of a mechanism's growth and dispersion becomes a story not only about forcing causes but also about forming causes—the causes that mould the productive mechanism of confession in a certain way, giving it a certain meaning. For Foucault's explanation is also concerned with the *transfer* of the mechanism of confession from the discourse of "sin and salvation" to the discourse of "bodies and life processes." Confession migrates from the landscape of meaning of Catholicism to that of psychoanalysis, and in doing so it changes radically, especially in its concrete effects (including the invention of homosexuality as an identity category).

To say this is, of course, to suggest that in the writings of Foucault one does find, despite his protests to the contrary, explanations—interpretive explanations, that is. His work is well known for introducing a "capillary" approach to social power, and for presenting us with certain dystopian interpretations of past and present social facts.[73] And

72. Foucault, *The History of Sexuality*, 61, 63.

73. For a discussion of Foucault's work in the context of the normative epistemic mode, see chapter 3, sections VI and VII.

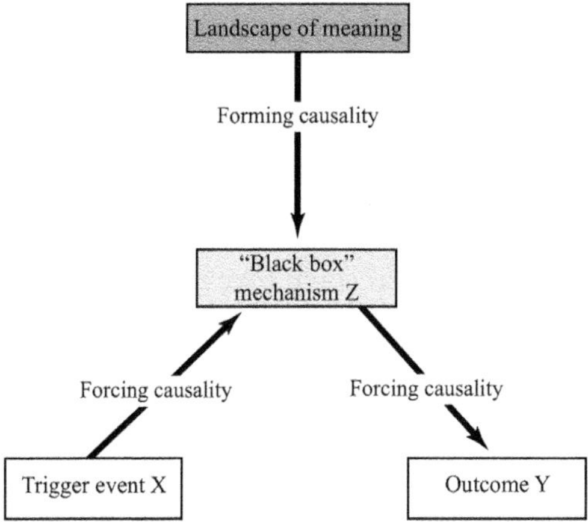

Figure 11: Meaning and mechanism

yet, if we examine his work on social practices like confession—and even more so, his early "archaeological studies"—I believe that what we find is the embedding of social processes into regimes of signification, which is to say, studies of how mechanisms occur upon landscapes of meaning (see fig. 11).

One could cite other examples of mechanisms embedded in meaning. Once we recognize forming causality as a different *kind* of social causality, we can see how it is repeatedly a part of social explanations, even if it is not presented in the terms of the Aristotle-inspired metaphor I am using here. Corrections to the new economic sociology suggest that that market mechanisms are not only embedded in social ties, but in social meanings;[74] political interests and ideologies are spread and consolidated via elaborate meaning work;[75] the decisions of female corporate executives are made on the terms of schemas of devotion.[76]

74. Fred Block, *Postindustrial Possibilities: A Critique of Economic Discourse* (Berkeley: University of California Press, 1990), 31–32; Frederick Wherry, *The Culture of Markets* (Cambridge: Polity Press, forthcoming); Lyn Spillman, unpublished manuscript.

75. Matthew Norton, "A Structural Hermeneutics of 'The O'Reilly Factor,'" *Theory and Society* 40, no. 3 (2011): 315–46.

76. Mary Blair-Loy, *Competing Devotions: Career and Family among Women Executives* (Cambridge, MA: Harvard University Press, 2003).

Both motivations and mechanisms, then, are given concrete form by signification. As a result the analysis of their causal effects is embedded within the interpretation of meaning. An implication of this is that landscapes of meaning, upon which mechanisms and motivations occur, are for the investigator a different (and prior) dimension along which causal arguments must be made. The effects of formal causes are, like other effects, drawn out through comparison and/or counterfactual reasoning ("it could have gone differently"). But the interpretation of landscapes of meaning, through the pluralist use of theory (as examined in chapter 4), historicizes these counterfactual arguments and renders them dependent, ultimately, on the in-depth knowledge of cases. For, in the interpretive epistemic mode, the counterfactuals of a given case or set of cases emerge from the *holistic* knowledge of the meanings active in a case. The interpretation of the history of a given landscape of meaning is itself the source of knowledge about what other meanings might have been available to certain motivated actors or what other discursively embedded mechanisms would have "worked." In other words, the development of counterfactual and/or comparative argument as a part of causal argument is itself a hermeneutic process.[77] Having suggested this triad

77. The implication of counterfactual reasoning in causal claims is accepted in many, vastly different, epistemologies for social research (see, e.g., James J. Heckman, "The Scientific Model of Causality," *Sociological Methodology* 35 [2005]: 1–97; James Mahoney, "Path Dependence in Historical Sociology," *Theory and Society* 29, no. 4 [2000]: 507–48). In the view presented here, the historicity of social relations implied by forming causes means that social dynamics cannot be captured by the concept of an "open system," because such a conception could not capture the meaningful aspects of a given historical trajectory. This returns us to Fritz Ringer's account of Weber's approach to causality. Ringer identifies the direct connection between Weber's "singular causal statements" and his theory of subjectivity and social action. This is because Ringer takes seriously Weber's language about the unreality of ideal types. He thus argues that in Weber's form of causal analysis, the investigator draws upon theory to help construct the *imaginative counterfactuals* that allow singular causal claims to be made. The purpose of ideal types is precisely to set up an account of the course of events from which actual events diverge, thus allowing the investigator to consider how ideal-typical process A→B was modified by various events and interactions with other processes, to produce what actually happened, A'→B'—all *within the same case*.

Note here the contrast to Goldstone's realist method (discussed in chapter 2). In Goldstone, A→B would be differentiated from A'→B' only in so far as *theory pointed directly* to a mechanism or process that was present in the latter and absent in the former. In Ringer's interpretation of Weber, however, while ideal types can provide the basis for comparing cases (either by contrasting differing ideal types, or by showing how two cases deviate in different ways from a given ideal type), the "singular causal analysis" takes place precisely in the moment when the case is compared to the ideal-of meaning, motivation, and mechanism as a metaframework for historicized explanation in social research, it is perhaps now appropriate to consider the idea of interpretive explanation in relationship to the argument of this book as a whole.

XI

Gary Alan Fine once described culture as an "amorphous mist."[78] He and other sociologists of culture have, in the process of bringing the interpretation of cultures into sociology, repeatedly insisted upon the intangibility of meaning, and thus on the necessity of grounding the study of culture in the aspects of social life that are more obvious, observable, or familiar to sociologists (and thus are supposedly more real).[79] But the arguments made in this book would suggest that

typical version of itself. Thus causal explanation emerges from deep knowledge of a given case and the theoretical development of ideal types.

A similar argument—about counterfactuals deriving from detailed historical knowledge of the case under scrutiny—can be found in Geoffrey Hawthorn, *Plausible Worlds: Possibility and Understanding in History and the Social Sciences* (Cambridge: Cambridge University Press, 1991). For an adumbration of this view, one which perhaps connects the work of Weber and Dilthey, see Georg Simmel, *The Problems of the Philosophy of History: An Epistemological Essay* (New York: Free Press, 1977).

78. Gary Alan Fine, "Small Groups and Cultural Creation: The Idioculture of Little League Baseball Teams," *American Sociological Review* 44 (1979). See also Amin Ghaziani, "An 'Amorphous Mist'? The Problem of Measurement in the Study of Culture," *Theory and Society* 38, no. 6 (2009).

79. This issue ranges far and wide in sociology, and is a point of focus for debates—both written and oral—that occur between members of the large section on the sociology of culture of the American Sociological Association. A variety of grounds for the study of meaning have been proposed—the practicalities of action; the social circumstances in which ideologies develop; the demographic shifts to which changes in literary form respond; the social networks that shape belief; and so on. There seem to be two things going on in these discussions. First, a very strong impetus to return meaning to some sort of institutional ground, which perhaps seems real or "harder" for the simple reason that the theoretical articulation of "social structure" and "institutions" is so deeply embedded in sociological theory, method, and informal sociological lingo (despite various ingenious theoretical attempts to overcome the opposition between social structure and culture, or to posit a bidirectional causality between the two). Second, an intense desire to avoid the uncertainties that attend to interpreting subjectivity, and thus to move the study of culture toward supposedly more observable entities, even if these entities are themselves "culture" or "discourse" or "communication." See Isaac Reed, "Book Review: Ann Swidler, *Talk of Love: How Culture Matters*," *Theory and Society* 31, no. 6 (2002); Ann Swidler, "Culture in Action: Symbols and Strategies," *American Sociological Review* 51, no. 2 (1986); Ann Swidler, *Talk of Love: How Culture Matters* (Chicago: University of Chicago Press); Robert Wuthnow, *Communities of Discourse: Ideology and Social Structure in the Reformation, the Enlightenment, and European Socialism* (Cambridge, MA: Harvard University

it is the motivations and mechanisms, or to use those terms again, "agency" and "structure," that are better compared to an amorphous mist. Motivations and mechanisms are real, but their identification in theory is not enough to enable social explanation. For, the ontological components of the social only become concretely effective when they are given form by systems of signification and meaning. Landscapes of meaning are formal causes in so far as they give motivations and mechanisms shape and color, concreteness and character.

Consider again Lichterman's church volunteers. They all have biographies that have led to them having motivated projects in the world, in historical situations defined by structures. Confronted with welfare reform (a structural constraint if there ever was one!), they are motivated—they "want to help." And there may be some ways in which these motivated projects draw upon the religious biographies of those who possess them, and thus already differ in a way that Lichterman has to be careful to allow for.[80] But the truth of the matter is that these motivations are like melted bronze before it is poured into a cast and allowed to harden into a real statue. The cast is the meaningful context in which amorphous motives become effectively performed actions. Motives only harden into effective social forces—forces that, for example, create the social capacity to work for the public good[81]—when they are given a concrete form by meaning. The same point applies to Foucault's ritual of confession.

Press, 1989). Wendy Griswold, "The Devil's Techniques: Cultural Legitimation and Social Change," *American Sociological Review* 48 (1983): 668–80. For a criticism of this tendency in American sociology and the articulation of a "structural hermeneutics" in opposition to it, see Jeffrey Alexander and Philip Smith, "The Strong Program in Cultural Sociology: Elements of a Structural Hermeneutics," in *The Meanings of Social Life: A Cultural Sociology* (New York: Oxford University Press, 2003). For an overview of the whole problem, with particular attention to how culture intersects with practice and with institutions, see Roger Friedland and John Mohr, "The Cultural Turn in American Sociology," in *Matters of Culture: Cultural Sociology in Practice*, ed. Roger Friedland and John Mohr (New York: Cambridge University Press, 2004), 1–68.

80. Lichterman's examination of a group of evangelical volunteers addresses this issue. He considers how, in a fuzzy way, the motivations that evangelicals brought to the problem of welfare reform may have been different, and relied perhaps on different beliefs, molded by a lifetime of different experiences and discourses. However, even here Lichterman finds that the explanatory leverage given by something like a commitment to a "personal influence strategy" for social betterment is better conceptualized as "a style of evangelical *group life*" that "shaped the volunteers' way of reaching out." Lichterman, *Elusive Togetherness*, 144.

81. Paul Lichterman, "Social Capital or Group Style? Rescuing Tocqueville's Insights on Civic Engagement," *Theory and Society* 35, nos. 5–6 (2006).

Certain things can be said, in the abstract, about how power works in the repeated ritual of confession, and thus about how the mechanism of confession works. But confession is given its lifeblood, its shape and effectiveness, by the discursive formation through which it takes place. An investigation into confession that does not account for the meanings that attach to it may produce a highly precise model, and a model that is heuristically useful. But these models should not be mistaken for the reality to which they supposedly refer. For without an understanding of formal causality, the theorization of a mechanism only grasps a formless force, an amorphous mist.

And so, for interpretive social research our conclusion is this: it is not necessary for ethnographers observing interaction and talk, historians embedded in archival details, cultural sociologists pouring over newspapers or through LexisNexis, communications scholars of a humanist bent, and others usually described as "interpretive" to reject mechanistic causality, or to reject the much-maligned attempt to interpret "what is inside people's heads." But they must realize that what our theories tell us about how mechanisms work, and how people are motivated to do what they do, will only tell us about clouds and fog that have yet to become a storm. For the issue, in the end, is not whether or not social life *is* or *is not* "mechanistic." The issue is the *conceptual method* by which an interpretive investigator could posit a mechanism or a motive when analyzing her evidence. On the one hand, mechanisms—those powerful, repeated social processes that help us explain so many social outcomes—and motives—those human desires, drives, and interests that accompany almost any action-situation—provide a clear sense that generalized social theory can be useful for building explanations. Social mechanisms, when abstracted from meaning and modeled effectively in sociotheoretic discourse, offer a way to schematize social process. Motivations, when considered as the sorts of projects actors take into the world, offer a way to grasp the involvement of individual humans in the processes that determine their lives.

But these theories will not deliver the goods of explanation until they are combined with the theoretically pluralistic process of the interpretation of meaning, to which chapter 4 was devoted. Indeed that process must be primary if we are to move from generalized theory to explanation, because in social life, unlike in nature, the force of social life must have a form—an aesthetic, an emotional valence, a reference point, a trope, in short, an interpretable meaning—to be effective (see fig. 12). Social life does develop certain repeatable processes—order emerges in a neighborhood, in a commodity chain, in a world-system. And actors bring certain motives to situations—sometimes very predictable ones. But do we want to say that these social regularities and predictable aspects of the human mind, which emerge in certain times and certain places, are but the empirical expression of the underlying properties or tendencies of a social being, whose ontology is revealed to us in theory? I think not, because the intellectual operation of the theoretical formalization of mechanistic processes and motivational projects that takes place within the community of inquirers is, in the end, the development of heuristically useful abstract fictions to get at historically located truths.

Perhaps ethnographies provide the classic example of this. Even in highly localized, thickly descriptive ethnographies, we find that the regularity of social life is to be found in meaningful settings, and indeed emerges there. Often what makes an ethnographic anecdote useful and representative is that it reveals in a particularly perspicuous way some ***recurring*** aspect of social life in a given setting, and certain aspects of ethnographic settings are indeed quite regular and predictable. What is tragic about Tyree's violent "campaign for respect" in *Code of the Streets* is just how predictable it really is; how the actions of Tyree and the gang of boys he eventually joins are scripted by the code; how, though there may be contingencies about when and where the violence occurs, that violence is coming to Tyree is a near certainty, for that fifteen-year-old, at that time and place. Just

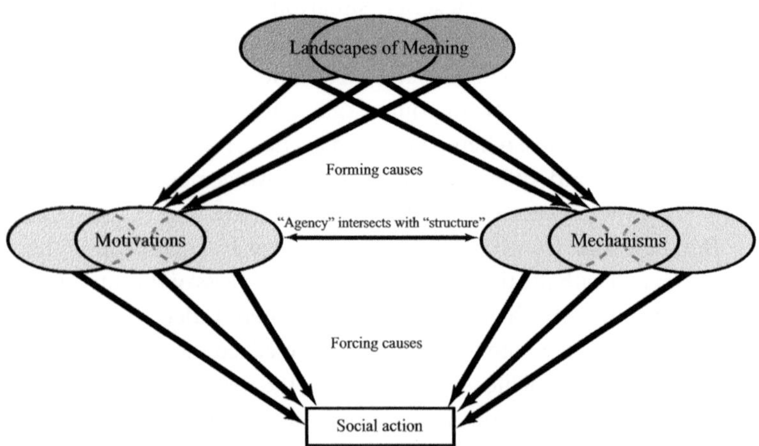

Figure 12: Forming causes, forcing causes, and social action

because we have (justifiable) hesitations about how generalizable Tyree's experience is, or how, exactly, it connects to changes in the political economy of the USA, does not mean that his experience was radically contingent, dependent entirely on chance, creativity, and agency. Quite the contrary—Tyree's trajectory upon moving in with his grandmother comes about as a result of his various motivations (to seek respect, to avoid further injury) and the regularized behaviors of violent gangs (defending turf, negotiating social relations through physical violence), embedded in the code of the streets, an encompassing semiotic system of masculinity, style, and honor.[82]

The point, then, is that the investigator must show the workings of forcing causes with constant reference to the meaningful context in which they occur. For, the processes of social life, the "how" of everyday interaction and negotiation, the organization of humans into effective working units, the development of specific capacities and powers to *move* the world, are formed by meaning. This is the underlying epistemological commitment of methodologies often deemed "interpretive," and to consider these methodologies as fundamentally set against the possibility of explanation is a mistake. Quite the opposite: methodologies are "interpretive" precisely in so far as they guide us toward this meaning-reconstruction, whereby social mechanisms are finally comprehended in their concrete, sometimes vicious power because the meanings that form them are brought to light. If to engage in this process of truth-making is going to be labeled a new sort of science, so be it. For the point is not to explain how interpretive epistemics lives up to the image of knowledge projected by the natural sciences and internalized by the social sciences, but but rather to comprehend how such an epistemics allows us to get the causal explanation right.

XII

The ultimate argument, then, is this: an essential aspect of social life *as such* is its dependence upon arrangements of meaning and representation, which themselves arrange and form the forceful causes of social action. But the possibilities for how meaning can construe or "form" social life are infinite, and can, in some cases, be highly idiosyncratic, because the meanings of symbols are arbitrary and conventional.

82. Elijah Anderson, *Code of the Street: Decency, Violence, and the Moral Life of the Inner City* (New York: W. W. Norton, 2000), 80–87.

Thus, because social life enacts meanings, its basic nature can never be fully specified, and instead must be understood as historically variable. So, theories of the social are at best heuristics that articulate the amorphous ontological mist of agency and structure in perspicacious ways. Only the theoretically informed interpreter of meanings can bring these terms out of abstraction. And so, perhaps instead of asking "What is the relationship between structure and agency?" we should ask how certain motivations and certain mechanisms enact and interpret the landscapes of meaning upon which they move, and by which they are formed. For, the nature of the social as such is that it is impossible to theorize, once and for all, the nature of the social as such. One must use theory to interpret meanings instead.

There is a fundamental connection between the investigator's interest in the causal dynamics of *concrete* sociohistorical reality,[83] the process of meaning-interpretation, and the plurality of theories of the social available to the working researcher. We have to interpret meaning to be able to specify our general theories of the social into true explanations. But to interpret meaning, as I argued in chapter 4, we need a plurality of social theories. The end goal of explanation can only be approached via an understanding of social causality as both historically specific and multidimensional. Hence the fate of the human sciences, wherein investigators must, sooner or later, deal with meaning. Plurality in theory, unity in meaning, historicity in explanation.

To the social researcher trained in naturalist ambition, meaning may appear elusive and epiphenomenal. But to the social actor, meaning is massively, unavoidably *real*, no matter how ultimately unrealistic its constructs, referents, or imaginings. The problem for the social researcher is, then, to interpret this meaning according to its causal consequences for social action. Max Weber set this out as the project for social theory and social research, in an era before realism and mechanism, and discourse and signification, were part of the language game of social theory. Perhaps we now have the conceptual resources to make this project our calling.

83. The idea of the human sciences being concerned with concrete social reality, in opposition to the more abstract natural sciences, appears in Hans Rickert but takes its classic form in Max Weber: "The type of social science in which we are interested is an empirical science of concrete reality. Our aim is the understanding of the characteristic uniqueness of the reality in which we move. We wish to understand on the one hand the relationships of the cultural significance of individual events in their contemporary manifestations and on the other the causes of their being historically *so* and not *otherwise*." Weber, *The Methodology of the Social Sciences*, 72.

Epilogue

I

The word 'theory' has its origins in the Greek *theoria*. Theoria was practiced when a person (the *theoros*) "made a journey or pilgrimage abroad for the purpose of witnessing certain events and spectacles."[1] The theoros traveled outside the boundaries of his city-state and attended—sometimes as an official civic representative—religious celebrations or athletic competitions. He (and it was, then, a he) observed these events and returned home, sometimes to discuss them with his own community. 'Theory,' then, has its various contemporary denotations and connotations at least in part because Plato and Aristotle drew metaphorical links between the practice of philosophy and the practice of theoria. In the twentieth century, the use of this link to the ancients, and discussion about the possible meanings of 'theoria'—both as a Greek practice and as a modern philosophical imperative—became part of the language of continental social theory, a sort of cipher by which to indicate the overall scope of a writer's

1. Andrea Wilson Nightingale, *Spectacles of Truth in Classical Greek Philosophy: Theoria in Its Cultural Context* (New York: Cambridge University Press, 2004), 3.

intention.[2] Jürgen Habermas did not refrain from the temptation to engage in this updated (and in some sense inverted) version of the *querelle des Ancients et des Modernes.*

In his inaugural lecture in Frankfurt in 1965, Habermas used an interpretation of theoria to reframe the distinction inherited from Max Horkheimer between "traditional" and "critical" theory. By linking theory to different human interests, and in particular by emphasizing the way the theoretical imagination could be connected to the human interest in emancipation, Habermas articulated the resistance to scientism that we now recognize as an essential characteristic of the revolution in social theory that took place in the 1960s and 1970s. In Habermas's view, the ancient ideal of *speculation* had been distorted in modern European philosophy when it was interpreted as disinterested, asocial thought. Echoing Horkheimer, he argued that modern advocates of radically antiempirical speculation were but the mirror images of positivism and scientism. But he went further, suggesting that the core impetus behind positivism—the distanced, objective gaze—had conquered almost all of the human sciences, even outside of behavioristic political science and neoclassical economics. "Historicism has become the positivism of the cultural and social sciences," he claimed.[3]

At its root, for Habermas, this problem stemmed from the "severance of knowledge from interest," and thus the loss of an essential piece of philosophical wisdom originally articulated in the theoros metaphor.[4] In Weberian language, his argument was that the total embrace of value-freedom in both empirical and theoretical work in the human sciences had vitiated the connection between values and truth that theory had once stood for. Thus "what was once supposed to comprise the practical efficacy of theory has now fallen prey to methodological prohibitions."[5] Both modern speculative philosophy and social scientific positivism had missed the essential point that, for the great Greek philosophers, abstract speculation was a process

2. Hans-Georg Gadamer, *Truth and Method* (New York: Continuum Publishing Company, 1989), 124–29, 453–56. Martin Heidegger, "Science and Reflection," in *The Question Concerning Technology and Other Essays* (New York: Harper & Row, 1977). Edmund Husserl, *The Crisis of European Sciences and Transcendental Phenomenology* (Evanston: Northwestern University Press, 1970), 282–87.

3. Jürgen Habermas, *Knowledge and Human Interests* (Boston: Beacon Press, 1971), 303.

4. Habermas, *Knowledge and Human Interests*, 303.

5. Habermas, *Knowledge and Human Interests*, 304.

deeply connected to humans' desire for emancipation from the forces that control them. Why should we know the world of pure forms? So that we can live better.

Habermas's specific contribution, then, was to cast doubt not only upon "bourgeois sociology," but also upon the ambitions for pure thought that stretched, in German philosophy, from Schelling to Husserl. Habermas extended and redeployed Horkheimer's position in two essential ways: he expanded its conceptual base to include a full analysis of communication and culture, and he extended the critique of "disinterested" theory to include the entire tradition of transcendental idealism *and* the "objectivist self-understanding of the hermeneutic sciences." The latter, he wrote, "defends sterilized knowledge against the reflected appropriation of active traditions and locks up history in a museum."[6] In other words, human scientists had only interpreted the world . . . and thus their theory was not *praxis*.[7]

I believe that this argument became iconic as it iterated itself, in varying versions, through an entire generation's worth of social theorists and their students. Consider literary theory in American universities, wherein the dominant figure was, for some time, Jacques Derrida. In the same years that Habermas was reworking his understanding of critical reason and social theory, Derrida engaged in an intellectual project radically different in its attitude toward the Western philosophical tradition but eerily similar in its attempt to revolutionize philosophy and the human sciences. In Derrida's view, formalistic and positivistic approaches to texts and to societies would be upended by the very exclusions that made them seem authoritative; the coherence of philosophy and of science was founded on contradiction. But a rupture was imminent, a rupture that would end the transcendentalist illusion that our best theoretical languages could point to pristine signifieds that sit outside the play of life and language.

6. Habermas, *Knowledge and Human Interests*, 316.

7. Austin Harrington has shown, conclusively in my view, that both Habermas and Gadamer misread Dilthey. As he writes with reference to the methodology of *verstehen*, "the fact that traditional interpretive methodologies do not generally thematize the researcher's relation to the object-domain in terms of normative 'dialogue' still provides no reason for regarding these doctrines as somehow misleadingly unreflexive and naïve, much less as covertly objectivist." Austin Harrington, "Objectivism in Hermeneutics? Gadamer, Habermas, Dilthey," *Philosophy of the Social Sciences* 30, no. 4 (2000): 493.

Derrida and Habermas have been subject to multiple interpretations, but one rather obvious implication of their work is that it was the duty of the theorist to resist the collapse of the critical possibilities granted by abstract thought into the advancing scientism of knowledge production in the postwar Western academy. For if this were allowed to happen, the critical capacity for the theorist to be a theoros who not only sees the world but also engages it would disappear. Hence the dispute about theoria: was the theoros, as distanced observer, the harbinger of objectivism and thus of a quiescence of thought, unable to disrupt the smooth functioning of a homogenized, ideologically justified, overrationalized modern world? Or was the theoros, as a fellow human being swept up in religious celebration, primed to become a political force upon his return home? Certainly, for Plato, the philosopher's ability to contemplate—and then verbalize imitations of—the Ideal Forms prepared him for political leadership. But what would this mean for radical democratic theory in a waning modernity? How, in a consumer society, would the real and the good be reconnected? How, in societies immersed in mass communication, could the virtuous life be lived, and with what political consequences? And so on.

It is in the context of this crisis of theory that the emergence and appeal of critical realism must be understood—and in particular the eloquent articulations of the emancipatory impulse by Roy Bhaskar, and the effective argumentation, by Margaret Archer and others, that the social sciences must resist colonization by rational choice theory.[8] Finally! Critical realism provides a perspective that links the capacities of science to the intellectual will necessary for the production of social critique in an overmediated, hypercapitalist world. And yet one wonders, at the same time, if this entire structure—of critical and traditional theory, praxis and scientism, disruption and reproduction, resistance and rationalization, pleasure and discipline—given to us by '68 and rearticulated in conferences around the globe, has outlived its utility. We might even consider the possibility that it is, at least in part, grounded on a misunderstanding of what research inspired by the "historical-hermeneutic sciences" is all about.

8. Roy Bhaskar, *Scientific Realism and Human Emancipation* (New York: Verso, 2009); Margaret S. Archer and Jonathan Q. Tritter, eds., *Rational Choice Theory: Resisting Colonization* (New York: Routledge, 2000).

II

In this book, I have tried to show that theory is a world of meanings, and useful meanings at that: when articulated with evidence it produces the maximal interpretations that, in my view, form the ultimate goal for knowledge in the human sciences. The semiotic scheme I developed for understanding these maximal interpretations was designed to comprehend realism and normativism as formats of interpretation that perform the fusion of theory and evidence in different ways, with different goals, and different results. But in applying this scheme to the meaning-centered mode of social investigation, I came to the conclusion that not only was "interpretivism" a different way of using theory, but also that our overall understanding of what theory can and should do for us is hampered by the classic opposition between theory-as-science and theory-as-(critical)practice. In terms of the Greek origins of the term 'theory,' then, what I am suggesting is that in focusing on the theoros as either observer or political force, we have missed an important aspect of the metaphor.

For the theoros is a stranger in a strange land. She has travelled across oceans, and first and foremost needs to *understand* what she sees. She brings with her the webs of meaning that constitute knowledge in her own community and the curiosities of her relations, friends, and colleagues, formed in countless dialogues that preceded the trip. She can share her curiosity with other strangers, from other city-states, who share her task. Prepared in this way by immersion in the meanings of theory, she observes and participates in the event. Upon her return, others in her community ask her to recount and interpret what it was she saw, and rearrange their webs of meaning as a result. Thus the theoros is the agent of understanding, the translator, the human avatar of Hermes, the *hermeneut.* I would submit that this is the ultimate purpose of the pluralistic, contentious language game of social theory—to allow the investigator to travel in mind and in text and through the analysis of evidence, and thus to comprehend and communicate the way social life works in other times and other places. Theory is the abstract construction of a mental ship; with it we can travel, with the explicit purpose of understanding. Curiosity and the will to understand must be primary, with explanation and critique to follow, for the actualization of understanding will rely on the traveler's sensitivities to idiosyncratic meanings, and not just on her logical brilliance. Theory, then, has to enable the comprehension of other signification systems, other social formations, other mechanisms pushing around other men and women, in other valleys.

One implication of this move toward the interpretive use of theory—and thus toward the idea that explanation and critique can both begin from the interpretation of meaning—is that we will have to dispense with one of the most common, almost taken-for-granted oppositions in contemporary social theory. In this opposition, the postpositivist, post-Marxist space of high theory is constituted by a division between work that is concerned (perhaps naïvely) with "meaning" and work that is concerned (perhaps obsessively) with "power." Some investigators dig into meanings and relegate power to outside the lifeworld, preferring, for example, to ignore the dynamics of colonial power in favor of comprehending the inner logic of a cockfight. Others are more suspicious, finding in minute shades of meaning the production of subjects. But this opposition—between Geertz and Foucault, between commentary and suspicion, between reproduction and disruption—depends conceptually upon the opposition between interpretation and explanation that I have tried to unravel in the previous two chapters. For only if we consider the interpretation of meaning to be somehow separate from the analysis of social causality can we justify the idea that to focus on power and practice is to avoid interpreting meaning. The concept of "forming causes" is designed, among other things, to make exactly this point. Power and causality are closely intertwined concepts for social research. For, effectivity in social life—for a person, organization, discursive formation, or whatever historically conditioned social force emerges upon and is formed by landscapes of meaning—is at its root the key to social power, whether that power is an emergent, capillary network of relations or the prerogative of the directors of a command economy. Thus if there are interpretive explanations—investigations into how meaning has concrete social *effects*—then there are interpretive studies of social power. Studies that show mechanisms actualized through meanings, the production of subjects via discourse and practice, the concretization of wills to power and moneyed interests through cultural formations: what do these studies do but grasp how meaning actually works upon people?

But this is, then, to suggest that the comprehension of how causality works in social life has to be thrown wide open if we are to comprehend the workings of social power. "Forming causes" are, in my view, only the very beginning of a project of historicized social explanation and theoretical pluralism.

III

But if meaning and power are to be interpreted together, what about the problems of interpretation itself? The very possibility of interpretive explanation is doubted by the hermeneutic tradition, and this doubt fuels the fire of those who would separate out the analysis of power and practice from the interpretation of meaning.

For if the metaphor of theoros as traveler captures the central point of hermeneutics, namely that the purpose of investigation is to "get to know the other," there are good reasons to be uncomfortable with the hermeneutic imperative so stated. On the one hand, in the epistemic crisis of Western anthropology, going into the field to comprehend the "native's point of view" has been identified as historically, socially, and intellectually entwined with Western colonialism. Getting to know the other was always already an act of power, and in so far as knowledge was successful, it aided domination. The traveler is, in a word, complicit. On the other hand, the tradition of hermeneutic philosophy has imprinted upon interpretation the existential near-impossibility of true understanding—suggesting that knowledge, particularly knowledge of human beings that claims scientific status, is deeply flawed at best. For hermeneutic philosophy, we cannot know or fully occupy another's horizon; interpretation is flawed and always in some sense a misrecognition. One of the overarching conclusions drawn—incorrectly, I believe—from this hermeneutic obsession with misrecognition and misunderstanding is that the best knowledge in the human sciences is dialogue and not explanation.

Release from these doubts will only come through the development of a plurality of abstract theoretical schemas, schemas that will succeed insofar as they augment the theoretical toolkit available to investigators who seek to construct deep interpretations of others' meanings. But to embrace this theoretical pluralism, it is necessary to reverse the tendency of thought that associates pluralism with epistemic relativism, for it is only because it is possible to construct better explanations that we need more theoretical tools with which to do so. It may indeed be impossible for the interpretivist, with her emphasis on concreteness, to differentiate with finality between the truth of two different theoretical schemas considered in the abstract.

But she can indeed differentiate between better and worse explanations of a certain set of social actions, and she can notice which theoretical schemas were particularly useful in constructing the better explanation, and for what conceptual reasons they were useful—what aspects of that meaningful swath of social life those theories allowed her to grasp. Such is the practical rationality of interpreters in search of maximal interpretations whose intellectual torque derives from their grasp of the forms and forces of social life.

IV

The philosopher of science Nancy Cartwright has developed the concept of a *dappled world* to describe how different philosophies of cause could be appropriate to different sciences; working primarily with reference to the natural sciences and to neoclassical economics, she has suggested that a given discipline or subdiscipline hunts for causes and explanations with the aid of laws that are simply not true when stated abstractly, but that serve as constructed "nomothetic machines" that allow analysis of concrete causal sequences to proceed.[9] The concept is suggestive of something slightly different from how she uses it, however. It suggests that the social world itself might itself be dappled because of the way signification is both arbitrary and conventional. The plurality of landscapes of meaning constructs a dappled world, one that has to be comprehended, and explained, via the interpretive use of social theory to create maximal interpretations. Is it any surprise that we would need multiple theoretical constructs, and a pluralistic conceptual method, to comprehend these multiple social realities?

The theoros traveled to other city-states and religious oracles; we use theory to travel throughout the dappled world of social life. It is this ability to travel and comprehend that makes Geertz's writing on cultural difference so deep and resonant, Bordo's critique of the discursive conditions for anorexic behavior so incisive, and Foucault's analysis of historical discontinuity so compelling. Pluralist in theoretical appropriation, interpretive analysis constructs meaning-centered explanation and invites rhetorically effective social criticism. But to achieve this pluralism, we must articulate our theories of social life

9. Nancy Cartwright, *The Dappled World: A Study of the Boundaries of Science* (New York: Cambridge University Press, 1999).

without the sort of ontological ambition that overrides hermeneutic sensitivity, and without the supports of either an account of human nature or a philosophy of history. Perhaps these ambitions and supports were the scaffolds without which we would not have social theory as it developed in the nineteenth century. In the latter half of the twentieth century the great deconstructionists and skeptics proceeded to take these scaffolds down. But in doing so did they debunk the utility of abstraction? Did they destroy the very possibility of causal explanation in the human sciences, or of the critique of ideology? Perhaps instead they merely revealed the way in which theoretical innovation could give dynamism to our comprehension of social life, even if theory's original ambitions and epistemic confidence derived from an unprovincialized Europe, an overconfident imagination set on universalizing our knowledge of "man." We work without this confidence, but what emerges in its place are myriad new possibilities for social knowledge.

For if it is the fate of the interpreter to be caught up between the universalist ambitions of each new theoretical scheme and the endless idiosyncrasies of human life as lived and experienced, so be it. It is not such a bad position to be in. The instructions for the traveler are, in the end, rather simple: build a good ship, bring as many books and maps as you can, and try to understand the people you meet, as a way to explain why they do what they do. That, in the end, is the all-too-human purpose of the human sciences.

Acknowledgments

Thanks to Jeffrey Alexander, teacher and mentor, for elucidating what metatheory is and how it works; for teaching me that the tasks of empirical sociology, social theory, and intellectual exploration can come together in a meaningful whole; and for introducing me to Dilthey and Saussure.

Julia Adams showed me the depth of historicity that could accompany sociological analysis; evidenced the intellectual capacities of theoretical pluralism; and taught me to read semiotics, Weber, and feminist theory together.

Braulio Muñoz and Robin Wagner-Pacifici started me down the road to this book at Swarthmore College.

Several colleagues, teachers, and friends engaged with the ideas expressed in the text during their development: Paul Lichterman, Lyn Spillman, Nina Eliasoph, Ron Eyerman, Philip Smith, John R. Hall, Peter Simonson, Emily Erikson, Seth Abrutyn, and Erika Summers-Effler. Thank you for your incisive criticism and conceptual labor.

Jake Lundberg, Sonali Chakravarti, and Daniel Gilbert were loyal companions in life and intellect.

My colleagues at the University of Colorado were exceptionally supportive, especially my senior faculty mentors Janet Jacobs and Jason Boardman.

Benjamin Lamb-Books provided excellent research assistance, and Danielle Lamb-Books turned my pen and pencil drawings into the diagrams herein.

Douglas Mitchell provided intellectual inspiration and energy as I moved the text to completion. The reviewers of the text for University of Chicago Press, as well as other anonymous reviewers, also provided important input. Katherine Frentzel provided excellent copyediting of the text.

Parts of this project were presented at the Sussman Lecture at Yale University, in colloquia in the sociology departments of the University of Colorado and the University of California, Davis, and to the Assistant Professor Sociology Working Group at the University of Colorado. The Department of Sociology and the College of Arts and Sciences at the University of Colorado generously provided the research semester that allowed me to complete the initial manuscript.

My parents Michael Reed and Jacqueline Ariail provided, and continue to provide, support and love. Ernesto was a constant canine companion throughout the writing of the text. Helen Reed will always be, via the memory of her strength and intellect, an inspiration.

. . . .

To my wife, Jennifer Bair, is owed the gratitude that can only be directed at one's dialectical other, an intertwining of opposition and recognition that resonates to the core of the soul and enhances the meaning of love. Intellectual argumentation with a loved one is the bread of life in an otherwise overaccelerated world; it makes it all worthwhile.

References

Abbott, Andrew. *Time Matters: On Theory and Method.* Chicago: University of Chicago Press. 2001.

Abbott, Andrew. "Against Narrative: A Preface to Lyrical Sociology." *Sociological Theory* 25, no. 1 (2007): 67–98.

Alexander, Jeffrey C. *Fin De Siècle Social Theory: Relativism, Reduction, and the Problem of Reason.* New York: Verso, 1995.

———. *Positivism, Presuppositions, and Current Controversies.* Berkeley: University of California Press, 1982.

Alexander, Jeffrey, and Philip Smith. "The Strong Program in Cultural Sociology: Elements of a Structural Hermeneutics." In *The Meanings of Social Life: A Cultural Sociology*, 11–26. New York: Oxford University Press, 2003.

Althusser, Louis, and Etienne Balibar. *Reading Capital.* New York: Pantheon Books, 1971.

Anderson, Elijah. *Code of the Street: Decency, Violence, and the Moral Life of the Inner City.* New York: W. W. Norton, 2000.

Archer, Margaret. "The Trajectory of the Morphogenetic Approach: An Account in the First-Person." *Sociologia: Problemas e Praticas* 54 (2007): 35–47.

Archer, Margaret, Roy Bhaskar, Andrew Collier, Tony Lawson, and Alan Norrie, eds. *Critical Realism: Essential Readingss.* New York: Routledge, 1998.

Archer, Margaret S., and Jonathan Q. Tritter, eds. *Rational Choice Theory: Resisting Colonization.* New York: Routledge, 2000.

Aristotle. *The Basic Works of Aristotle*. Edited by Richard McKeon. New York: Random House, 1941.

Bair, Jennifer. "On Difference and Capital: Gender and the Globalization of Production." *Signs* 36, no. 1 (2010): 203–26.

Bernstein, Richard J. *The Restructuring of Social and Political Theory*. New York: Harcourt Brace Jovanovich, 1976.

Bhaskar, Roy. *The Possibility of Naturalism: A Philosophical Critique of the Contemporary Human Sciences*. Philosophy Now. Atlantic Highlands, NJ: Humanities Press, 1979.

———. *The Possibility of Naturalism: A Philosophical Critique of the Contemporary Human Sciences*. 3rd ed. New York: Routledge, 1998.

———. *A Realist Theory of Science*. New York: Verso, 2008.

———. *Scientific Realism and Human Emancipation*. New York: Verso, 2009.

Biernacki, Richard. "After Quantitative Cultural Sociology." In *Meaning and Method: The Cultural Approach to Sociology*, edited by Isaac Reed and Jeffrery C. Alexander, 119–207. Boulder: Paradigm Publishers, 2009.

Blair-Loy, Mary. *Competing Devotions: Career and Family Among Women Executives*. Cambridge, MA: Harvard University Press, 2003.

Block, Fred. *Postindustrial Possibilities: A Critique of Economic Discourse*. Berkeley: University of California Press, 1990.

Bohman, James. *New Philosophy of Social Science*. Cambridge, MA: MIT Press, 1993.

Boltanski, Luc, and Laurent Thévenot. *On Justification: Economies of Worth*. Princeton: Princeton University Press, 2006.

Bordo, Susan. "Anorexia Nervosa: Psychopathology as the Crystallization of Culture." In *Unbearable Weight: Feminism, Western Culture, and the Body*, 139–64. Berkeley: University of California Press, 2003.

Borofsky, Robert. "Cook, Lono, Obeyesekere, and Sahlins." *Current Anthropology* 38, no. 2 (1997): 255–65.

Bourdieu, Pierre. *In Other Words: Essays toward a Reflexive Sociology*. Cambridge: Polity Press, 1990.

———. *Science of Science and Reflexivity*. Chicago: University of Chicago Press, 2004.

Bourdieu, Pierre, and Loïc J. D. Wacquant. *An Invitation to Reflexive Sociology*. Chicago: University of Chicago Press, 1992.

Boyer, Paul, and Stephen Nissenbaum. *Salem Possessed: The Social Origins of Witchcraft*. Cambridge, MA: Harvard University Press, 1974.

Brown, Elizabeth A. R. "The Tyranny of a Construct: Feudalism and Historians of Medieval Europe." *American Historical Review* 79 (1974): 1063–88.

Burawoy, Michael. *Ethnography Unbound: Power and Resistance in the Modern Metropolis*. Berkeley: University of California Press, 1991.

Butler, Judith. *Gender Trouble: Feminism and the Subversion of Identity*. New York: Routledge, 1999.

Calhoun, Craig. “Habitus, Field, and Capital: The Question of Historical Specificity.” In *Bourdieu: Critical Perspectives*, edited by Craig Calhoun, Edward LiPuma, and Moishe Postone, 61–88. Chicago: University of Chicago Press, 1993.

Campbell, Colin. *The Myth of Social Action*. New York: Cambridge University Press, 1996.

Cartwright, Nancy. *The Dappled World: A Study of the Boundaries of Science*. New York: Cambridge University Press, 1999.

Chakrabarty, Dipesh. *Provincializing Europe: Postcolonial Thought and Historical Difference*. Princeton: Princeton University Press, 2000.

Cohen, Ira J. *Structuration Theory: Anthony Giddens and the Constitution of Social Life*. Houndmills, Basingstoke, Hampshire: Macmillan, 1989.

Collier, Andrew. *Critical Realism: An Introduction to Roy Bhaskar's Philosophy*. New York: Verso, 1994.

Collins, Harry. *Tacit and Explicit Knowledge*. Chicago: University of Chicago Press, 2010.

Collins, Randall. *Interaction Ritual Chains*. Princeton: Princeton University Press, 2004.

———. “On the Microfoundations of Macrosociology.” *American Journal of Sociology* 86, no. 5 (1981): 984–1014.

Cosgrove, Denis. *Social Formation and Symbolic Landscape*. Madison: University of Wisconsin Press, 1998.

Crapanzano, Vincent. *Hermes' Dilemma and Hamlet's Desire: On the Epistemology of Interpretation*. Cambridge, MA: Harvard University Press, 1992.

Cruickshank, Justin. *Critical Realism: The Difference It Makes*. London: Routledge, 2003.

———. *Realism and Sociology: Anti-Foundationalism, Ontology, and Social Research*. Routledge Studies in Critical Realism 5. London: Routledge, 2003.

———. “A Tale of Two Ontologies: An Immanent Critique of Critical Realism.” *Sociological Review* 52, no. 4 (2004): 567–85.

———. “The Usefulness of Fallibilism: A Popperian Critique of Critical Realism.” *Philosophy of the Social Sciences* 37, no. 3 (2007): 263–88.

Danto, Arthur C. “Deep Interpretation.” *Journal of Philosophy* 78, no. 11 (1981): 691–706.

Darnton, Robert. *The Great Cat Massacre and Other Episodes in French Cultural History*. New York: Basic Books, 1984.

Davidson, Donald. “Actions, Reasons, and Causes.” In *The Essential Davidson*, 23–36. New York: Oxford University Press, 2006.

———. “Causal Relations.” *Journal of Philosophy* 64 (1967): 691–703.

———. “Problems in the Explanation of Action.” In *Problems of Rationality*, 101–16. New York: Oxford University Press, 2004.

Day, Mark. “Explanatory Exclusion, History, and Social Science.” *Philosophy of the Social Sciences* 34, no. 1 (2004): 20–37.

Dean, Mitchell. *Critical and Effective Histories: Foucault's Methods and Historical Sociology*. New York: Routledge, 1994.

Demetriou, Chares. "The Realist Approach to Explanatory Mechanisms in Social Science: More than a Heuristic?" *Philosophy of the Social Sciences*. 39, no. 3 (2009): 440–62.

Dening, Greg. "Review." *William and Mary Quarterly* 54, no. 1 (1997): 253–59.

———. "Sharks That Walk the Land: The Death of Captain Cook." *Meanjin* 41 (1982): 427–37.

Dilthey, Wilhelm. "The Construction of the Historical World in the Human Studies." In *Dilthey: Selected Writings*, edited by H. P. Rickman, 170–245. New York: Cambridge University Press, 1976.

———. *Selected Works, Volume 4: Hermeneutics and the Study of History*. Princeton: Princeton University Press, 1996.

Dray, William H. "'Explaining What' in History." In *Readings in the Philosophy of the Social Sciences*, edited by May Broadbeck, 343–48. New York: Macmillan, 1968.

Du Bois, W. E. B. *The Souls of Black Folk*. New York: W. W. Norton & Company, 1999.

Durkheim, Emile. *The Elementary Forms of the Religious Life*. New York: Free Press, 1995.

———. *The Rules of Sociological Method*. New York: Free Press, 1982.

———. *Suicide: A Study in Sociology*. New York: Free Press, 1966.

Eco, Umberto. *A Theory of Semiotics*. Bloomington: Indiana University Press, 1976.

Eley, Goeff. "Nations, Publics, and Political Cultures: Placing Habermas in the Nineteenth Century." In *Habermas and the Public Sphere*, edited by Craig Calhoun, 289–339. Cambridge, MA: MIT Press, 1992.

Emirbayer, Mustafa. "Manifesto for a Relational Sociology." *American Journal of Sociology* 103, no. 2 (1997): 281–317.

Emirbayer, Mustafa, and Ann Mische. "What Is Agency?" *American Journal of Sociology* 103, no. 4 (1998): 962–1023.

Engelskirchen, Howard. "The Aristotelian Marx and Scientific Realism: A Perspective on Social Kinds in Social Theory." Ph.D. diss., State Universtity of New York at Binghamton, 2007.

Etzioni, Amitai. "Creating Good Communities and Good Societies." *Contemporary Sociology* 29, vol. 1 (2000): 188–95.

Evans, Peter B., Dietrich Reuschemeyer, and Theda Skocpol. *Bringing the State Back In*. New York: Cambridge University Press, 1985.

Fairclough, Norman. *Discourse and Social Change*. Cambridge: Polity Press, 1992.

Fairclough, Norman, Bob Jessop and Andrew Sayer. "Critical Realism and Semiosis." In *Realism, Discourse, and Deconstruction*, edited by Johnathan Joseph and John Michael Roberts, 23–42. New York: Routledge, 2004.

Fine, Gary Alan. "Small Groups and Cultural Creation: The Idioculture of Little League Baseball Teams." *American Sociological Review* 44 (1979): 733–45.

Foucault, Michel. *The History of Sexuality: An Introduction*. New York: Vintage Books, 1990.

———. "Nietzsche, Genealogy, History." In *The Foucault Reader*, edited by Paul Rabinow, 76–100. New York: Pantheon Books, 1984.

———. "What Is an Author?" In *The Foucault Reader*, edited by Paul Rabinow, 101–20. New York: Pantheon Books, 1984.

———. *The Order of Things*. New York: Vintage Books, 1970.

Fraser, Nancy. "Michel Foucault: A 'Young Conservative'?" *Ethics* 96 (1985): 165–84.

Friedland, Roger, and John Mohr. "The Cultural Turn in American Sociology." In *Matters of Culture: Cultural Sociology in Practice*, edited by Roger Friedland and John Mohr, 1–70. New York: Cambridge University Press, 2004.

Friedman, Jonathan. "Captain Cook, Culture, and the World System." *Journal of Pacific History* 20 (1985): 191–201.

———. "No History Is an Island." *Critique of Anthropology* 8 (1988): 7–39.

Gadamer, Hans-Georg. *Truth and Method*. 2nd ed. New York: Continuum Publishing Company, 1989.

Gandhi, Leela. *Affective Communities: Anticolonial Thought, Fin-De-Siecle Radicalism, and the Politics of Friendship*. Durham: Duke University Press, 2006.

Gardiner, Patrick, ed. *Theories of History*. New York: Free Press, 1959.

Geertz, Clifford. *Available Light : Anthropological Reflections on Philosophical Topics*. Princeton: Princeton University Press, 2000.

———. "Deep Play: Notes on the Balinese Cockfight." In *The Interpretation of Cultures*. New York: Basic Books, 2000.

———. "Thick Description: Toward an Interpretive Theory of Culture." In *The Interpretation of Cultures*. New York: Basic Books, 2000.

Ghaziani, Amin. "An "Amorphous Mist"? The Problem of Measurement in the Study of Culture." *Theory and Society* 38, no. 6 (2009): 581–612.

Giddens, Anthony. *The Constitution of Society*. Berkeley: University of California Press, 1984.

———. *Social Theory and Modern Sociology*. Cambridge: Polity Press, 1987.

Ginzburg, Carlo. *Clues, Myths, and the Historical Method*. Baltimore: Johns Hopkins University Press, 1986.

Glynos, Jason, and David Howarth. *Logics of Critical Explanation in Social and Political Theory*. New York: Routledge, 2007.

Goldstone, Jack. "Comparative Historical Analysis and Knowledge Accumulation in the Study of Revolutions." In *Comparative Historical Analysis in the Social Sciences*, edited by James Mahoney and Dietrich Rueschemeyer, 41–90. New York: Cambridge University Press, 2003.

Goldthorpe, John H. *On Sociology*. 2nd ed. Stanford: Stanford University Press, 2007.

———. "Sociological Ethnography Today: Problems and Prospects." In *On Sociology, Volume 1: Critique and Program*, 61–90. Stanford: Stanford University Press, 2007.

Goodwin, Jeff. "How to Become a Dominant American Social Scientist: The Case of Theda Skocpol." *Contemporary Sociology* 25, no. 3 (1996): 293–95.

Gorski, Philip. "The Poverty of Deductivism: A Constructivist Realist Model of Sociological Explanation." *Sociological Methodology* 34 (2004): 1–33.

Green, Donald P., and Ian Shapiro. *Pathologies of Rational Choice Theory: A Critique of Applications in Political Science.* New Haven: Yale University Press, 1994.

Griswold, Wendy. "The Devil's Techniques: Cultureal Legitimaiton and Social Change." *American Sociological Review* 48 (1983): 668–80.

Gross, Neil. *Richard Rorty: The Making of an American Philosopher.* Chicago: University of Chicago Press, 2008.

Habermas, Jürgen. *Knowledge and Human Interests.* Boston: Beacon Press, 1971.

———. *Legitimation Crisis.* Boston: Beacon Press, 1975.

———. "Modernity versus Postmodernity." *New German Critique* 22 (1981): 3–14.

———. *The Philosophical Discourse of Modernity: Twelve Lectures.* Cambridge, MA: MIT Press, 1987.

———. *The Structural Transformation of the Public Sphere: An Inquiry into a Category of Bourgeois Society.* Studies in Contemporary German Social Thought. Cambridge, MA: MIT Press, 1989.

———. *The Theory of Communicative Action.* Boston: Beacon Press, 1987.

Hacking, Ian. *Representing and Intervening: Introductory Topics in the Philosophy of Natural Science.* New York: Cambridge University Press, 1983.

———. *The Social Construction of What?* Cambridge, MA: Harvard University Press, 1999.

———. *Historical Ontology.* Cambridge, MA: Harvard University Press. 2002.

Hall, John R. *Cultures of Inquiry: From Epistemology to Discourse in Sociohistorical Research.* Cambridge: Cambridge University Press, 1999.

Harding, Sandra, ed. *Can Theories Be Refuted? Essays on the Duhem-Quine Thesis.* Hingham, MA: D. Riedel, 1976.

———. "Is There a Feminist Method?" In *Feminism and Methodology: Social Science Issues*, edited by Sandra Harding. Bloomington: Indiana University Press, 1987.

Harré, Rom. "Social Reality and the Myth of Social Structure." *European Journal of Social Theory* 5 (2002): 111–23.

Harré, Rom, and Grant Gillett. *The Discursive Mind.* Thousand Oaks, CA: Sage Publications, 1994.

Harré, Rom, and E. H. Madden. *Causal Powers : A Theory of Natural Necessity.* Oxford: B. Blackwell, 1975.

Harrington, Austin. "Objectivism in Hermeneutics? Gadamer, Habermas, Dilthey." *Philosophy of the Social Sciences* 30, no. 4 (2000): 491–507.

Harvey, David. *The Condition of Postmodernity: An Enquiry into the Origins of Cultural Change.* Oxford: B. Blackwell, 1989.

Hawthorn, Geoffrey. *Plausible Worlds: Possibility and Understanding in History and the Social Sciences.* Cambridge: Cambridge University Press, 1991.

Hedström, Peter. *Dissecting the Social: On the Principles of Analytical Sociology.* Cambridge: Cambridge University Press, 2005.

Hedström, Peter, and Richard Swedberg, eds. *Social Mechanisms: An Analytical Approach to Social Theory.* New York: Cambridge University Press, 1998.

Hegel, Georg Wilhelm Friedrich. *Phenomenology of Spirit.* Translated by A. V. Miller. New York: Oxford University Press, 1977.

Heidegger, Martin. "Science and Reflection." In *The Question Concerning Technology and Other Essays.* New York: Harper & Row, 1977.

Heinemann, Evelyn. *Witches: A Psychoanalytic Exploration of the Killing of Women.* New York: Free Association, 2000.

Hekman, Susan. "Action as a Text: Gadamer's Hermeneutics and the Social Scientific Analysis of Action." *Journal for the Theory of Social Behavior* 14, no. 3 (1984): 333–54.

———. "Weber's Concept of Causality and the Modern Critique." *Sociological Inquiry* 49, no. 4 (1979).

Hempel, Carl. *Aspects of Scientific Explanation and Other Essays in the Philosophy of Science.* New York: Free Press, 1965.

———. "The Function of General Laws in History." In *Theories of History,* edited by Patrick Gardiner. New York: Free Press, 1959.

Henderson, David. "Norms, Normative Principles, and Explanation: On Not Getting Is from Ought." *Philosophy of the Social Sciences* 32, no. 3 (2002): 329–64.

Henderson, David K. *Interpretation and Explanation in the Human Sciences.* SUNY Series in the Philosophy of the Social Sciences. Albany: State University of New York Press, 1993.

Hesse, Mary. "The Hunt for Scientific Reason." *PSA: Proceedings of the Biennial Meeting of the Philosophy of Social Science Associaiton* 2 (1980): 3–22.

Honneth, Axel. *Disrespect: The Normative Foundations of Critical Theory.* Cambridge, MA: Polity Press, 2007.

———. *The Struggle for Recognition: The Moral Grammar of Social Conflicts.* Cambridge, MA: Polity Press, 1995.

Honneth, Axel, and Hans Joas. *Social Action and Human Nature.* New York: Cambridge University Press, 1988.

Hübner, Kurt. *Critique of Scientific Reason.* Chicago: University of Chicago Press, 1983.

Hughes, H. Stuart. *Consciousness and Society: The Reorientation of European Social Thought, 1890–1930.* New York: Vintage Books, 1961.

Husserl, Edmund. *The Crisis of European Sciences and Transcendental Phenomenology*. Evanston, IL: Northwestern University Press, 1970.

Jameson, Fredric. *The Geopolitical Aesthetic: Cinema and Space in the World System*. Bloomington and London: Indiana University Press and the British Film Institute, 1992.

———. *Postmodernism: or, the Cultural Logic of Late Capitalism*. Post-Contemporary Interventions. Durham: Duke University Press, 1991.

Jay, Martin. "The Debate over the Performative Contradiction: Habermas versus the Poststructuralists." In *Philosophical Interventions in the Unfinished Project of Enlightenment*, edited by Axel Honneth, Thomas A. McCarthy, Claus Offe, and Albrecht Wellmer, 261–79. Cambridge, MA: MIT Press, 1992.

Joy, Lyn S. "Scientific Explanation from Formal Causes to Laws of Nature." In *The Cambridge History of Science: Early Modern Science*, edited by Katharine Park and Lorraine Daston, 70–105. New York: Cambridge University Press, 2006.

Katz, Jack. "From How to Why: On Luminous Description and Causal Inference in Ethnography (Part I)." *Ethnography* 2, no. 4 (2001): 443–73.

———. "From How to Why: On Luminous Description and Causal Inference in Ethnography (Part 2)," *Ethnography* 3, no. 1 (2002): 63–90.

King, Anthony. *The Structure of Social Theory*. London: Routledge, 2004.

King, Gary, Robert O. Keohane, and Sidney Verba. *Designing Social Inquiry: Scientific Inference in Qualitative Research*. Princeton: Princeton University Press, 1994.

Lakoff, George, and Mark Johnson. *Philosophy in the Flesh: The Embodied Mind and Its Challenge to Western Thought*. New York: Basic Books, 1999.

Lerner, Berel Dov. *Rules, Magic, and Instrumental Reason: A Critical Interpretation of Peter Winch's Philosophy of the Social Sciences*. New York: Routledge, 2002.

Leupntiz, Deborah. "Beyond the Phallus: Lacan and Feminism." In *The Cambridge Companion to Lacan*, edited by Jean-Michel Rabate, 221–37. New York: Cambridge University Press, 2003.

Levey, Geoffrey Brahm. "Theory Choice and the Comparison of Rival Theoretical Perspectives in Political Sociology." *Philosophy of the Social Sciences* 26, no. 1 (1996): 26–60.

Levi-Strauss, Claude. *The Raw and the Cooked: Mythologiques, Volume 1*. Chicago: Chicago University Press, 1983.

Lichterman, Paul. *Elusive Togetherness: Church Groups Trying to Bridge America's Divisions*. Princeton: Princeton University Press, 2005.

———. "Social Capital or Group Style? Rescuing Tocqueville's Insights on Civic Engagement." *Theory and Society* 35, nos. 5–6 (2006): 529–63.

Little, Daniel. "Explaining Large-Scale Historical Change." *Philosophy of the Social Sciences* 30, no. 1 (2000): 89–112.

———. *Understanding Society*. PDF available at http://understandingsociety.blogspot.com.

———. *The Scientific Marx.* Minneapolis: University of Minnesota Press, 1986.

———. *Understanding Peasant China: Case Studies in the Philosophy of Social Science.* New Haven: Yale University Press, 1989.

Longino, Helen. *The Fate of Knowledge.* Princeton: Princeton University Press, 2002.

Luhmann, Niklas. *Microfoundations, Method, and Causation: On the Philosophy of the Social Sciences.* New Brunswick, NJ: Transaction Publishers, 1998.

———. *Social Systems.* Stanford: Stanford University Press, 1995.

Lyne, John R. "Rhetoric and Semiotic in C. S. Peirce." *Quartely Journal of Speech* 66, no. 2 (1980): 155–68.

MacIntyre, Alasdair C. *After Virtue: A Study in Moral Theory.* Notre Dame, IN: University of Notre Dame Press, 1981.

———. *Against the Self-Images of the Age: Essays on Ideology and Philosophy.* London: Duckworth, 1971.

———. "The Intelligibility of Action." In *Rationality, Relativism, and the Human Sciences,* edited by J. Margolis, M. Krausz, and R. M. Burian. Boston: Martinus Nijhoff Publishers, 1986.

MacIver, Robert M. "The Imputation of Motives." *American Journal of Sociology* 46, no. 1 (1940): 1–12.

———. *Social Causation.* Social Science Series. Boston: Ginn and Company, 1942.

Mahajan, Gurpeet. *Explanation and Understanding in the Human Sciences.* Delhi: Oxford University Press, 1997.

Martin, John Levi. "What Is Field Theory?" *American Journal of Sociology* 109, no. 1 (2003): 1–49.

Marx, Karl. "Economic and Philosophic Manuscripts of 1844." In *The Marx-Engels Reader,* 2nd ed., edited by Robert C. Tucker, 67–125. New York: W. W. Norton, 1978.

———. *Grundrisse.* New York: Penguin, 1973.

———. *The Karl Marx Library, Volume 1.* New York: McGraw-Hill, 1977.

Maxwell, Grover. "The Ontological Status of Theoretical Entities." *Minnesota Studies in the Philosophy of Science* 3 (1962): 3–27.

McAdam, Doug, Sidney Tarrow, and Charles Tilly. *Dynamics of Contention.* New York: Cambridge University Press, 2001.

McCarthy, George E., ed. *Marx and Aristotle: Nineteenth Century German Social Theory and Classical Antiquity.* Savage, MD: Rowan & Littlefield Publishers, 1992.

McCarthy, Thomas. "Private Irony and Public Decency: Richard Rorty's New Pragmatism." *Critical Inquiry* 16, no. 2 (1990): 355–70.

Merton, Robert K. *Social Theory and Social Structure.* Enl. ed. New York: Free Press, 1968.

———. "Three Fragments from a Sociologist's Notebooks: Establishing the Phenomenon, Specified Ignorance and Strategic Research Materials." *Annual Review of Sociology* 13 (1987): 1–28.

Meyer, Susan Sauve. "Aristotle, Teleology, and Reduction." *Philosophical Review* 101, no. 4 (1992): 791–825.

Mills, C. Wright. "Situated Actions and Vocabularies of Motive." *American Sociological Review* 5, no. 6 (1940): 904–13.

———. "Language, Logic, and Culture." *American Sociological Review*. 4, no. 5 (1939): 670–80.

Moore, Barrington. *Social Origins of Dictatorship and Democracy: Lord and Peasant in the Making of the Modern World*. Boston: Beacon Press, 1967.

Nagel, Ernest. *The Structure of Science: Problems in the Logic of Scientific Explanation*. New York: Harcourt, 1961.

Nagel, Thomas. *The View from Nowhere*. New York: Oxford University Press, 1986.

New, Caroline. "Feminism, Critical Realism and the Linguistic Turn." In *Critical Realism: The Difference It Makes*, edited by Justin Cruickshank, 57–74. New York: Routledge, 2003.

Nightingale, Andrea Wilson. *Spectacles of Truth in Classical Greek Philosophy: Theoria in Its Cultural Context*. New York: Cambridge University Press, 2004.

Norton, Matthew. "A Structural Hermeneutics of 'The O'Reilly Factor.'" *Theory and Society* 40, no. 3 (2011): 315–46.

Obeyesekere, Gananath. *The Apotheosis of Captain Cook: European Mythmaking in the Pacific*. Princeton and Honolulu: Princeton University Press and Bishop Museum Press, 1992.

———. "'British Cannibals': Contemplation of an Event in the Death and Resurrection of James Cook, Explorer." *Critical Inquiry* 18, no. 4 (1992): 630–54.

Ortner, Sherry. "Theory in Anthropology since the '60s." *Comparative Studies in Society and History* (1984): 126–66.

Ortner, Sherry B. *Making Gender: The Politics and Erotics of Culture*. Boston: Beacon Press, 1996.

Outhwaite, William. *New Philosophies of Social Science: Realism, Hermeneutics, and Critical Theory*. New York: St. Martin's Press, 1987.

Parsons, Talcott. *The Structure of Social Action: A Study in Social Theory with Special Reference to a Group of Recent European Writers*. New York: McGraw-Hill Book Company, 1937.

Parsons, Talcott, Edward Shils, and Neil J. Smelser. *Toward a General Theory of Action: Theoretical Foundations for the Social Sciences*. Abridged ed. New Brunswick, NJ: Transaction Publishers, 2001.

Peirce, Charles Saunders. "Of Reasoning in General." In *The Essential Peirce: Selected Philosophical Writings*, vol. 1. Bloomington: Indiana University Press, 1998.

Popper, Karl, and John C. Eccles. *The Self and Its Brain*. Boston: Routledge & Kegan Paul, 1977.

Porpora, Douglas. "Sociology's Causal Confusion." In *Revitalizing Causality: Realism About Causality in Philosophy and Social Science*, edited by Ruth Groff, 195–204. London: Routledge, 2007.

Putnam, Hilary. "Meaning and Reference." *Journal of Philosophy* 70, no. 19 (1973): 699–711.

———. "The Meaning of Meaning." In *Minnesota Studies in the Philosophy of Science*, vol. 7, edited by Gunderson. Minneapolis: University of Minnesota Press, 1975.

———. "Why There Isn't a Ready Made World." *Synthese* 51, no. 2 (1982): 141–67.

Ragin, Charles. *Fuzzy-Set Social Science*. Chicago: University of Chicago Press, 2000.

———. *Redesigning Social Inquiry: Fuzzy Sets and Beyond*. Chicago: University of Chicago Press, 2008.

Rappaport, Roy A. *Ritual and Religion in the Making of Humanity*. Cambridge Studies in Social and Cultural Anthropology. Cambridge: Cambridge University Press, 1999.

Reed, Isaac. "Book Review: Ann Swidler, *Talk of Love: How Culture Matters*." *Theory and Society* 31, no. 6 (2002): 785–94.

———. "Justifying Sociological Knowledge: From Realism to Interpretation." *Sociological Theory* 26, no. 2 (2008): 101–29.

———. "Why Salem Made Sense: Culture, Gender, and the Puritan Persecution of Witchcraft." *Cultural Sociology* 1, no. 2 (2007): 209–34.

———. "Review Essay: Social Theory, Post-post-positivism, and the Question of Interpretation." *International Sociology* 23, no. 5 (2008): 665–75.

Reed, Isaac Ariail. "Epistemology Contextualized: Social-Scientific Knowledge in a Post-Positivist Era." *Sociological Theory* 28, no. 1 (2010): 20–39.

Reed, Isaac Ariail, and Benjamin Lamb-Books. "Hermeneutics and Sociology: Deepening the Interpretive Perspective." In *New Directions in Sociology: Essays on Theory and Methodology in the 21st Century*. Edited by Ieva Zake and Michael DeCesare. Jefferson, NC: McFarland, 2011.

Reiss, Julian. "Causation in the Social Sciences: Evidence, Inference, and Purpose." *Philosophy of the Social Sciences* 39, no. 1 (2009): 20–40.

Richardson, Alan. "Robert K. Merton and Philosophy of Science." *Social Studies of Science* 34, no. 6 (2004): 855–58.

Ricouer, Paul. "The Model of the Text: Meaningful Action Considered as a Text." *Social Research* 38 (1971): 529–62.

———. "What Is a Text? Explanation and Understanding." In *Hermeneutics and the Human Sciences: Essays on Language, Action, and Interpretation*. New York: Cambridge University Press, 1981.

———. "Hermeneutics and the Critique of Ideology." In *Hermeneutics and the Human Sciences: Essays on Language, Action, and Interpretation*. New York: Cambridge University Press, 1981.

Ringer, Fritz K. *Max Weber's Methodology: The Unification of the Cultural and Social Sciences*. Cambridge, MA: Harvard University Press, 1997.

Risjord, Mark W. *Woodcutters and Witchcraft: Rationality and Interpretive Change in the Social Sciences*. SUNY Series in the Philosophy of the Social Sciences. Albany: State University of New York Press, 2000.

Rorty, Richard. "Inquiry as Recontextualization: An Anti-Dualist Account of Interpretation." In *The Interpretive Turn: Philosophy, Science, Culture*, edited by David R. Hiley, James Bohman, and Richard Schusterman, 59–80. Ithaca: Cornell Univeristy Press, 1991.

Roth, Paul. "Interpretation as Explanation." In *The Interpretive Turn: Philosophy, Science, Culture*, edited by David R. Hiley, James Bohman, and Richard Schusterman. Ithaca: Cornell University Press, 1991.

Runciman, W. G. *A Critique of Max Weber's Philosophy of Social Science*. Cambridge: Cambridge University Press, 1972.

———. *A Treatise on Social Theory*. 3 vols. Cambridge: Cambridge University Press, 1983.

Ruttenburg, Nancy. *Democratic Personality: Popular Voice and the Trial of American Authorship*. Stanford: Stanford University Press, 1998.

Ryan, Mary P. "Gender and Public Access: Women's Politics in Nineteenth Century America." In *Habermas and the Public Sphere*, edited by Craig Calhoun, 259–87. Cambridge, MA: MIT Press, 1992.

Sahlins, Marshall. "Captain Cook at Hawaii." *Journal of the Polyneisan Society* 98 (1989): 371–425.

———. *How "Natives" Think: About Captain Cook, for Example*. Chicago: University of Chicago Press, 1995.

Salmon, Wesley. *Causality and Explanation*. New York: Oxford University Press, 1998.

———. *Scientific Explanation and the Causal Structure of the World*. Princeton: Princeton University Press, 1984.

Salzinger, Leslie. *Genders in Production: Making Workers in Mexico's Global Factories*. Berkeley: University of California Press, 2003.

Sayer, R. Andrew. *The Moral Significance of Class*. New York: Cambridge University Press, 2005.

Schudson, Michael. "Was There Ever a Public Sphere? If So, When? Reflections on the American Case." In *Habermas and the Public Sphere*, edited by Craig Calhoun, 143–63. Cambridge, MA: MIT Press, 1992.

Scott, Joan W. "The Evidence of Experience." *Critical Inquiry* 17, no. 4 (1991): 773–97.

Searle, John. "Social Ontology: Some Basic Principles." *Anthropological Theory* 6, no. 1 (2006): 12–29.

———. *The Construction of Social Reality*. New York: Free Press, 1995.

Sewell, William H., Jr. "The Concept(s) of Culture." In *Beyond the Cultural Turn*. Edited by Lynn Hunt and Victoria E. Bonnell. Berkeley: University of California Press, 1999.

———. "Ideologies and Social Revolutions: Reflections on the French Case." *Journal of Modern History* 57, no. 1 (1985): 57–85.

———. *Logics of History: Social Theory and Social Transformation*. Chicago Studies in Practices of Meaning. Chicago: University of Chicago Press, 2005.

———. "Theory of Action, Dialectic, and History: Comment on Coleman." *American Journal of Sociology* 93, no. 1 (1987): 166–72.

———. *Work and Revolution in France: The Language of Labor from the Old Regime to 1848*. Cambridge: Cambridge University Press, 1980.

Simmel, Georg. *Essays on Interpretation in Social Science*. Totowa, NJ: Rowman and Littlefield, 1980.

———. *The Problems of the Philosophy of History: An Epistemological Essay*. New York: Free Press, 1977.

Skocpol, Theda. "Cultural Idioms and Political Ideologies in the Revolutionary Reconstruction of State Power: A Rejoinder to Sewell." *Journal of Modern History* 57, no. 1 (1985): 86–96.

———. *States and Social Revolutions: A Comparative Analysis of France, Russia, and China*. Cambridge: Cambridge University Press, 1979.

Smith, Christian. *Moral Believing Animals: Human Personhood and Culture*. New York: Oxford University Press, 2003.

Spillman, Lyn. "Causal Reasoning, Historical Logic, and Sociological Explanation." In *Self, Social Structure, and Beliefs: Explorations in the Sociological Thought of Neil J. Smelser*, edited by Jeffrey Alexander, Gary T. Marx, and Christine L. Williams, 216–34. Berkeley: University of California Press, 2004.

———. *Solidarity in Strategy: Making Business Meaningful in American Trade Associations*. Unpublished manuscript.

Steinmetz, George. "Critical Realism and Historical Sociology. A Review Article." *Comparative Studies in Society and History* 40, no. 1 (1998): 170–86.

———. *The Devil's Handwriting: Precoloniality and the German Colonial State in Qingdao, Samoa, and Southwest Africa*. Chicago Studies in Practices of Meaning. Chicago: University of Chicago Press, 2007.

———. "Odious Comparisons: Incommensurability, the Case Study, and 'Small N's' in Sociology." *Sociological Theory* 22, no. 3 (2004): 371–400.

Stoddart, David R. "Captain Cook and How We Understand Him." *Geographical Review* 87, no. 4 (1997): 537–41.

Swartz, David. *Culture and Power: The Sociology of Pierre Bourdieu*. Chicago: University of Chicago Press, 1997.

Swedberg, Richard. "Max Weber's Interpretive Economic Sociology." *American Behavioral Scientist* 50, no. 8 (2007): 1035–55.

———. *The Max Weber Dictionary: Key Words and Central Concepts*. Stanford: Stanford University Press, 2005.

Swidler, Ann. "Culture in Action: Symbols and Strategies." *American Sociological Review* 51, no. 2 (1986): 273–86.

———. *Talk of Love: How Culture Matters*. Chicago: University of Chicago Press, 2001.

Taylor, Charles. "Interpretation and the Sciences of Man." In *Philosophy and the Human Sciences: Philosophical Papers, Volume 2*. New York: Cambridge University Press, 1981.

Thacher, David. "The Normative Case Study." *American Journal of Sociology* 111, no. 6 (2006): 1631–76.

Thompson, E. P. *The Poverty of Theory and Other Essays*. New York: Monthly Review Press, 1978.

Tilly, Charles. "To Explain Political Processes," *American Journal of Sociology* 100, no. 6 (1995): 1594–610.

Toulmin, Stephen. *The Uses of Argument*. New York: Cambridge University Press, 2003.

Townsley, Eleanor. "'The Sixties' Trope." *Theory, Culture, and Society* 18, no. 6 (2001): 99–123.

Turner, Jonathan. "In Defense of Positivism." *Sociological Theory* 3, no. 2 (1985): 24–30.

———. "Returning to 'Social Physics': Illustrations from the Work of George Herbert Mead." *Current Perspectives in Social Theory* 2 (1981): 187–208.

Vaidyanathan, Brandon, Michael Strand, Austi Choi-Fitzpatrick, and Thomas Bushman. "Causality in Contemporary American Sociology: An Empirical Assessment." Unpublished manuscript.

Vaisey, Stephen. "Motivation and Justification: A Dual-Process Model of Culture in Action." *American Journal of Sociology* 114, no. 6 (2009): 1675–715.

Van Fraassen, Bas C. "A Re-Examination of Aristotle's Philosophy of Science." *Dialogue* 19 (1980): 20–45.

———. *The Scientific Image*. New York: Oxford University Press, 1980.

Wallerstein, Immanuel. *The Modern World-System*. New York: Academic Press, 1974.

Wallerstein, Immanuel, Calestous Juma, Evelyn Fox Keller, Jürgen Kocka, Domenique Lecourt, V. Y. Mudkimbe, Kinhide Miushakoji, Ilya Prigogine, Peter J. Taylor, Michel-Rolph Touillot. *Open the Social Sciences: Report of the Gulbenkian Commission on the Restructuring of the Social Sciences*. Stanford: Stanford University Press, 1996.

Walzer, Michael. *Interpretation and Social Criticism*. Cambridge, MA: Harvard University Press, 1993.

———. *Spheres of Justice: A Defense of Pluralism and Equality*. New York: Basic Books, 1983.

Warner, Michael. *The Letters of the Republic: Publication and the Public Sphere in Eighteenth-Century America*. Cambridge, MA: Harvard University Press, 1990.

Warnke, Georgia. *Justice and Interpretation*. Cambridge, MA: MIT Press, 1994.

Weber, Max. *Economy and Society: An Outline of Interpretive Sociology*. Berkeley: University of California Press, 1978.

———. *The Methodology of the Social Sciences*. New York: Free Press, 1949.

———. *The Protestant Ethic and the Spirit of Capitalism*. Translated by Talcott Parsons. Mineola, NY: Dover Publications, 2003.

Weiner, Jonathan M. "The Barrington Moore Thesis and Its Critics." *Theory and Society* 2, no. 3 (1975): 301–30.

Wherry, Frederick. *The Culture of Markets*. Malden, MA: Polity Press, 2011.

Whitney, Elspeth. "International Trends: The Witch 'She'/the Historian 'He': Gender and the Historiography of the European Witch-Hunts." *Journal of Women's History* 7, no. 3 (1995): 77–101.

Winch, Peter. *The Idea of Social Science and Its Relation to Philosophy*. New York: Humanities Press, 1958.

Wuthnow, Robert. *Communities of Discourse: Ideology and Social Structure in the Reformation, the Enlightenment, and European Socialism*. Cambridge, MA: Harvard University Press, 1989.

———. *Meaning and Moral Order: Explorations in Cultural Analysis*. Berkeley: University of California Press, 1987.

Zald, Mayer. "Sociology as a Discipline: Quasi-Science and Quasi-Humanities." *American Sociologist* 22, nos. 3–4 (1991): 165–87.

Index

Printed and bound by CPI Group (UK) Ltd, Croydon, CR0 4YY

09/06/2025

14685692-0002